Turning Point

Enlightening Essays on Life

Part 1

Turning Point

Enlightening Essays on Life

Part 1

SWAMINARAYAN AKSHARPITH
Ahmedabad

Turning Point

Enlightening Essays on Life

Part 1

Inspirer: HDH Pramukh Swami Maharaj

Previous Prints: 2004, 2006, 2008, 2010
3rd Edition: 1st Reprint: July 2013

Copies: 5,000 (Total: 34,000)

Price: ₹60/-

ISBN: 978-81-7526-421-2

Published & Printed by
Swaminarayan Aksharpith
Shahibaug, Ahmedabad-4, India

Website: www.baps.org

CONTENTS

PERSONALITY DEVELOPMENT

HEALTH

PREFACE

Dr S. Radhakrishnan, a former president of India, emphasizes the fundamental need for spiritual growth in his introduction to *Mahatma Gandhi – Essays and Reflections,* "The greatest fact in the story of man on earth is not his material achievement, the empire he has built and broken, but the growth of his soul from age to age in its search for truth and goodness. Those who take part in this adventure of the soul, secure an enduring place in the history of human culture."

From the cradle to the grave man aspires for five things: (1) everlasting happiness, (2) infinite knowledge, (3) immortality, (4) sovereignity and (5) freedom. But we script our own miseries and failures through moral misconduct, spiritual ignorance and laziness.

The eternal truths evade us because of our mundane pursuits and joys! But these truths strike a conscious note in times of tragedy, failure and illness. We are then spurred to seek the Divine for solace, happiness and the fundamental truths so essential for personal stability and growth.

Turning Point, Enlightening Essays on Life, Part 1, through its wide range of enlightening and empowering essays, seeks to awaken and elevate the readers to a higher level of knowledge, wisdom and spiritual living. They provide an opportunity to reflect upon and also introduce a change in our spiritual, social and health aspects of life.

We acknowledge the divine inspiration of guru Pramukh Swami Maharaj and the labour and devotion of BAPS sadhus and devotees in contributing to this excellent publication of enlightening essays.

- Swaminarayan Aksharpith

SPIRITUALITY

1 VEDIC SOCIETY: I

Gujarati Text: Sadhu Viveksagardas
Translation: Sadhu Vivekjivandas

Our dependence on material things increases by the day as we identify ourselves more and more with the motto "Minimum effort, maximum comfort." How tragic it is that we chose to lose our individuality and become captives of materialism.

When Mahatma Gandhi was battling against heavy odds, he sought Tolstoy's advice. Tolstoy said, "Go back to your religion."

This is exactly what we should do to reaffirm our spirits. Our holy scriptures like the Vedas, Upanishads, Bhagavad Gita and many others have illuminated our path to human and spiritual excellence. Together with moral injunctions, they lay emphasis on worship, love, peace and duty to both God and society. This first part focuses on character as a means to happy living.

Who Is Virtuous?

Two thousand five hundred years ago Bhagwan Buddha met a Brahmin named Sonadanda while walking in the streets of Shravasti. Soon they entered into a discussion as to what constitutes a virtuous man. Sonadanda enumerated five qualities. He said, "One who has beauty, is born of high caste, possesses infinite knowledge, character and profound wisdom is a man of true virtue."

Buddha questioned, "It is very rare to find in a man all these qualities! Tell me, couldn't an ugly man be virtuous?" Sonadanda was quick to grasp the purport of Buddha's question and replied, "Beauty, birth in a high caste and knowledge are not the essential ingredients of a virtuous man, but character and wisdom cannot be dispensed with."

Our rich heritage is full of shining examples of men and women who, by virtue of their character and wisdom, have become the hallmark of spiritual excellence.

Sage Ashtavakra and Kubja were by no means handsome, yet we respect them and draw inspiration from their virtuous lives. Beauty is by no means a measure of character.

The valiant Karna has said, "A person is born in a higher or lower caste by the wish of God." The character of Sage Vasishtha, Narad Muni, Shabri, Raidas and many others, though born of low caste, spoke amply about their nobility. Ravan, a Brahmin by caste, was swamped with evil notions and actions. Duryodhan, too, was of noble birth but no one today calls their son Duryodhan or Ravan. Hence, the belief that one born in aristocracy as an attribute of a virtuous person fails to convince.

Knowledge of scriptures, too, plays a tertiary role while describing a virtuous man. The milkmaids of Vrindavan were by no means pundits yet they have been hailed as Shrutis of the Vedas. We have had many lofty souls who possessed little or no extraordinary knowledge. Pujya Yogiji Maharaj had scant education but he had the power to touch the hearts of thousands by virtue of his profound saintliness and divinity. The acclaimed scholar of the Shrimad Bhagavad Gita, the late Pandurang Shastri, voiced his feelings when he met Yogiji Maharaj, "What Yogiji Maharaj has learnt only a handful today have been able to accomplish. He has learnt Brahmavidya."

Source of Virtue – Vedas

The Vedas are divine revelations recorded by our ancient seers. They prescribe how man can ensure happiness here and hereafter. Character and wisdom, that make a man virtuous, find their source in the Vedas.

Even our modern scientific theories, inventions and discoveries can be traced to the Vedas. The science of that age was seen through the eyepiece of spirituality and so it was utilized for peaceful and spiritually elevating purposes.

The late Shri Bharati Krishnatirthji, former Shankaracharya of Puri, discovered mathematics from the Vedas. His book, *Vedic Mathematics* includes 14 fundamental aphorisms through which problems in modern mathematics can be speedily solved. This book is now a standard textbook in several countries.

The Vedas have also thrown light on medicine, astronomy, chemistry and other branches of science. These subjects were taught in our ancient *gurukuls;* but emphasis was laid primarily on spiritual knowledge as a means for *moksha.* Both *apara vidya* (material knowledge) and *para vidya* (spiritual knowledge) were taught in our *gurukuls.*

Parã yayã tadaksharamadhigamyate

"*Para vidya* is that knowledge which takes us to Akshardham."

This had been the prime objective of education during the Vedic times. The inspirations from *para vidya* charged people to fare successfully through the straits of joy and happiness in life. They could effortlessly detach themselves from the forces of attachment, hatred, jealousy, ego, greed and anger.

Vedic Education

After having completed their studies disciples would take back with them a lofty message during a farewell convocation. The guru would place his hands on the student's shoulder and say,

Satyam vada, dharmam chara, svãdhyãyãnmã pramdaha,
Ãchãryãya priyam dhanamãhrutya prajãtantum mã vyavachchhetsihi;
Satyanna pramaditavyam, dharmanna pramaditavyam,
kushalãnna pramaditavyam, bhutyai na pramaditavyam,

svãdhyãya-pravachanãbhyãm na pramaditavyam.
Matrudevo bhava, pitrudevo bhava,
ãchãryadevo bhava, atithidevo bhava;
Yãnyanavadyãni karmãni, tãni sevitavyãni no itarãni,
Yãnyasmãkam sucharitãni, tãni tvayopãsyãni.
Esha ãdeshaha; Esha updeshaha, Eshã vedopanishat;
Etadanushãsanam evamupasitavyam.

"Dear child, always speak the truth, be bound morally, never refrain from studying the Vedas, don't offer money earned at the expense of hurting another's conscience to your guru, never be negligent in speaking the truth, never be negligent in observing dharma, never be negligent in good deeds and never be negligent in matters of personal progress. Recite the Vedas and deliver discourses. Respect your mother and father as gods, and likewise behold your guru and guests. Perform good deeds. Model your life after whatever good you've seen in this ashram. This is my message, the quintessence of the Vedas and Upanishads. This is my loving command, so you must obey."

The students, fortified by this sublime knowledge, would enter the portal of family living. Their learning played a major role in striking a balance in life. Their learning was conveyed from generation to generation, not merely through speech but also through example. These sages saw to it that their character was never tarnished by material desires.

The son of Brihaspati, Kachchha, desired to learn the 'Sanjivani Vidya' (knowledge that merits one with the power to revive a dead man). Shukracharya, their opponent, was the only one who could teach him the 'Sanjivani Vidya.' Shukracharya agreed. During those years of learning, Devyani, daughter of Shukracharya, fell in love with Kachchha. She proposed to him but Kachha refused. He said, "I cannot marry you because a guru's daughter is like a sister to all his students." But Devyani, overwhelmed with love pressed Kachchha to marry her. Again

Kachchha refused and didn't for one moment think of sacrificing his character to please Devyani. The beautiful Devyani, though hurt, rushed to seek her father's aid. Shukracharya, in a tide of sympathy, ignored his duty and summoned Kachchha. He insisted that Kachchha accept Devyani's hand in marriage. Kachchha politely refused. The guru, vexed at his disobedience, threatened him, "If you do not marry my daughter you shall forget the Sanjivani Vidya." But Kachchha remained undeterred. He remained firm, saying, "Gurudev! I would rather relinquish my Sanjivani Vidya than be a stigma to the very order of discipleship." He left the guru's ashram forgetting the Sanjivani Vidya, but adding a feather in the cap of the tradition of true discipleship.

Ram Rajya

Shri Ram, Sita and Lakshman were spending their days in exile in the forests. Sita was abducted by Ravan. While Ravan was on his way to Lanka, Sita threw some of her jewellery as a lead on Mt. Rishyamuk. Sugriv found some of them and kept them with him. In their search for Sita, both Ram and Lakshman came to the mountain. Sugriv, on their enquiry, brought Sita's jewellery and narrated what he had seen. Shri Ram gave the jewels to Lakshman to see if he could recognize them. Lakshman failed to identify Sita's earrings and a necklace, but when he saw her anklet he burst out joyfully, "This is mother Sita's anklet."

Ram asked him why he hadn't recognized Sita's earrings (*kundal*) and bracelet (*keyur*). In reply Lakshman answered,

Nãham jãnãmi keyuram, nãham jãnãmi kundalam,
Nupuram eva jãnãmi, nityam pãdãbhivandanãt.

"I have never seen mother Sita's earrings and her bracelet but while touching the dust of her holy feet everyday I had noticed these anklets."

For 14 long, testing years when only three individuals

lived and moved together in the forests, we find Lakshman serving both Ram and Sita with unswerving discipline. The epic Ramayan eloquently drives home a lesson of respect bordered with discipline. Lakshman attributes his nobility by saying,

Pitã yasya shuchimurto mãtã yasya pativratã,
Ubhãbhyãmeva sambhrutaha tasya no chalate manah.

"One's mind is never soiled by evil thoughts when one is born of pure noble parents."

Bharat bitterly refused the kingship acquired for him by his mother at the cost of Ram's exile. He lived a hermit's life during the entire 14 years. Sita went through the furnace of fiery trials - Ram having banished her - yet she entertained no ill feeling for Ram. On the contrary, like a flower that still offers fragrance when crushed, Sita said,

Bhuyo yathã me janannãnterapi,
Twamev bhartã na cha viprayogaha.

"O Ram, may you be my husband birth after birth."

The famous poet Kalidas describes the Raghu clan, "The descendants of the Raghu clan were noble and pure from birth." The Ram Rajya was indeed a noble empire established by luminous souls.

India's Glorious Society

The power of Sati Savitri's fidelity for her husband, Satyavan, saved him from the death noose of Yamraja. Nachiketa, the shining star of India's youths, remained resolute in acquiring the eternal knowledge and thus refused the pleasure of wealth and women offered by Yamraja.

Shravan's loving service to his aged parents, King Harishchandra's unparalleled sacrifice for truth, King Rantidev's charity of food after a spartan 49-day fast, the humility of King Ambarish and the valorous Arjun who saved himself from the infatuation of Urvashi's charms by calling her 'mother' are just a few of the many fragrant flowers that have bloomed in the garden of India.

The distinguished economist, the late Nani Palkhivala, with respect to Vedic Society, says, "Citizens were ranked in the society not by wealth or power but by the virtue and character they possessed."

"Is This Man?"

On the sands of time, the element of negligence has painted an ugly picture on our noble structure of character. Today we find theology has lost its appeal and technology has taken the lead. Metaphysics has been stripped of its prefix and now mere physics remains. Human values have degraded to alarming levels.

Alvin Toffler, author of *The Third Wave*, points out that after the Agricultural Revolution, the 17th century saw the birth of a second wave beginning with the Industrial Revolution. The second wave has left our society in a medley of mounting problems. We now live in a diseased society suffering from the virus of hatred, social tensions, corruption, crippling strikes and union agitation, energy crises, pollution, unemployment, loneliness, frustration, etc. The list is endless.

On 6 August 1945 man dropped the devastating atomic bomb on his own kind. It was the day when he relinquished his humanity and raised a cloud of doubt, "Is this man?"

2 VEDIC SOCIETY: II

Gujarati text: Sadhu Viveksagardas
Translation: Sadhu Vivekjivandas

Man is both a rational and a social animal. He lives in what we call a society, shaped by a wall of spiritual and moral regulations. If he breaks this wall and grazes in the pastures of free living, he courts his own ruin. He sins to a pitiful existence akin to that of animals.

Henry Ward Beecher describes the three planes of human living evident in our world, "Man at the bottom is an animal, midway a citizen, and at the top, divine. But the climate of the world is such that only a few reach the top."

Radhakrishnan, the renowned Indian philosopher and President of India observed that man has learnt to fly like a bird in the air, swim like a fish in water but failed to walk on earth as a sane human being.

The late J. Krishnamurti stressed, "Leave man by himself. He needs no guru!" But the truth is that a man does need a guru to pilot his ship through the rough seas of life. His life needs to be governed by dharma.

Man has often been likened to a bird confined in a cage. He has been born to live in a cage of moral disciplines. But, since he finds the restrictions uncomfortable he makes attempts to escape and fly wherever he pleases. Eventually, when he becomes saturated with dissatisfaction he returns to his cage. For a caged bird, home is none other than the cage itself. Its walls are by no means a hindrance or a challenge to his freedom. Who would say that the roots of a tree, which moor it to the ground, are a hindrance to the tree when they are the very means through which it is nourished? The strings of a sitar are tied from one end to the other but when plucked they speak the language of music. Similarly dharma binds man and when observed it speaks the language of happiness.

When you buy a domestic machine you'll find a manual describing how to use it. After having followed each step from the manual the machine will operate correctly. Likewise to operate the human machine correctly, whose supreme function is to worship God, we need a 'manual'. These 'Manuals of Mankind', called Yagnavalkya Smruti and Manu Smruti, have been prescribed by our Vedic sages. Bhagwan Swaminarayan in his code of conduct, called Shikshapatri, shows the ideals of manhood and means to ultimate liberation from verses 11 to 121. If we abide by the instructions from these manuals we would be contributing to the re-establishment of a Vedic society - fragrant in character and peaceful.

Man's Monstrosity!

During the Stone Age our ancestors fought and battled with stones and fists, in the Iron Age, they wielded swords and lances and presently we take pride in inventing powerful and sophisticated bombs. Man's instinct to kill his own kind out of hatred, enmity and fear has spurred him to invent an amazing arsenal of lethal weapons.

Do the boons of modern science speak of man as being civilized? No! At the most it shows that he has become modern! In a time where modernity is hailed and encouraged and spiritual values are scoffed at do we not find that peace evades man? He seeks the fleeting peace in addictions and indulgence and when this sickens him, he contemplates a final escape from all misery - suicide. An opulent area in Chicago earned its name, 'Suicide Belt', when it hit the headlines for its alarming suicide cases. And what's more surprising is the French publication called *Suicide Manual,* which guarantees a successful suicide!

Achievement of Science - Death

The Vedic civilization, Roman civilization, Babylonian civilization, Mesopotamian civilization and the Egyptian civilization were all born to ameliorate human society. The remnants of the Mohenjodaro civilization in India, from over 4,500 years ago, has revealed the ingenuity and strong character of its people. Today, however, the story is different. We find ourselves holidaying on the shore of a 'Neutron Age'. An age where man's value has been relegated to mere nothingness. This sad fact is reflected in the invention of the neutron bomb - a bomb that destroys all life but saves what man has created.

Swami Vivekanand describes, "Each soul is potentially divine," but do we not find that, "normal man has proved himself to be a monster may times over". The orgy of violence and destruction unleashed by Idi Amin stripped Uganda of its dignity and prosperity. It is at such junctures in human history that the eternal words of the Vedas become more relevant:

Manuhu bhava!
Brother, become a 'man'.
Pumãn pumãnsam paripãtu vishvataha!
Man protects his own kind in all ways.
Mitrasyãham chakshushã sarvãni bhutani samikshe!
I look at all things with an eye of friendship.
Sarve bhadrãni pashyantu!
May all be blessed with auspiciousness.

Our first objective should be to become a 'man'. We should give priority in directing our thoughts and actions in the process of self-making. Garfield was once asked, "Do you want to be an engineer or a doctor?" He replied, "First I want to be a man."

Today we have many doctors and engineers but very few men.

Addictions

To sedate his consciousness from self inflicted miseries man vainly pursues the momentary elation he derives from addictions. It is indeed a woeful tale that he makes little effort to delight in the pool of *atmic* happiness. He arrogantly lifts his glass of liquor and proclaims, "It gives me a kick." How right he is. His addiction 'kicks' him out of his home, his society and the world. One who remains subdued under the influence of intoxicants fails to grasp the poetry of life.

We call our society a 'Free Society' but the naked fact is that this 'Free Society' of ours is under the slavish influence of vices and addictions.

A growing part of our society has come to accept lewd entertainment catered in hotels, on the big screen and television and in magazines as a part of enjoyment in life. Many parents set a bad example for their children by sipping liquor and paging through pornographic magazines.

"Living in sin is an accepted way of life in Sweden," says a leading Swedish newspaper. The consequences of this tremendous erosion of morals have damaged and even destroyed the various edifices of culture throughout the world. The generations that follow degenerate in the prevailing immoral environment.

We spend billions in cleaning our rivers and keeping the air we breathe free from pollution but rarely do we focus our attention in combating our inner pollutants.

We Need Pure People Today!

To usher a silent revolution of self-purification we need the mighty leadership and strength of a God-communion sadhu. An advert in a Texas daily read, 'Wanted Holy Men.' We all need holy men.

During Pramukh Swami Maharaj's visit to Rochester, USA, the Mayor, while presenting the Key to the City, said, "Our culture is like a worthless glittering gem whereas yours is a priceless jewel. I humbly request you to tell your people to remain wedded to your ideals. And this I shall take to be your people's greatest contribution for the progress of America."

Some progressive streams in Christianity, like the Mormons ban their adherents from smoking and drug taking. The Seventh Day Adventist Church insists on a vegetarian diet and an addiction-free life.

In a suburb of Lancaster, Pennsylvania, the Amish and Mennonites still follow the lifestyle their forefathers had lived. Rather than accept the blessings of science and technology they have chosen to live in simplicity. They use oil lamps to illuminate their homes, plough their land with horses and wear traditional clothes similar to what their forefathers wore. They are a hard-working and a God-fearing people. Through all these years their community has remained steadfast in their simple lifestyle and profound faith in God.

The story of how the Jews, in spite of their fiery trials and tribulations, displayed their granitic religious faith is very inspiring. Today we find its people dotted throughout the world, taking pride in their faith and customs. They have survived the cultural 'melting pot' in America and have held their banners high with added gusto. Many Jewish people wed their daughters only to bridegrooms who know Hebrew. If India should pass a law that a Hindu bride should be betrothed only to a bridegroom knowing Sanskrit, there would be a revival of our glorious Ram Rajya culture, because the roots of our culture lies in our rich and inspiring Sanskrit language.

3 VEDIC SOCIETY: III

Gujarati text: Sadhu Viveksagardas
Translation: Sadhu Vivekjivandas

- In the 1980s, the Prime Minister of Singapore, Lee Kuan Yew, having observed a sharp drop in the moral values in his country, introduced a campaign to spread the ideals of Confucianism. Cham Longe, a minister, in spite of furious public opposition, shut down one of the city's red-light areas.
- In the 1980s, the Prime Minister of Malawi, Dr Banda, bitterly denounced ball-dances and mini-skirts in his country.
- In Thailand, to maintain its Buddhist culture every student, by law, has to spend at least six months as a Buddhist monk.
- In many countries we find more and more people taking to vegetarianism through the efforts of vegetarian societies that have sprung up rapidly during the last few years. Advertisements on the hazards of smoking and drinking alcohol have inspired thousands in recent years to give them up altogether. If such a campaign against the evils of society is kept up, the dark clouds hovering on our horizon will get dispersed.

Arnold Toynbee, an eminent British historian, foresaw a surge in oriental values that would lead to the revival of the West. He said, "It is already becoming clear that a chapter which had a Western beginning will have to have an Indian ending if it is not to end in the self-destruction of the human race. At this supremely dangerous moment in human history, the only way of salvation for mankind is the Indian way."

Max Mueller, the German philosopher and Indologist, deeply impressed by Indian Culture, said, "If I were to look over the whole world to find out the country most richly endowed with all the wealth, power and beauty that nature can bestow, in some parts a very paradise on earth, I should point to India.

"If I were asked under what sky the human mind has most fully developed some of its choicest gifts, has most deeply pondered on the greatest problems of life and has found solutions to some of them which will deserve the attention even of those who have studied Plato and Kant, I should point to India.

"And if I were to ask myself from what literature we, here in Europe, we who have been nurtured most exclusively on the thoughts of the Greeks and Romans and of the Semitic race, the Jewish, may draw that corrective which is most wanted in order to make our inner life more comprehensive, more universal, in fact a more truly human life, not for this life only, but a transfigured and eternal life, again I should point to India."

Indian culture had spread its wings to far off countries. Even today we still find Hindu culture in countries like Thailand, Burma, Japan, Kampuchea, Latin America and scores of other places.

The last few decades have been witness to an increasing demand for Indian thought and culture in the West. Thousands of institutions teaching Indian languages, yoga, philosophy, traditions, arts, crafts and culture have sprung up. Indeed, one such school, St. James' High School in Kensington, London, has been overwhelmingly successful. The school teaches Sanskrit to its young primary and secondary pupils. The administrators believe that Vedic culture ranks among the noblest of all cultures; one that, if sincerely adhered to, could forge peace in our world. The immortalizing nectar of Vedic Culture is locked in our Sanskrit language. And it is with this objective that St. James' School has been teaching Sanskrit to its pupils from the age of five to seventeen. It is a compulsory subject for all students. And a point worth appreciating is that all its teachers are required to know Sanskrit and be free from any addictions whatsoever.

While we find the West drawn towards the splendour of Indian Culture, India on the contrary, allows its sails to be filled by the winds of materialism blowing from the West. The late Nani Palkhivala, an eminent Indian economist, pertinently points out, "India is like a donkey who doesn't know what it is carrying." It forgets that its Vedic Culture is the mother hen of all cultures. We have forgotten that we are the sons of a noble culture. Our situation is like the donkey described in the following *shlok,*

"Yathã kharshchandanbhãrvãhi bhãrasya vettã na tu chandansya."

"When a sack of sandalwood is placed on a donkey, the beast of burden merely takes it to be another load."

The Modern 'Tripur'

In the Shrimad Bhagvat we find the story of a demon, Mai, who presented three gigantic flying machines to his demon brethrens. Each of the machines, one of gold, another of silver and the third made of iron, were the size of a large city. Wherever these flying machines attacked they pulverized the existing moral and spiritual structure and established their own materialistic hierarchy. When the demons started to spread his net of evil and materialism, God stalled their efforts and destroyed the three flying machines and from that day he has been hailed as 'Tripurari'.

Today, we find these three flying machines locked on a path of destruction. Let us have a look at the way in which these flying machines, namely the gold, silver and iron are destroying our culture.

We can relate the 'Gold' machine to our affluent society, with particular reference to its materialism. Today this disturbing torrent of materialism in our world has swept many Indians from their moral and spiritual grounds. Their comfy homes have no home mandirs for worship and devotion. And instead of their shelves being packed with inspiring scriptures like the Bhagavad Gita, Upanishads, Vachanamrut and other inspiring texts, we find magazines and paperbacks on romance and suspense. Their dining tables are often littered with bottles of beer.

If you happen to wear some traditional Indian clothes you may well be derided for being rural and backward. Parents are often proud of their children's fluency in English and indifferent to their ignorance of their native language. Sanskrit pundits are scoffed at and termed as 'vediyas'. The ennobling stages of practising our 16 *sanskars* have now become extinct. This is indeed in sharp contrast to our forefathers.

In olden times our people in India remained steadfast in their faith and morals. They refused to remove their sacred thread and *tilak* and *chandlo* in spite of heavy persecution. Today the picture is quite different! In an Independent India these auspicious signs and customs are dying away. We are now witnessing an influence of the 'Gold' machine on the cultural landscape of India.

The 'Silver' flying machine ushers an eat, drink and be merry philosophy as the prime objective of life. Those under the influence of the 'Gold' machine wallow in a greater degree of mundaneness than the 'Silver' machine society.

The 'Iron' flying machine fans the fires of murder, prostitution, stealing, corruption and a host of other evils.

We find that India, like many other countries, is morally, ablaze. These flying machines are wreaking havoc and destruction on our culture. Out of these three machines, any one of them descends on hundreds of people everyday to destroy their moral and spiritual ethos. It behoves upon us to be alert from being crushed by the influence of any of these three lethal machines.

Traditions Are Being Strangled!

In recent years we have seen the birth of the disco age in India. It has created a wave of frenzy among the young generation. This particular mode of entertainment has also entered the religious arena. Our sacred and auspicious mantra, 'Hari Aum', has now become a part of many disco songs. We find disco dances held under the false pretext of worship in the presence of a *murti* of Ganapati. During the Navratri festival, disco dances, with a *murti* of Mataji, have now become a source of distasteful entertainment rather than worship. The spiritual element in our festivals has begun to fade. During great holy festivals like Janmashtmi and Shivratri people are busy gambling in a game of cards and intoxicating themselves with bhang.

Where other religions are inexorably making efforts to preserve their culture, we have been wilfully trying to remain untouched by ours. Our interests have become more mundane and gross. We steer our efforts according to the prevailing winds in society. We find people spending lavishly on antiques to add lustre to their homes but how many furnish their homes with a *murti* of God and our cultural values – the most valuable antiques of all.

Everyone must have observed insects attracted by the light of a lamp. They cannot resist the infatuation towards the light in spite of them seeing their brothers perish. Likewise, the Eastern Hemisphere, in spite of seeing the miseries and frustrations that overwhelm the affluent lifestyle are still irresistibly drawn towards the inevitable pit of unhappiness.

The unhealthy times have left our society crippled of its morals and drained of its spiritual vitality. It is during such times of estrangement from righteousness that God comes to our rescue and repairs the moral fabric of society.

4 VEDIC SOCIETY: IV

Gujarati text: Sadhu Viveksagardas
Translation: Sadhu Vivekjivandas

Three Sources of Virtue

Our scriptures, mandirs and sadhus have, for centuries, played a paramount role in ennobling and redeeming our society. Even today, whatever virtues and spiritualism people have derived in India and the world over can be traced to these three indispensable fountainheads. In the absence of any of these three our world would have long ago plunged into a nightmarish darkness of evil and suffering.

How have our Vedic scriptures, mandirs and sadhus been lightening the burden of our mounting sin and suffering in society?

Scriptures

Our scriptures have conferred inspiring boons, some of which have become a part of our daily life. For example, the role we have come to naturally accept in our ties with our mother, sister and wife find their origin in our scriptures. Our scriptures seek to enlighten us through inspiring messages and stories of heroes wedded to truth and endowed with character. They have also chronicled the cruel fate of men and women who strayed and defied the injunctions of God. Ravan's lust for Sita spelled his doom. His vast empire based on wealth and power perished with him.

Mandirs

Like the scriptures, our glorious mandirs have always acted

as beacons of inspiration. They have contributed a significant share in shaping our lives both physically and spiritually. A mandir in a town or a village invariably inspires its congregation to wash or to take a bath before entering its sacred precincts for worship. Mandirs have come to incorporate and sought to encourage the skill and imagination of its sculptors and architects. They have become mediums which preserve our traditions in art and sculpting. It is under that large stone canopy, in front of the deity, that people feel humble and flood their hearts with the poetry of divine love. Is it not true that at the altar of God man often stands on the threshold of a vision that he is merely an instrument in his divine play?

He is also made aware of the fact that to come near God, the choicest devotee of God should be his ideal. That he should attain the eternal state of *akshar-rup* to enjoy the privilege of offering supreme devotion to God.

With these noble inspirations and many more, his miseries evaporate; he once again becomes charged to battle the frustration and tensions of daily life.

Mandirs have also ideally played a pivotal role in uniting India. More than 3,500,000 mandirs in India have knitted the cultural and spiritual strands of the Indian people to produce a beautiful tapestry of a united India.

Three hundred mandirs in Mauritius, along with festivals, have kept the spirit of Hinduism alive among the descendents of Hindus who migrated there 300 years ago.

Fish of the Earthly Lake

The third and final source of virtues are the sadhus and sages of our country. They have appropriately been sung of as the fish in the lake of *sansar*. Like the fish that strive to keep our rivers and lakes clean and fresh, sadhus persevere in cleansing our society of its garbage of corruption, addictions and immorality.

Very often we have seen that government fails to enforce a law to stop people from drinking. In spite of heavy penalties and punishments people keep on drinking. Where the law has often failed, the sadhus have triumphed with their patient and loving efforts.

We hear the world clamouring for good doctors, proficient lawyers, good policemen... and to these let us add genuine sadhus. It will be the bona fide sadhus who will cure our diseased souls, combat evil and discipline our unruly elements. They share their goodness for the happiness and spiritual progress of mankind. Remember man does not live by bread alone. Fulfilling the physical and educational hunger of a child is in itself not enough. He is unlike an animal that is satisfied when provided with food and water. He is born with a mission to shape a destiny for himself that will take him beyond the frontiers of our fleeting pleasures and fragile existence. And to achieve this, dharma, the bestower of happiness, is one of the fundamental needs. If this food is not provided he vainly searches for an illusory happiness in drugs, addictions and licentiousness. This dharma - the bread of the soul - is provided by the bona fide sadhus of our society.

Custodian of Culture

If it hadn't been for the priceless blessings of our scriptures, mandirs and sadhus our Vedic culture would have become a thing of the past. The sadhus' presence as custodians and propagators has enabled us to avail ourselves of benevolence and vast treasures. Whenever these three sources have been ignored, or have been in peril, the very backbone of our cultural framework has come dangerously close to snapping.

Two hundred years ago, the immense pressures of corruption, hypocrisy, animal sacrifices and scores of other evils sought to pulverize the edifice of Indian Culture. This catastrophe was however averted with the advent of Bhagwan

Swaminarayan in 1781. Under the banner of dharma he vigorously crusaded against the social evils that plagued the society of his day. He was successful in wiping out the *sati* practice, female infanticide, and animal sacrifices in *yagnas*. Besides this, he transformed hard-core criminals into humble, peace-loving disciples. During his earthly journey of 49 years he sang the glories of our scriptures, initiated over 500 into the highest saintly order of *paramhansa* and built six lofty mandirs. His teachings appealed to all, laying particular stress in identifying oneself with Brahma as a requirement for supreme devotion to Parabrahma.

Revival of Vedic Society

To share these rare gems of Bhagwan Swaminarayan's teachings, His Divine Holiness Pramukh Swami Maharaj moves amid the masses of today. Wherever he goes he ushers in a wonderful revolution. Young and old, poor and rich find themselves enriched after meeting him. Thousands living in the tribal areas are abstaining from vices and addictions and have adopted a healthier, more prosperous mode of living. Besides worship and prayer they have also taken to preaching Swami's noble message to others in their areas.

Under Swamiji's effort and inspiration thousands of youth and children's centres, fragrant with character, faith and sacrifice have blossomed. His dynamic efforts have evoked a tremendous amount of goodness. He has established over 500 mandirs in India and abroad. The beautiful Shri Swaminarayan Mandirs in London, Nairobi, Houston and Chicago, and the Akshardham monuments in Gandhinagar and New Delhi have inspired millions with morality and pride in India's glorious heritage.

Seven hundred sadhus, the majority of whom have been initiated by Swamiji, have added momentum to his noble mission. They harness their knowledge and talents to sow the seeds of Satsang. Swamiji, too, tirelessly moves, reviving and rebuilding the towns, villages and individuals that have been hit by the material culture of the three flying machines of gold, silver and iron. His immense compassion and selfless love have effected miracles of man-making. Let us also become worthy of his abundant grace by imbibing his message, "Exemplify morality and promote a morally sound society."

5 THE VEDAS

Sadhu Anandswarupdas

- Jean Le Mee in *Hymns from the Rig Veda* describes the immortality of the Vedas, "Precious or durable materials - gold, silver, bronze, marble, onyx, granite - have been used by most ancient people in an attempt to immortalize their achievements. Not so, however, with the ancient Aryans. They turned to what may seem the most volatile and insubstantial material of all - the spoken word - and out of this bubble of air, fashioned a monument which more than thirty, perhaps forty centuries later stands untouched by time or other elements. For, the Pyramids have been eroded by the desert winds, the marble broken by earthquakes and gold stolen by robbers, while the Veda remains, recited daily by an unbroken chain of generations, travelling like a great wave through the living substance of mind."
- A.C. Bose, an Indian philosopher, says in his book *Vedas Indian Inheritance*, "If great poetry is the combination of what have been called the 'emphasis of sound' and the 'emphasis of sense', if it unites imagery and melody into a complete whole, then there is no truer or greater poetry than we find in the finest of Vedic verses."

What are the Vedas? The word Veda is derived from the Sanskrit root 'vid' which means 'to know'. Therefore Veda literally means 'knowledge'. As the core of this knowledge is concerned with the Ultimate Eternal Reality, God, the Vedas came to mean the 'Supreme Knowledge' or the 'Knowledge of

God'. Because God is infinite and eternal, the 'knowledge of God' is also infinite and eternal. Therefore the Vedas, i.e., 'knowledge of God', are inexhaustible and exist eternally. Portions of this knowledge were 'seen' and 'heard' by hundreds of Hindu sages and seers in their supranormal consciousness. They were direct revelations from God. Thus they are called *apaurusheya,* i.e., not of human origin. For centuries, these experiences were passed down from generation to generation through an elaborate oral tradition to prevent any distortion. They were later recorded to form the Vedic literature. Vedic literature is the secondary meaning of the word Vedas.

Tradition holds that the great sage Vyas compiled these lofty intuitive experiences at the beginning of the present age; the dark age, Kali Yuga (about 3000 BCE). He classified them into four great works: the Rig Veda, the Yajur Veda, the Sama Veda and the Atharva Veda. Each of these great works has three main divisions: the Samhitas, the Brahmanas and the Aranyakas. Most of the famous Upanishads are found in the Aranyakas. The Samhitas are mostly written in the form of poetry or hymns whereas the Brahmanas are in prose. The Rig Veda contains 10,552 hymns, the Sama Veda 1,875, the Yajur Veda 1,975 and the Atharva Veda 5,987, making a total of 20,389 hymns. We may loosely say that the Samhitas and the Brahmanas deal mainly with rituals, the Aranyakas with meditation and the Upanishads with supreme knowledge.

Many portions of the Vedas describe various types of offerings (*yagnas*). The purpose of this offering is to purify the mind to receive the knowledge of God, which we find primarily in the Upanishads. Besides this, various other hymns are recited on different occasions to sanctify persons, things, and the departed souls of the dead. Certain portions of Yajur Veda and Atharva Veda deal with man's life, protection from enemies, kings and politics.

If we wish to describe the Vedas in a nutshell, we may say that they are infallible and the highest authority. Almost all other Hindu religio-philosophical texts trace their origin to the Vedas.

The truths enshrined in them are eternal, uncreated, extrasensory and even beyond the comprehension of the human mind. According to the Vedic sages, at the highest mystical and spiritual level, when the self is purified through discipline, these truths are 'seen' or 'heard' directly, followed by an immediate experience of God. Although the Vedic sages felt that these experiences could never be expressed adequately through words they have done so for there was no better medium of conveying them.

Many religious beliefs can be found in the Vedas. Because the Vedic people frolicked in the lap of nature, many a time they have personified, deified and worshipped the different forces of nature like water, fire, wind, etc. Later on, they accepted God as the Supreme Being, the creator of nature and the source of goodness and truth. Consequently they laid emphasis on the necessity of worshipping God. This led to the development of media like ritualism and sacrifices (*yagnas*). Sometimes ritualism is subordinated and a direct union with God is urged.

The goal of human life is to seek union with him. There are many ways to achieve this, but self-sacrifice and discipline are pre-requisites of such a union. One should totally dedicate one's life to God. Note that this does not mean that one should negate the responsibilities of a family life. A spiritual life lived rightly also encompasses within its fold the social responsibilities of a householder.

The perception of order in the natural world led the Vedic people to the concept of 'Rita'. 'Rita' is the Eternal Law that maintains order in the universe.

There should also be order in our lives. Our lives are

governed by the Law of Karma according to which 'As you sow, so shall you reap', so everyone is responsible for his actions and their consequences. God is the dispenser of the fruits of karma. Moral norms and self-discipline are considered to be the foundations of an individual's life and a healthy society thereof.

There are many who accept that Brahma is the Ultimate Reality, and that the individual self *(atma)* and Brahma are one. But Bhagwan Swaminarayan has a different stand on the basis of the Vedas. He preached Parabrahma to be a reality higher than even Brahma. He says: "Parabrahma is distinct and separate from Brahma. He is the supporter, inspirer and cause of Brahma. With this knowledge of Brahma, the spiritual aspirant should identify himself with Brahma, and worship Parabrahma as his Lord, upholding the ideal of the servitor-mentor relationship. Realization of such knowledge brings ultimate salvation."

It is very difficult to grasp the full import of the Vedas, but it breathes out the message of peace and harmony:

Let your aim be one and single,
Let your hearts be joined in one,
The mind at rest in unison
At peace with all, so may you be.

(Rig Veda 10.191.4)

6 MURTI PUJA

Sadhu Anandswarupdas

When was murti puja born?
What do the major religions say about murti puja?
Does it play an important role in shaping our lives?
This article deals with some salient aspects
of murti puja – image worship.

Mysterious are the ways in which people are sometimes drawn towards image worship. Thakorbhai Patel, an eminent gynaecologist, was elected the Mayor of Vadodara City in the late 1960's. During this term, he contracted a fatal disease. An abscess in his liver threatened to kill him. He was also bleeding internally. As an expert medical doctor he knew, rather too well, that he would breathe his last within a few days.

It is one thing to speak of death but altogether different when a person comes face-to-face with it.

Thakorbhai became desperate. He wanted help. Someone suggested the name of Yogiji Maharaj, a very humble and pious sadhu. But Thakorbhai had no religious inclinations. Far from it, he fancied that an idol is no more than a piece of stone, God a myth and sadhus a burden on society.

Nevertheless, with the survival instinct at play, he went to meet Yogiji Maharaj with a doubting mind and a longing heart. Yogiji Maharaj consoled him, gave him sanctified water and advised him to drink it daily. Thakorbhai was overwhelmed by his utter simplicity, transparent purity and selfless love. So he willingly accepted the humble gift.

The first spoonful of the sanctified water stopped his

bleeding. With some more spoonfuls his disease was cured. He was amazed. Although what occurred was contrary to his years of experience, something beyond his ken, he said, "I am a changed man. Now I have come to believe in image worship and God, not so much because I was miraculously saved, but because I experienced the Divine in Yogiji Maharaj."

Belief in image worship is born, nourished and consolidated by the contact of a God-communion sadhu. Not all are fortunate like Thakorbhai and come across a sadhu like Yogiji Maharaj. So naturally they have questions about image worship. They want to know more about it.

The precise date of the beginnings of image worship is not known. However, the earliest spiritual texts of the world, the Vedas, refer to it, both covertly as well as overtly. The seed of image worship lies certainly in the idea of a personal God, that is, God having a form.

A spiritual aspirant not only loves God but also experiences love from him. However, one can only love or experience love from someone who has a living form. So, it obviously follows that God has a form, that is, he is personal. The aspirant also believes that this God, is infinite, all-powerful, all-merciful, all-pervasive, all-knowing and the fountainhead of all goodness. You may question how God, who is infinite, can have a form? But the aspirant is not worried by this query, for he believes that God is above all contradictions. For him, it is only love that matters.

Humans need something that they can adore and worship. Thus we have the rituals and the worship of symbols and idols, that mediate between man and God.

Benefits of Image Worship

Ultimate redemption of the soul is possible only through the service of God or a God-communion sadhu, who is present on this earth in human form. But it requires spiritual insight to know and understand them. Sages and seers have, therefore, enjoined image worship. This is never misleading. In fact this kind of worship purifies the senses and mind to such an extent that the worshipper can readily perceive the difference between a true sadhu and an impostor.

Purification of the Senses and Mind

The senses are purified because the body is involved in worship. And the mind is purified because the worshipper, while worshipping the idol, does not take it to be a piece of stone but mentally attributes to it the qualities of God. The more he thinks of it the purer he becomes. Purification corresponds to concentration. It is easy to concentrate when the image is in a human form. Image worshippers, therefore, prefer such an idol.

Queries Regarding Image Worship

Some people ask, "How can an infinite God reside in an image?" This question would not arise at all were they to believe that God is omnipresent. Since, if God is present everywhere, he cannot be absent from an idol.

There are others who ask, "How is it that the presence of God is more pronounced in an idol than other things?" For a moment let us forget other things and consider human beings. It is a fact that God's presence is more in some people than others. Otherwise, how would you account for saintly people like Mirabai and Tulsidas, Eknath and Tukaram, Gunatitanand Swami and Bhagatji Maharaj? When ordinary people come into contact with such sadhus, God within them starts manifesting. The more the contact, the greater is the manifestation and the more the presence of God is felt. Such sadhus, who have the power to make the presence of God felt in human beings, also have the power to invoke God in an image.

The history of religion is replete with incidents wherein the idol has responded to the loving calls of the devotees. No less are such incidents even in the history of the Swaminarayan Sampraday.

Premanand Swami was garlanded by the idol of Bhagwan Swaminarayan when he was engrossed in singing his glory. Yogiji Maharaj had frequent talks with the idol. We too can see the actual presence of God in an image, provided our hearts are pure.

Image Worship in Some Major Religions of the World

Hinduism believes in image worship. For Hindus it is a wonderful technique devised by divine personages to assist devotees to reach God.

Buddhism doesn't believe in God. So the subject of image worship holds no meaning. Nevertheless, we see thousands of images of its founder, Gautam Buddha, being worshipped akin to a personal God. This is also true of Jainism, in which images of Mahavir are worshipped.

Christianity does not believe in image worship. But a lot of image worship has crept into its main division, namely, Roman Catholicism. Even the next major division, Protestantism, holds churches as more sacred than other places. And for them the Bible has a special significance. The Catholics, therefore, charge them with the defect of Bibliolatry. They in turn charge the Catholics with the flaw of Mariolary, because there are images of Mary in churches. They are adored, respected and worshipped.

Islam strongly condemns image worship. Worship of any form is considered sinful by the Muslims. But they don't think so when they kiss their most sacred shrine, the black Kaaba stone. Wherever they pray they have to visualize mentally that they are standing before the Kaaba. They believe that the millions of kisses stamped on it by them will stand up as witnesses for their benefit, on the Day of Judgement. Isn't this also a kind of image worship?

Thus, in the major religions of the world we perceive at least some kind of image worship.

Swami Vivekanand was bold enough to say that every spiritual leader is an idolater as he has not fully realized God and his soul. And this is quite true, for it is impossible to conceive of God without associating him with some form or the other.

When such exalted souls practice image worship, why shouldn't we?

7 GOD EXISTS: I

Sadhu Atmaswarupdas

Does God Exist?

It is a million dollar question that has exercised man's mind for ages. Of course, the question has been answered time and time again. However, doubts continue to persist about the existence of God. Perhaps it would be appropriate to examine the reasons for such doubts so that the problem can be tackled at the very root.

Causes for Doubts About God's Existence

The foremost cause for such a doubt is man's ego, which prevents him from accepting an authority above himself. That would mean playing second fiddle to God. The inflated ego does not permit one to accept God as a divine, superior power.

Abraham Lincoln had echoed the same feeling saying: "We have been recipients of the choicest bounties of Heaven... but we have forgotten God... we have vainly imagined that all these blessings were produced by some superior wisdom and virtue of our own. We have become too proud to pray to God that made us... I set apart 30th April 1863, as a day of national humiliation, fasting and prayer."

Another reason is that with the advances in science and technology, people have become sceptical about their belief in God. They ask such questions as: "We cannot see God so how can we accept him? God cannot be proved through experiment in a laboratory, so how can we accept his existence?" Such people forget that there are many things in the world which are beyond reason. Someone said that a mind all logic is like a knife all blade which makes the hand that uses it bleed. Yet, such doubts never leave the minds of rational people.

Yet another cause for atheism is the fanatical attitude of some religions. Their fanaticism leads them to denounce other religions, thus hurting the feelings of the followers of such religions. Man looks to religion as the uniting force of humanity, but such fanatics, who constantly strike a discordant note, engender disbelief in God among the more sensitive people.

Association with impostors is also another cause for losing faith in God. In the name of religion, they bank on man's inherent fear of God and try to exploit credulous people to serve their selfish ends. However, when these innocent people come to know of the impostors' misdeeds they tend to lose faith in God. They simply cannot stand 'cheating' in the name of religion. The consequence of this is that people then develop disbelief in the words of even true saints and sages, who are the upholders of religion and belief in God.

Atheism also develops in one who constantly reads literature that tends to undermine the belief in and existence of God.

The base natures of man, passion, anger, greed, egoism and jealousy also prevent people from accepting the authority of even God-realized persons. Hence, doubts about the very existence of God always linger on in their minds.

Finally, one thing is certain. Even great scholars of religious texts fail to understand the true glory of God as they ascribe human failings even to God, just as they themselves have such shortcomings.

Having examined the causes for atheism, let us examine the basic qualifications required to develop faith in God.

How Can We Develop Faith in God?

Certain basic attributes must be nurtured if we are to

develop faith in God. They are as follows:

1. If we can understand the glory of God then we will start believing in the divine (Vachanamrut, Gadhada II 16).
2. We can be convinced of God's existence through inference. We can see flames, smoke and clouds rising up in the sky, but we cannot see the wind that causes them to rise. So, we can certainly infer the existence of wind from this phenomenon. Similarly, God can be inferred from his works.
3. We can be certain of God's existence provided we tread the path of God-realization. Yogi Krishna Prem, a Vaishnav sadhu, once explained to his friend, "The Grand Trunk Road leads to Delhi. How do you know? Tread on it and you will know." Thus, mere theorizing does not help us to develop faith in God; one has to practice the various disciplines.

Perseverance is another requisite to realize God. K.M. Munshi, the founder President of Bhartiya Vidya Bhavan, once wrote, "I took 16 years to gain a degree, and yet another 12 years to become a good lawyer. But in matters of religion, I wanted immediate results." You cannot get mangoes the day after sowing a seed. It takes time. But once one has that vision, it is as E. Schroedinger, a Nobel laureate in Physics, said, "We know when God is experienced that this is an event as real as an immediate sense perception or as one's own personality."

Once a disciple asked his guru, "Have you seen God?" The guru replied, "Yes, I have seen God." The disciple became impatient and said, "Then show me God." The guru promised that he would show him God. After a few days, the residents of the ashram happened to go to a nearby lake for a bath. The guru also accompanied them. The enquiring disciple was also with them. They all plunged into the lake. After a while, the guru went near the disciple, caught hold of his head and submerged it under water. The disciple struggled hard to surface above the water. But the guru continued to hold him under water. After an intense struggle the disciple managed to loosen the guru's grip. When he came out, he began to gasp for breath. In a couple of minutes he came round and charged the guru with trying to kill him. The guru pretended not to hear the complaint. On the contrary, he asked the disciple, "What were you doing under water." The disciple, in a fit of anger, retorted, "Good heavens! You seem to be least bothered about my life. Didn't you see how frantically I had to struggle to loosen your grip on my head? How can you be so cruel?" The guru again asked him, "But why did you struggle so frantically to loosen my grip?" The disciple retorted, "Why not? It was a matter of life and death for me. Had I not struggled so hard, I would have died." The guru then told the disciple, "Just as you struggled so hard to save your life, have you undertaken an equally frantic struggle to see God? If you do so, then God will certainly reveal himself to you."

The moral of the story is that we have to make an effort to realize God.

Also, there are some things which lie beyond the intellect. Bertrand Russell in his book *What I Believe* confesses, "In the near future when the volume of evidence will increase quantitatively, we shall have to revise our opinion and come in line with the findings of religion which are so often branded as trash." Even Pascal has said, "The heart has reasons of its own, which the head can never understand." Jean Jacques Rousseau, the 18th century French philosopher, opines, "Above the logic of the head is the feeling of the heart." The Bible says, "Blessed are the pure in heart for they shall see God." Bergson has rightly directed our attention to the possibilities of intuition as a conveyor of direct knowledge. When the heart is thoroughly purified, one develops a sixth sense, i.e., intuition of a purified heart, through which comes the experience of supersensory realities that lie beyond the intellect. The Taittiriya Upanishad has underlined the principle thus: "*Yato vãcho nivartante aprãpya manasã saha.*" That is, "The mind and speech cannot approach God and return to their empiric state."

In the Bhagavad Gita, when Shri Krishna manifested before Arjun in all his glory, Arjun just could not look at him until he was granted divine vision by Krishna.

During the 1977 satsang tour abroad by His Divine Holiness Pramukh Swami Maharaj, a press reporter asked him in an interview: "Why can't we see God?" Back came the reply from Swamishri, "We do see him but just can't believe him to be God."

Bhagwan Swaminarayan has explained the same in his discourses called the Vachanamrut, "A diamond can be cut only by a diamond; it can never be cut by anything else. Similarly, the conviction of God can only be cultivated through God. In the same way, the darshan of God is also possible only through God, but it is not possible through the *mãyik indriyas* and *antahkarans*" (Gadhada I 51).

Thus, God is beyond our understanding, but through his grace, we can know him.

The next point which goes a long way in nurturing our faith in God is belief in the scriptures and the God-communion Sadhu.

Bhagwan Swaminarayan says that the scriptures are the source of prevalence of dharma. One who has not read the scriptures, even unknowingly conforms to the rules laid down in the scriptures and acts accordingly with his mother, sister, wife, daughter, etc. These relations and its definitions have been born out of the scriptures and one holds them to be true and behaves with one's relations according to the code of behaviour so laid down. The scriptures are therefore the great and only authority. But one who does not respect these scriptures and acts according to his own conception is a heretic. And one who takes the authority of the scriptures has a strong foundation for the path of God-realization (Vachanamrut, Sarangpur 13).

Bhagwan Swaminarayan says that scepticism develops when one reads scriptures which deny God. The company of believers in such scriptures is also sure to turn one into an atheist. However, if one desires to drive out such sceptic influence from one's mind, one should read holy scriptures like the Shrimad Bhagvat, etc. (Vachanamrut, Gadhada I 68).

He goes on to say further that the sadhu in whom the vital redemptive attributes *(nishkam, nirlobh, nisswad, nissneh,* and *nirman)* are displayed is said to have established rapport with God. Therefore, his words should be taken as the ultimate truth, and the knowledge of God that he infuses in the disciples is the ultimate knowledge and the eternal truth (Vachanamrut, Gadhada III 27).

His Divine Holiness Yogiji Maharaj was often found talking to the *murti* of God. Once, an enquiring aspirant asked, "Swami, we can hear you talking to the *murti* of God. But, does God ever respond?" Swamishri said, "Of course, he invariably talks to me." The aspirant asked further, "Why is it then that we can never hear that voice?" Swamishri replied, "Well, it is like connecting a telephone call to someone. At my end you can hear my part of the conversation, but can you hear what the party at the other end is saying?" Thus, through the association of a sadhu who is in direct rapport with God one can realize God.

Finally, one should keep away from the vilifying influence of atheists for they deny the authority of God and the scriptures. One should pray to God to protect one from such influence (Vachanamrut, Gadhada I 48).

1. Effect Points to the Cause

After seeing a sword weighing two hundred kilos, one can imagine the strength of the warrior who can fight with such a sword; similarly, one can visualize God's greatness through his works.

Often we wonder: Who is the sculptor that gave such vivid shapes to the various living creatures? Who is the music maestro who taught the birds their love-song to beckon their mates? Who is that chemist who put juice in the fruits and fragrance in the flowers? Who is the artist who painted the designs on the leaves of the various trees and filled colour into the lovely butterflies? Who is the engineer who designed a cow's stomach such that grass is transformed into milk? Who is the manufacturer who made wood out of carbon dioxide and water? Indeed, such miracles must have a miracle-maker behind them.

Besides, there are infinite galaxies coursing through the cosmos. Yet they do not meet with accidents. The sun also never fails to rise regularly every day. No barriers prevent the overflow of water from an ocean, yet, it remains within its boundaries! No doubt, there must be a controller to regularize all such activities!

Thus, we can infer from such observations that a creator-cum-controller is a must, and that is God!

2. Scientific Arguments and Illustrations for the Existence of God

There are various rational arguments posed to deny the existence of God. Some of them are dealt with and explained as follows:

(1) Some people argue, "How do I believe in God when I cannot see him?" Ramkrishna Paramhansa explains by giving an example, "You see many stars in the night sky but not when the sun rises. Can you then say that there are no stars in the heaven of day? So, O man, because you cannot see the Almighty in the days of your ignorance do not say that there is no God. If a mirror is covered by dust I cannot see my image in it. The moment the dust is wiped off, the image is there. The mirror image and the

face are the same but the dust obstructed visibility. Similarly, the dust of *maya* (ignorance) obstructs our view of God."

Since I cannot see your brain, am I to assume you don't have one? More and more powerful instruments are needed to unravel the mysteries of the physical sciences. That being so, is it not scientific to accept that mysteries of the Divine can be understood only by sharper and sharper spiritual perceptions?

To cite another example, none of us has seen electricity, however, when the switch is turned on and the lights blaze forth, we say there is an electric current in the line. Thus, though we do not see electricity, we infer its existence through its working. The same is the case with God whose working proves his existence.

(2) Yet some people argue, "Can you prove the existence of God with certainty as is done in laboratory experiments?"

But the sceptics forget that there are many things in science which have no proof yet they are accepted as true. For example, nobody has ever obtained the square root of minus one. But, science has decided to call it 'i' and proceeds to apply it. Even without this proof, there are so many applications of 'i' in the theory of Analytical Functions which lead to fruitful results. Hence, absence of any experimental proof cannot be a criterion for the non-existence of anything.

Further, Planck gave the Third Law of Thermodynamics: "Entropy of a perfect crystal at absolute zero (temperature) is zero." There is no proof for it as none has yet been able to reach absolute zero temperature. However, it has many practical applications.

Thus absence of experimental proof is no criterion for the denial of anything, least of all God!

8 GOD EXISTS: II

Sadhu Atmaswarupdas

3. A Whale of a Tale – The Dilemma of Dolphins and Duckbills

Many scientists swear by the theory of evolution. However, there are many inconsistencies to this theory which shake its very foundation.

Most evolutionists claim that life began in the sea. They insist that all living forms 'gradually' migrated from the sea, came on the land or took to the air.

Let us take the case of dolphins. Evolutionists say, "The past of the whales is extremely obscure. All we know is that sometime... some smallish, four-footed land animals began a series of extraordinary rapid evolutionary changes. In the geologically short span of 50 million years they learned to swim instead of walk, and to reproduce offspring which were able to swim from the moment they left the womb."

But how can anyone prove all this? Can it be proven? Is there any fossil record? Are these ideas plausible? How could they 'gradually' change their habitat in such a drastic manner? What caused these changes? We are told in positive terms that these creatures evolved from land animals. What kind of land animals? No one knows. No fossil remains of the land ancestors of the whale have been discovered as yet! There is a yawning gap in fossil records.

One evolutionist admitted, "As the science of oceanography progresses, we may find the whale's complete skeletal record on the ocean's bottom. Until then the guesses are further apart than those for man's evolutionary record."

The ideas about man's evolution are admittedly guesses.

Some of them are pretty wild. Guesses concerning the past of whales are even wilder!

After adapting to a life on land, the ancestors of porpoises, for unknown reasons, went back to the sea. Just what the land animal was like no one can be sure, for the 'missing link' in the evolutionary chain is lost.

Baby dolphins are born underwater. They are gently nudged to the surface by their mothers. They must somehow open and breathe through their brand-new little air vent at just the right moment. A second too soon or too late and the babies would drown.

Remember again, that the very first migration; the very first deep dive; the very first attempt to capture fish for a meal: the very first use of salt water; the very first underwater birth; the very first voluntary control of breathing – these and myriad more fantastic firsts all had to occur at the same time! At the very instant the first dolphin swam.

And from these fantastic abilities, do scientists see great thought and planning? Do they observe great design and intricate creation? Do they stand in awe of the great mind it took to produce and put into action such huge creatures?

Not at all. They see only the creature not the Creator. They are only the material creation – not its producer, designer, sustainer and ruler.

The evolutionists theorize that, given enough time, virtually anything can happen. Do explosions in print presses produce the unabridged dictionary? Do tipper trucks dumping a load of bricks produce palatial mansions, complete with carpets, appliances, chandeliers, and rare paintings? Do city dumps produce typewriters – which falling together accidentally type out the *Encyclopaedia Britannica?*

Yet these are some of the very arguments used by evolutionists in college classrooms today! But why do evolutionists 'beat about the bush' in their guesses about the 'evolution' of whales and dolphins? They have to do it, otherwise they will be disloyal to their theory.

Whales and dolphins are certainly mammals. But there is an even more enigmatic mammal – the unbelievable platypus of Australia. This creature confounds the evolutionists.

The Unbelievable Platypus

"Bizarre." "Monstrous Misfit!" "Unbelievable." "An impossible patchwork creature!" This is what the evolutionists say of the duckbilled platypus. They have a tough time explaining its evolution and existence.

Native to Australia, the platypus appears to be a 'patchwork' animal because evolutionists like to see some sort of comparison or inter-relationship in all living things. In trying to relate the platypus to various other animals, evolutionists have not been able to stop short of at least four or five widely differing creatures nowhere near each other in the purely fanciful 'evolutionary tree'.

Its tail is muscular and flat, like that of a beaver's. It is covered with fur instead of scales! The 'shoulder' is definitely reptilian.

Then there's the strange looking 'bill'. While the ducks have a fairly hard and bony bill, the bill of the platypus is like pliable skin filled with highly sensitive nerves.

Since the little animal suckles its young, it is classified as a mammal. But it seems it lays eggs! The eggs are reptilian in nature, and are covered with a skin-like texture, instead of a hard shell. And the little platypus doesn't really 'suckle' its young, but actually secretes the milk from a mammary opening which then drips from the hair of the underbelly, and the young lap the milk from the hair!

Despite the duck-like bill, beaver-like tail, snake-like eggs, venom fang, otter-like forefeet, and suckling characteristics of mammals, the little creature has only a single ventral opening for elimination, mating and birth – just like reptiles! The story does not end here since it is warm-blooded, unlike reptiles. Further, it stores food in cheek pouches, like some mammals; but unlike mammals, it has no exterior ear, only an opening into its hearing apparatus which is located inside!

No wonder evolutionists get 'mixed up' when they attempt 'scientific' classification – which could either be mammal, bird, or reptile! The platypus simply does not fit the evolutionary scheme of things.

Even more amazing, there is nothing transitional about the platypus. It is highly intelligent and remarkably built to fit its environment.

No fossils have yet been found in any continent which reveal the lineage of the platypus prior to the last few million years in Australia itself.

All fossil platypuses found so far look exactly like the 'modern' platypuses.

The platypus is another of those serious obstacles to the evolutionary theory – a living creature that has no living counterparts and no close relatives in the fossil record. Therefore, science calls this little creature 'a living fossil'.

Why, having once begun to enjoy the advantages of large brains and maternal care, were the monotremes (the platypus comes under them) not pushed on through the ages by the same forces of selection and survival that shaped the other animals? There is no answer to this recurrent riddle of evolution.

The platypus waves his bill at evolutionists in pity. It almost appears as though God made the platypus just to confuse the evolutionists!

But those of us, who have the intelligence, ought to be able to understand from the creation around us, that God does exist.

Both the dolphins and duckbills are classified as mammals.

Both share extremely unusual characteristics. Both these mammals confound the evolutionary family tree.

4. Scientists Claim Chemical Combinations Produce Life

If this were so, then we should be able to raise corpses to life by injecting various chemicals into their bodies! But it is not the case because it is God who has created life.

5. Faith Is the Key to Knowledge

We need to realize that many things have to be accepted in good faith. They do not call for proof. For example, we are told that taking poison can be fatal. But we never try it for ourselves, for, in that case, we would very possibly not live to see the results of such an experiment. Most of us may not have seen anyone die due to poison. Yet, if given the chance to swallow poison, we would simply abstain from the act. This is due to an inner conviction that poison kills. Have we ever thought over the reason or proof for such a fact? Certainly not. Still we do hold the statement to be true.

Besides, if we are asked, "How do you know that such and such a person is your father? Have you any proof of it?" Our simple reply would be, "My mum told me so." We would be dubbed foolish if we were to seek proof of our parentage. The fact is a matter of faith in the words of one's mother.

So, we do accept many things in good faith. But, when it comes to God, our ego bars us from accepting his existence!

Some Examples of God's Creation

(1) The Human Faculty of Reasoning

The evolution theory cannot explain the highly developed reasoning power of human beings. It must be God and none else who has endowed human beings with great intelligence.

(2) The Instincts of Living Entities

(i) The Eel

It is noted that when the eel is ready to lay eggs, it goes all the way from European waters to the Bermuda Islands in the western Atlantic. As soon as the eggs are laid, the mother dies. However, it is a great surprise indeed that the newborn eels reach the very European waters from where their mothers had migrated. The distance covered by the newborn eels is two thousands miles and yet they do not lose their way.

Similar is the case with American eels. They also come to the Bermuda Islands for laying eggs, then the mothers die. However the newborn fish head straight for American waters from where their mothers had migrated.

Though the European eels and American eels gather together, there is never any mixing up resulting in newborn American eels heading for Europe, or newborn European eels heading for America.

This is due to the instinct in eels endowed by God's grace. It is he who is the unmistakable guide to the eels.

(ii) The Weaver Bird

An experiment was conducted on some weaver birds. They were confined to the four walls of a room without material for building their nests. The offspring were removed to other confined rooms where they could not build nests. This experiment was extended till the fifth generation. Then the weaver birds of the fifth generation were let out in the open. And to everyone's surprise these birds built nests exactly like any other weaver birds! How was this knowledge of nest building passed on to the fifth generation? They call it instinct, which in other words, implies that God revealed it to the weaver birds. Hence, presence of the instinct of nest building ability indicates God's hand.

(iii) The Calf

A newly born calf, immediately and unmistakably, after getting up, heads for the udder of the mother for suckling. Who has provided it with the knowledge that its food is in its mother's udder in the form of milk? Certainly it is God's grace that has revealed to a newborn calf the udder of its mother as the source of milk.

Science fails to explain all these three and similar phenomena logically. God's existence is the only explanation for these and other such extraordinary events.

(3) Theory of Creation of Earth as a Chance Phenomenon

Let us examine this chance theory in the light of the facts which clearly refute it. Cressy Morrison, former president of the New York Academy of Science, says:

(i) The earth rotates on its axis at an approximate speed of 1,000 miles an hour. If, by chance, its rotational speed were 100 miles per hour, what would have been the result? Well, the duration of the day as well as of night would have been 10 times longer. In that case, exposure during daytime to the intense heat of the sun would have destroyed vegetation. Vegetation that could have survived the sunlight during the long day would have to stand equally long nights. The chill of the nights would have caused this vegetation to wither away. Thus the world would be stripped of all vegetation! This disastrous effect, thanks be to the grace of God, has been averted because the rotational speed of the earth has been set at the appropriate speed for vegetation to flourish. The Chance Theory would simply not allow a world flourishing with vegetation. There is, for sure, design and meticulous planning behind every phenomenon that occurs in nature.

(ii) The temperature on the surface of the sun is about 12,000°F. If its temperature was to be, by chance, half of this, then no human being could survive the resulting cold on earth. If its temperature was one-and-a-half times its present temperature, then we would all have been burnt to ashes due to the resulting heat. But the fact that the temperature of the sun is appropriate and conducive to human survival on earth, clearly indicates that creation is designed to definite patterns and is not haphazard, as the Chance Theory claims.

(iii) Imagine the moon being 50,000 miles away from earth. The consequence would be that there would be high tides in the oceans of the earth twice a day. The high tides would be so enormous that the land mass of the earth would be submerged under those tides twice daily! The fact that it simply does not happen, vouches for the intelligent creation of earth and the moon. No wonder, then, that the Chance Theory has no chance of succeeding in explaining creation.

(iv) Besides, if the oceans were a little deeper than they are at present, then all the supply of carbon dioxide and oxygen in the world would have been exhausted! It is due to God that the world has not become a graveyard!

(v) If our atmosphere were a little less dense than it actually is, then the falling meteors would still be ablaze when reaching the earth. They would set fire to the world!

Hence, life has not developed as a result of chance. There certainly is a Supreme Controller – God.

(4) Some Atheists Say That the Universe Works 'Automatically'

But they fail to realize that even the most automatic creations of man – the computer – requires a maker, an operator, and a maintainer! Then how can the vast universe carry on automatically as suggested by some atheists? Undoubtedly, we have to accept the fact that there is certainly a great creator and controller of everything. Hence logic leads us to accept the existence of God as that Supreme Creator and Controller.

(5) Animal and Plant Balance

We wonder how this balance is effected. We are indeed amazed to find how those animals and plants which multiply at an alarming rate have not filled the world!

There is some power fixing a limit on the size of rapidly reproducing and growing insects. For example, bees. Providence has seen to it that the respiratory passages among them are restricted in size. This checks an undue size. If there was no such limitation, then we would have had bees the size of a lion roaming about! In that case, man would simply not have survived. We have to thank God for this.

(6) The Genes

So unspeakably tiny are they that, if all the genes of all living people in the world could be collected together, there would be less than a thimbleful. Yet these ultra microscopic genes are the absolute keys to all human, animal and vegetable characteristics. Thus the fantastic genes indicate that they are the creation of God.

9 GOD EXISTS: III

Sadhu Atmaswarupdas

6. Prayer

A.H. Compton, Nobel Laureate, in his book *The Cosmos of Arthur Holly Compton*, writes, "When we pray to our fatherly God, it is a common experience that we receive courage and strength to do deeds of friendliness towards his children. It is hard to think of receiving strength, without imagining a being that gives us strength."

Even Alexis Carrel, Nobel Prize winner in Medicine, says in his book *Reflections on Life*, "The existence of God explains, better than any hypothesis, the results of prayer, the phenomenon of mysticism and the sense of the holy."

There are innumerable instances in which prayers to God have worked miracles. We shall cite a few of them:

(i) George Mueller, a British citizen, had no means of support. However, he felt an ardent urge to serve the cause of orphans. Through his prayers to God he received seven million dollars. From that he founded five great orphanages and other institutions in Bristol, England.

(ii) The story of Apollo 13 is also ample proof that 'someone' answers our prayers. The explosion damaging the fuel tanks jeopardized the entire mission and the lives of the astronauts. NASA appealed to 200 million Americans to pray to God for the safe return of the astronauts. They realized that science had limited power to bring the spacecraft and its crew back from the moon to earth. Their prayers were answered by God and the astronauts returned safely on earth.

(iii) Many Russians are widely known to be atheists.

However, during World War II, all the churches in Russia used to be full of people praying for the safe return of their near and dear ones from the war fronts.

(iv) Dr Smiley of England innovated a novel way of curing his patients. He employed priests who regularly prayed to God for the quick recovery of patients. His work spanning over four decades has revived faith in God among many of his patients. And, it has worked wonders. There have been rapid recoveries among patients. God responds to our inner pleadings in the form of prayers.

(v) Even Mahatma Gandhi, the father of the Indian nation, used to say that India gained freedom from British rule by the power of prayer to God.

7. Atheists Turned into Theists

The most convincing arguments can be had from the outstanding transformations of previously confirmed atheists into theists:

(i) Count Charles, a German officer during World War I, was a confirmed atheist. He rejected all talk about God and his existence. He lay dying in a French hospital. The nurse in the hospital looking after him was also a German. She asked the officer again and again if she might call a priest, but the officer always refused. Finally, the nurse said, "I will pray for you." The officer laughed and told her it was useless to pray for him.

The nurse replied, "No, I will continue praying for you. I have been praying for a certain person for the past sixteen years and I shall still keep praying for him." The officer then enquired, "Is it your brother or your father you are praying for?" "No," said the nurse, "I am doing it as a special favour to the mother of this person. She is a German Countess and her young son, the man I am praying for, left home and joined the army. He had been a pious, young boy, but when he left home, he forgot all about God and religion. I am praying to keep my promise made to his mother. Poor woman! She does not even know where her son is now. It would be wonderful for her to see him changed again for the better."

The man stared at her and his face lit up. His eyes shone brightly, and tears rolled down his cheeks. He got up on his bed and asked, "Are you talking of Countess Beata, my mother?" The nurse was surprised to hear this and could only murmur, "Then you are Count Charles, that same young man I have been praying for! Do you want a priest?" "Yes," said the young man, "Today, God's mercy and your prayers have saved me." From that moment he became a firm believer in God.

(ii) An Arab and an Englishman were crossing a desert. The Arab prepared to offer his prayers to Allah in the evening. The Englishman did not believe in God. So he asked the Arab not to waste his time in such a futile act. He said, "There is no sign of God. Have you ever seen or talked to God?" The Arab did not utter a single word in reply.

At night they camped together in the desert. Early in the morning, the Englishman woke up first. When he came out of the camp, he saw the footsteps of a camel in the sand. Soon after, the Arab woke up and came out. The Englishman told the Arab, "A caravan seems to have passed by at night." The Arab asked, "How do you know that? Did you see the caravan or talk to the men?" The Englishman said, "I have seen the footsteps of a camel, hence it is the sign of a caravan." Immediately, the Arab said, "I also see the sign of God in the golden rays of the sun and in the cool moonlight. Hence, I conclude that there must be God." The Englishman realized his mistake and started to believe in God and offer prayers to him.

(iii) A German surgeon was also one such atheist. Once, his son had severe abdominal pain. On investigation it was found that he had to be operated upon for appendicitis. The father preferred to perform the surgery. Though he had performed delicate cardiac and other operations, the simple appendicitis operation failed and the boy died. That time, the German surgeon realized that though he was an experienced surgeon there was someone else who was the saviour. His failure in the operation marked a turning point in his life. He began to believe in the existence of God as the saviour.

(iv) Once, there was an old man travelling by train to Paris. Sitting opposite him was a young scientist bubbling with enthusiasm, for he had been selected to do his research work in one of the most renowned research institutes in France, the Louis Pasteur Institute of Research. Only a few scholars were chosen for the assignment.

During that journey, the young man saw the old man, sitting opposite him, telling the beads of his rosary. The young man was an atheist. He thought science had all the answers to the various problems of the world and that there was no creator – no God. When he saw the old man telling his beads, he said, "Look here, old man, you seem to be really ignorant. You still believe in God when science has made such great strides. Even the great scientists of our times have denied the existence of God. In spite of that, you still seem to stick to outdated beliefs."

The old man said, "Well, is that so? Are even the great scientists of our times denying the existence of God? I am afraid, I did not know that. Please explain to me their viewpoints in detail so that I can be properly guided and enlightened by their intelligent arguments."

The young man said, "Look here, gentleman, I can quote and narrate a thousand incidents to prove that God does not exist. However, Paris is drawing nearer and I have to reach the research institute on time. Nevertheless, if you care to give me your address, I shall personally drop in and convince you that God does not exist. The old man readily agreed to meet him some time later. Then, he gave his own visiting card to the young man. The man read the address and he was stunned. For, the card read: "Louis Pasteur, Director, Louis Pasteur Institute of Research."

The young man felt highly embarrassed. He was ashamed to have talked so bluntly with Louis Pasteur, one of the great scientists of his time. It was indeed a great paradox that he had been claiming an atheistic viewpoint on the authority of the great scientists when one of the great scientists, Louis Pasteur, held such firm faith in God.

This transformed the young man. He decided to emulate the pious example of Louis Pasteur, who was also to be his guide in his doctoral work. From that day onwards he began to believe in the existence of God.

(v) Dr Jung, one of the great psychologists of the 20th century has also said, "In my darkness...I could have wished for nothing better than a real live 'Guru', someone possessing superior knowledge and ability, who would have disentangled me from the involuntary creations of my imagination." It is very true that our mundane intellect prevents us from accepting the authority and existence of God.

(vi) Narendranath was a young, educated man who had many doubts about God's existence. However, when he met Ramkrishna Paramhansa, all his doubts melted away. For, when asked by Narendra if he had seen God, Ramkrishna Paramhansa replied immediately, "I see God as clearly as I see you." This put an end to Narendra's doubts and soon he became a completely changed man and became known the world over as Swami Vivekanand.

(vii) Dr Thakorbhai Patel, the ex-Mayor of Vadodara, was also an atheist. But he says, "I did not believe in God, I looked upon the idols consecrated in mandirs as mere stones. However, when I saw His Divine Holiness Yogiji Maharaj, I had the feeling

God certainly must exist. Otherwise, such divine bliss emanating from Yogiji Maharaj would be inexplicable. On the word of Yogiji Maharaj, I was prepared to accept the existence of God."

8. Great Personalities Vouch for God

(i) Sir Isaac Newton's discovery of the Law of Gravitation is indeed one of the great discoveries of all times. However, when he was profusely felicitated by people the world over for his tremendous contribution towards the advancement of science, he humbly said, "I am merely picking pebbles on the seashore while the vast ocean of knowledge lies beyond." The fact that he had made real progress in science did not deter him from accepting God's great work - Creation!

(ii) Thomas Alva Edison's genius led to the invention of the light bulb. But he spoke out for God, saying, "I am highly indebted to the Almighty for having inspired my intellect to discover this."

Indeed great scientists have always hailed the greatest scientist of all - God!

(iii) Dr Alexander Fleming discovered penicillin. People extolled him as a great scientist. But he was modest enough to say, "It is God who has created penicillin. I have merely found the use for it."

(iv) Dr Isaac Bashevis Singer, the American Nobel Prize Winner for literature in 1978, says, "I am thankful to God for each story, each idea, each word, each day."

(v) Dr Von Braun, the Deputy Associate Administrator of NASA, designed the Saturn V rocket to propel the Apollo spacecrafts. But he also felt the need for God when he said, "For only with God reinstated in the heart of the world will He provide us with ethical guidance through the dangers of technological revolution."

(vi) On the currency of USA, a country which has made

tremendous material progress, we still find written: "In God We Trust."

(vii) The UK Parliament begins its session invariably with the prayer: "O God, you are the ruler of this world. Please give us the wisdom to be able to rule with justice."

(viii) Dr Jung, one of the great psychologists of the twentieth century, also expresses his experience that in his sixty years of practice as a psychologist he had yet to come across a single person who had faith in God and yet needed mental treatment.

(ix) Once, when Swami Vivekanand was due to deliver a discourse in a congregation, an atheist went well before time and wrote on the blackboard 'God Is Nowhere.'

When Swami Vivekanand came to the hall to deliver his speech, he read the sentence. He simply separated the words, 'Now' and 'Here' from the word 'Nowhere' and re-wrote the same sentence 'God is Now Here.' The gathering accorded him a thunderous applause. Even the atheist who had written the first sentence joined in the applause. It kindled faith in God in his heart.

Conclusion

Thus we have examined many ideas which reinforce our faith in God. Despite these, and other rational arguments, we tend to doubt the existence of God. Even many ardent devotees still have traces of scepticism. But the highest faith is vouchsafed by a God-communion Sadhu, so that the trace of scepticism which remains suppressed within us disappears entirely. He realizes all that is written in the scriptures is true, as revealed by Bhagwan Swaminarayan in Vachanamrut, Ahmedabad 1.

Further, Bhagwan Swaminarayan says that this state of realization can be attained only in the company or by the grace of a realized Sadhu who has attained rapport with God (Vachanamrut, Gadhada I 60).

His Divine Holiness Pramukh Swami Maharaj is such a God-communion Sadhu. So let us fully consolidate our faith in God through service and association with him.

Thus, in the final analysis, it is essential for all to associate with a God-realized Sadhu to assert unfailingly, and with firm affirmation, that God Exists.

10 LIMITATIONS OF PERCEPTION

Sadhu Brahmaviharidas

Two friends were walking down a country lane.

One believed in God; the other did not. Said the atheist to the theist, "We have had God and religion for thousands of years and yet evil thrives in this world. Hatred, crime, war and immorality is getting harsher than ever. What good has been your God or your religion?"

The theist kept quiet and digested the raw rancour with a smile. They strolled on. Once again the atheist swung his sword of sarcasm, "With so much unrighteousness around, what good has your God and religion done?"

And again, the theist walked silently on. Then they saw a young boy splashing in a muddy puddle. He was covered all over by mud. Hinting at the boy, the theist turned to his friend and asked, "Tell me, what good has soap been to this world. We've had it for so long..."

"But you have to use it!" snapped the atheist.

"Exactly! You have to use religion, accept God and his teachings in your life to see the benefits."

The dialogue finishes here.

But as is the case with many non-believers, some would argue, "I can see the soap. I can see its foam and suds; and its cleansing process. But, with God, I can't see him with my eyes! Only when I know God through my senses will I accept him."

Our inability to understand the existence and nature of God through material senses has given added momentum to atheistic cults. Belief in God is often attacked as 'primitive', 'out-of-fashion', 'only for the weak-minded and not for the modern and scientific brains'.

As the so-called modern, scientific understanding is based on knowledge acquired through material senses, God is rejected.

But is it the fault of God if our scientific senses are too feeble; insufficient, inaccurate and inadequate to know the glory of his being?

Careful analysis shows that knowledge gained through the material senses is defective. There are a lot of discrepancies. First of all, the senses themselves are limited and thus imperfect. Second, we easily become illusioned. Third, we make mistakes. And fourth, we lack experience.

Let's have a closer look at these four limitations.

1. Imperfect Senses

Human senses, though powerful, are not powerful enough. There is much we can't see! Much we can't hear! Even to get accurate information about the external world, our senses have physiological limits, or 'thresholds of perception'.

Take the eye, for example. A human eye cannot see through walls; it is blind to x-rays, ultra-violet rays and infrared! We can only see a tiny fraction of the total electromagnetic spectrum. An electromagnetic wave can range from one quadrillionth of a metre up to 100 million metres in length. And of this immense array of energy, we can see only the wavelengths between 400 and 750 millimicrons (a millimicron is a billionth of a metre). This we call the visible spectrum. And anything outside this range is invisible. Our visible spectrum is shockingly small and shrinks to near insignificance when compared to the vast section of waves that remain invisible.

Our eyes can see only 0.00000000000035% (3.5×10^{-13}) of what there is to see. To visualize this infinitesimal figure, if we take the population of one earth as 6 billion and collect 2 million such earths; out of the total number of people before us (2 million x 6 billion) we would see only 42! This is the stunning limitation of the human eye!

And in this frail band of vision lies our wonderful world of colours.

Our hearing is limited as well. No human ear can hear the dog whistle! Its frequency is beyond the range of human hearing. Sound waves are measured in hertz (cycles per second). Our hearing extends from 20 Hz up to 20,000 Hz. And we are deaf to any vibration above or below this range.

Each of our remaining senses exhibits similar limitations.

So our senses are limited, imperfect. But what of scientific instruments! Can't they help us get more perfect knowledge! Not really.

Nobel prize-winning physicist, Eugene Wigner points out, "Even if we photograph the stars, we must eventually 'take in' by our senses what the photograph shows. Furthermore, without our senses, we could not handle a photographic camera. Clearly, all knowledge comes to us ultimately through our senses."

So even if refined by instruments, ultimately, whatever knowledge we gain through sense perception is no more perfect than our imperfect senses.

2. Illusions

Even within our limited range of perception, we suffer from illusions. You only have to ask a magician and he'll demonstrate how easy it is to deceive a person through illusions. He has hundreds up his sleeve.

Our eyes are most easily illusioned.

Many of us have seen mirages on a hot summer day. As you drive down the highway you see what looks like small puddles of water ahead of you. But in reality they are just illusions.

As school kids we studied refraction in physics. If you fill up a glass beaker with water and partially immerse a pencil in it, the part of the pencil in the water appears bent - an illusion due to refraction of light.

If you stand between railway tracks at ground level and look at the tracks as they stretch ahead, they don't seem to be parallel. They appear to converge and meet at a distant point. But we quickly realize that our eye is lying.

The sense of touch is also highly susceptible to illusion. If you cool your right hand sufficiently in water at 5°C and then dip it in a trough of water at 15°C, the water will feel 'warm'. But if your left hand has been preconditioned in 20°C water, then the trough of 15°C will feel 'cool'. Though the water is the same, it simultaneously feels both 'warm' and 'cool'.

With regards to our sense of hearing most of us have been fooled at least once. We have turned to what sounded like someone calling out our name, only to find out in embarrassment that it was a fault of hearing or a trick of the ear!

Spooky or strange sounds and uncanny noises are also sound illusions, which the ear bears when the mind is scared.

Taste. The tongue lies not only through words. If after having eaten a sweet chocolate or some sugary foodstuff, you drink tea; the tongue reports an absence of sugar. But in reality, the tea does have sugar. It is an illusion of taste!

Try tasting an orange after tasting sugar, the orange will taste sweet. Try the orange after a lemon, and the same orange will taste sour!

In short, all our senses, apart from being limited in power are subject to illusions.

Some illusions are apparently caused by odd imperfections in our sensory apparatus. As the famous painter Vincent Van Gogh reached the end of his life, he began depicting shining objects (such as the sun) as if they were surrounded by concentric rings of colour. For a long time art critics were convinced that Van Gogh had "broken through a new level of reality" by letting his imagination run free. If this were the case, then we might say that Van Gogh was hallucinating the circles around the sun that he so often painted. But we now suspect that Van Gosh suffered from a dreadful disease that was systematically destroying his nervous system. One of the symptoms of this particular illness is that the person's vision becomes cloudy and all bright lights have halos around them. It is likely, then, that Van Gogh was suffering from the same kind of illusion that you can experience if you look at a streetlight on a foggy night, or watch a full moon through a thin layer of colours.

3. Mistakes

With our imperfect senses and our illusion-prone mind, mistakes are inevitable. 'To err is human.'

The Challenger space shuttle was definitely the best production of top brains in science. Yet something went wrong. What began as a spectacular space expedition ended in a nightmarish fireball. Some unknown mistake had been made. A mistake that shook NASA and brought tears to humanity. Sadly, such mistakes have been a part of human history.

Dr R.C. Gregory, Director of the Brain and Perception Laboratory at the University of Bristol, England, says, "Science with all its dramatic successes, had from its beginning also generated wildly incorrect accounts; stars were believed to be pinpricks in a crystal ball, electricity and heat as fluids, the brain as an organ to cool the blood... These are dramatic deviations from what we now see as truth; and when invented they were deviations from what then appeared true."

The tragedy of mistake-making has haunted humanity. Everybody knows that there was a time when Aristotle claimed that the earth was stationary, the centre of the universe and the sun revolved round the earth. It passed unquestioned, until Copernicus, and then Galileo focussed his telescope towards the heavens to prove Aristotle wrong. The list of our past mistakes is appalling; the earth was considered to be flat and all matter as 'solid'. But today, the earth is a globe and nothing seems to be 'solid'. At subatomic levels, everything is forces, and more forces.

In another instance, three astronomers recently discovered a significant mistake in the Hubble Constant, an equation used as a cosmic yardstick to measure enormous distances in the universe. The Hubble Constant - named after astronomer Edwin P. Hubble - has undergone so many corrections since he first formulated it that many astronomers now laughingly call it the 'Hubble Variable'.

As new frontiers of knowledge are explored, man changes his old views. In the light of higher knowledge our old theories, howsoever dear to us, have to be rehashed or replaced. Is it not possible then, that when higher wisdom dawns upon us that the 'no God' theory will have to be dumped in the junkyard of human mistakes?

4. Lack of Experience

Behind many mistakes is lack of experience. It makes us professional mistake-makers. Whatsoever we undertake to study, without the necessary experience in the subject, we are always likely to misunderstand or not understand at all. If Einstein himself knocks on your door and presents to you his prized paper on relativity theory, will you be in a position to understand it?

Never: If Physics is like hieroglyphics to you and you know nothing of the subject.

No: Even if you know physics but have not the requisite depth.

Yes: If you are equipped with enough insight in physics and are thoroughly grounded in it.

How likely is a man, ignorant of science and mathematics, to appreciate the formula $E=mc^2$? Even if the scientists themselves demonstrate all the proofs, will he follow the logic of the proofs?

Thus, it is plain logic that to read a book in Chinese, one must first be trained in the Chinese language.

And if someone who has no idea of what a number is demands to be logically shown that two plus two is four, it can't be done. Similarly, if a spiritual ignoramus demands that God be logically demonstrated to him, his very request is illogical!

And given the proof of God, would he, a materialist know how to read it?

Even if God himself were to appear before him, he would fail to understand him, for he lacks sufficient spiritual experience!

Conclusion

We can logically conclude that the perfect, infinite personality of God cannot possibly be understood by our limited, illusion-ridden, inaccurate and inexperienced senses.

Does it mean that we can never know God?

No. Even with all these handicaps, there is still a way to realize the Supreme.

The colossal gap between us and God can be bridged. This bridge is the genuine Sadhu who is infallible in spiritual wisdom; who is in constant communion with the Supreme at one end and in humanly touch with us on the other. He links us mortals with the Immortal. He guides us and acquaints us with spiritual *sadhana*. And through his company and training a person rises above the material limitations. This process of rising is known as divinisation.

Bhagwan Swaminarayan explains that when a person undergoes genuine spiritual training under the care and company of an enlightened Sadhu, who reveals to him the glory of God, his senses and mind become divine. Graced with such a divine vision, he is able to see God in human form and develops a firm conviction about his supremacy. Otherwise it is impossible to see God with the material senses (Vachanamrut, Gadhada I 51).

Bhagwan Swaminarayan further describes in Vachanamrut, Sarangpur 2 that when a person thus realizes God, his power of perception transcends all barriers and he can hear everything being said in any corner of the cosmos and see everything anywhere in the multiple universes.

There cannot be more convincing words than God's own. And once you've tasted the bliss of God, doubts disappear like darkness before the sun.

Addressing a packed audience, an atheist vociferously defied God with proof after proof. His mastery of words and logic left everyone stunned. He arrogantly challenged from the stage.

"Can anyone contradict me? Or wishes to attempt proving God to me?"

A heavy hush engulfed the listeners.

Then an old man limped up onto the stage with anxious faces monitoring him as he took his stance before the microphone.

Surprisingly he said nothing. Instead, he took out an orange from his pocket and began peeling. Minutes ticked by. Everybody was intent on listening to his defence. Yet he quietly, with bent head, kept on peeling.

The atheist breathed fire, "Old man have you nothing to say? Or have your ideas suddenly vanished and you can't find words?"

While the atheist ridiculed him, the old man finished peeling the orange. He waved a hand and broke his silence. Then placing a segment of the juicy orange in his mouth and sucking it with delight, he turned to the atheist and said, "Can you tell me the taste of this orange?"

"How can I? I haven't eaten it," he retorted.

The old man faced the audience.

"Can anybody describe how this orange tastes?"

Silence.

"Scientists, sociologists, professors and people of much greater intelligence than me are present here, and yet, nobody knows the taste of this orange. Only he who eats it knows the taste. It is the same with God. Only he who has experienced him and tasted his bliss knows that he exists forever."

So, for a person who genuinely wants to know God, God is nearer than his own heart, God is as clear as sunshine.

11 RELIGION AND YOUTH

Sadhu Atmaswarupdas

Youth is the spring of life, the symbol of vigour, dynamism and enthusiasm. It has tremendous potential. It depends on how the potential is utilized. If channelized properly, it can work wonders. If not, it can wreak havoc!

The River Tapi, in the city of Surat, Gujarat, India, often used to overflow, destroying human life and property. The floods had devastating effects. However, the authorities looked into the matter, thought it over and then built the Ukai Dam. Today hundreds of thousands of acres of land benefit through irrigation, and electricity is generated from hydro-electric power. The river has been tamed and its benefits reaches millions. The youth, too, have a colossal amount of energy. If it is properly channelized for constructive work, a great deal of good can follow. As Pramukh Swami Maharaj says, "If a boat is in the sea, there is no problem. But if the 'sea' is in the boat, there are nothing but problems." Likewise, if youth power is properly oriented it is fine. If not, only problems are created.

Religion is needed to make the life of youth more purposeful and goal-oriented. It can inspire in them a new vigour, a new direction and a new vision. When Rabindranath Tagore, the Nobel Laureate and famous Bengali poet, was a child he was not aware that he had poor eyesight. One day, while playing with his pals at school, a friend dropped his spectacles. Picking them up, Tagore tried them on. To his utter surprise, everything he saw became much clearer and well-focussed. The spectacles provided the right eye correction and gave him new sight, free from blur. He welcomed the change with mixed feelings. On the one hand he was elated for he could see so clearly for the first time in his life, and on the other hand, the fact that he had been deprived of the beautiful vision all those years made him curse himself for the great loss. He wished he had acquired spectacles much earlier. Tagore narrates this incident from his life and explains that the spectacles represent faith in God. So long as one has not acquired the spectacles, one's myopic state persists, presenting a blurred vision in life. But once the spectacles of faith are put on, one can behold an altogether different world - a world as it really is - full of beauty, variety and bubbling with inspiration and awe. Then we shall attain the vision to realize that all creation is an outstretched finger pointing towards God.

It is generally held that the youth are not religious. But this is not so. In fact, the youth are religious provided religion is youthful, that is, religion bereft of blind faith, superstitions, malpractices and fanatic dogmas, religion that brings people together and promotes the meeting of hearts. The youth hear that religion is a 'way of life'. But in reality, he finds that people seem to be religious only within the four walls of the mandir or place of worship. Elsewhere, they do not hesitate to transgress any and even all the moral and spiritual values on which religion is based. The young cannot reconcile such double standards. It bites them to the bone.

During the Spanish conquest of Mexico under Hernando Cortez in the early 1500s, a resistance leader named Hatney was captured after a fierce battle and sentenced to be burned alive. After tying him to the stake, his captors urged him to accept their religion, so that at his death his soul might be given an entrance into heaven. He asked his tormentors if they expected to go to this place. On being told that they did, he cried out, "Then I will not accept to go to a place where I would find men so cruel!"

The majority of youth want to understand religion from a

'rational' viewpoint. The reason chiefly being education, which sharpens the scrutiny and logical understanding of things. One cannot hammer religious beliefs into the youth. Hence there is the need to provide old wine in a new bottle; the age old traditions and teachings should be put in a palatable form.

A believer and a sceptic were once walking on a quiet lane.

The sceptic said, "Look at the trouble and misery in the world after thousands of years of religion. Of what good has religion been?"

His companion remained tight-lipped, because he couldn't think of an answer. However, on walking further, he noticed a child, filthy with grime, playing in the gutter.

He said, "We've had soap for a long time yet look how dirty that child is. Of what value is soap!"

The sceptic protested, "But soap can't do any good unless it is used?"

"Exactly!" replied the believer. "Religion is not of much good if not honestly practised."

Life is full of crises, trials and tribulations. It is religion that can pull one through them. An ordinary car would get stuck in muddy terrain but a car with four-wheel-drive will pull through. Similarly, one's faith in the all-powerful God relieves one of all tensions and stresses that follow from one's ego-propelled endeavours. The youth need God all the more in view of the fact that they suffer from despair, dejection and hopelessness. Religion provides new drive and hope in life. It tells us that where the desert ends, green grass grows. It gives the hope that day follows night. Religion links one to God. And peace floods the soul when God rules the heart. This is its greatest benefit.

Peace is something everyone aspires for, but peace cannot be bought in the market place. The root of peace and bliss is God. Faith in God is the only answer to our quest for peace. A person can do without food for several weeks, he may even do without water for a while but he cannot do without air for even a few minutes. Religion is the very breath of life. It sustains. It was faith in God that sustained the youthful Gandhi during his anti-apartheid struggle in South Africa, that provided strength to the young Shankaracharya during his debates and that spurred Swami Vivekanand to hold aloft the spiritual torch of India in the West.

So, reinforced with a religious faith, attended by honest and sincere practice of moral and spiritual values, the tremendous potential of youth can move mountains.

During World War II, General Douglas MacArthur helped the Filipinos recapture their country, Philippines, in 1942. Grateful for his assistance when all had seemed lost, the government in Manila later directed its armies to begin a tradition of calling out MacArthur's name at every parade roll call. Each company designated one officer who would respond by answering 'present in spirit'. That symbolic gesture helped to ensure that the dedication and courage of the general would live on in the hearts of the soldiers long after MacArthur was gone. If Philippine soldiers can gain great encouragement by remembering MacArthur, how much more can the youth be heartened by remembering God, who guides, strengthens and enlightens us all.

12 NAM-JAP

Sadhu Shriharidas

In this age of conflict and anxiety chanting the holy name of God is the solution to all our problems and worries.

A few years ago a rich man saw Pramukh Swami Maharaj absorbed in chanting God's name with a pair of cymbals in his hands. He was greatly impressed. He had never witnessed a person so happy in his entire life. He felt that no amount of money could buy the bliss Swamiji was seen to be experiencing. He asked Swamiji, "How can we ever experience the happiness you so abundantly enjoy?" The reply was short and to the point, "Absorb yourself in chanting God's name. This will forge an armour that will make you invincible to all miseries."

While reading this article you are probably aware or unaware of the cacophony of sounds and myriad visions around you; the next door neighbour's blaring radio or hi-fi system, the screaming television in the next room, a simmering row across the street or a catchy poster on your way to office or college. All these and a lot more infiltrate and influence your character, mode of thought and health.

When anyone shouts, "Scorpion! Scorpion!", "Snake! Snake!", you instinctively jump in fright. When someone calls you names or heaps insults you find it painful to bear. You become inflamed and uneasy. When someone praises you, you feel happy.

The spectrum of human reactions to the words and things around us is endless. If such situations can arouse feelings of fear, anger, joy, then what of chanting or hearing God's name

– the purest and greatest of all names? The mere saying of the word 'apple' conjures an image of it and a lot more. Similarly, chanting God's name creates an image or awareness of God. We become 'apple-conscious' on saying the word apple, similarly we become 'God-conscious' on chanting God's name *(nam-jap)*.

During the two World Wars soldiers marching to the front chorused or whistled patriotic songs. This bolstered their fighting spirit and numbed their anxieties. The slaves in the cotton fields of America sang songs to kill the monotony of work and blunt the persecution from their masters. In this age of conflict and anxiety, chanting the holy name of God is the panacea to all our problems and worries. A popular verse from the Brihadnaradiya Puran, pointed out by Chaitanya Mahaprabhu, says:

Harer nãma Harer nãma Harer nãmaiva kevalam,
Kalau nãstyaiva nãstyaiva nãstyaiva gatiranyathã.

The above verse means that in Kaliyuga there is no other means to *moksha* than chanting the name of God. The words 'Harer nama' (i.e., the Lord's name) are mentioned three times to emphasize the importance of singing God's name.

All our sufferings stem from the delusion that "I am the body." Our true identity is *atma* (or soul). Believing what you are not (i.e., a case of mistaken identity) incurs misery and frustration. You'll find misery coming your way when you believe you are a leader, even though you are not, or when you believe you know about lots of things, when in reality you don't. Living in false identity stifles your peace and happiness. To support this consider the example of a thief who is about to do his work. He is never at ease. He is always vigilant lest he should get caught. But if he behaves normally, his true self, he is free from the fear of getting caught. To realize who we really are, our true identity, and extricate ourselves from the delusion that "I am the body," and all the reactions that go with it, we need to chant the name of God. *Nam-Jap* ultimately strikes a spiritual dialogue between the chanter and God.

Pingala, a woman of loose morals in the time of King Bhartruhari, underwent a miraculous change through hearing God's name. The story says a thief presented a parrot to her. The parrot kept singing the name of "Ram, Ram." Out of her fondness for the parrot her conscience began to ring with the Lord's name. Though she was unaware of Shri Ram's glory, the holy name induced a union with God. By the virtue of God's name she was freed from sin.

The story of Ajamil in the Shrimad Bhagvat is another testament to the power of God's name. Ajamil was initially a pure, disciplined Brahmin. His downfall came about when he inhaled a fragrant flower from a prostitute. As a result he became fond of her. She became everything to him. He slipped from his daily routine of worship and lapsed in his morals. He left his lawful wife and married the prostitute. He had several children out of which the youngest, Narayan, was very dear to him. Years later the servant of Yama (god of death) came to claim his soul. Ajamil was destined to damnation if he hadn't uttered Narayan – his son's name. In calling his son (Narayan) God forgave all his sins because 'Narayan' is also God's name and redeems whoever utters it.

The Lord's name chanted knowingly or unknowingly, correctly or incorrectly (as was the case for Valmiki who chanted "Mara, Mara' instead of "Ram, Ram") plays its purifying role. Gunatitanand Swami says, "I shall redeem anyone who knowingly or unknowingly chants the name of Swaminarayan." Just as fire or acid burns anyone ignorant of its burning property, similarly, God's name destroys sins regardless of one's ignorance. It would however be pertinent to note that one who chants with faith and understanding supercedes the former.

When the valiant Ram returned to Ayodhya he was

accorded a hero's welcome. A grand coronation was arranged. Guests from all corners were invited. Vibhishan (brother of Ravan) and his followers were also invited. After the occasion the guests returned to their kingdoms. Vibhishan decided to stay behind. His followers, however, wished to return to Lanka. But there was a major problem stopping them from going. The stone bridge to Lanka had submerged in water, leaving them with no hope of returning home. Vibhishan solved their dilemma.

He took a leaf and without their knowledge wrote the name of 'Ram' and wrapped it in a cloth. "Take this cloth," Vibhishan said, "and a way shall be opened to you." The followers did as their new king had instructed. They entered the waters and to their surprise the ocean waters became knee-deep. They waded towards Lanka. Midway, one of them opened the cloth to see its contents. Seeing only a dry leaf, he laughed. On closer inspection he saw the name of 'Ram' written on it. This made him laugh all the more. "How could the name of Ram make the ocean knee-deep!" And with this thought his faith subsided. The ocean waters rose and they all perished in the deluge.

Nam-jap has a marked effect on health. Dr Benson of Harvard University cited an interesting aspect of *jap*. In a 1976 issue of *Span* magazine, he says that experiments show that metabolism in a human changes when he retires for the night. Blood pressure and other body processes operate without any fluctuations. The individual awakens fresh and invigorated. This particular situation can also be attained through 20 minutes of *jap,* twice during the day. Chanting God's name corrects all erratic body processes, thus enabling good health.

In the Skand Puran (written by Sage Vyasji) we find a verse that reads: "I pray to the infinitely powerful Lord whose holy name and remembrance relieves me of all mental and physical afflictions."

In Vachanamrut, Loya 6 Bhagwan Swaminarayan

emphasizes the importance of *jap* by questioning an assembly of sadhus and devotees, "While meditating on God, countless different waves of vicious thoughts arise in the mind, just as large waves arise in the ocean. When such thoughts do arise, how can they be suppressed?"

Shriji Maharaj answers his own question, "When such vicious thoughts arise, one should stop the meditation, and should clap and chant 'Swaminarayan, Swaminarayan' aloud, without shame. One should pray to God, 'O Lord! You are a friend of the meek! You are an ocean of mercy!' Also, one should remember a great sadhu of God, like Muktanand Swami, and pray to him too. As a result of this, all disturbing thoughts will be eradicated and peace will prevail. Apart from this, there is no other method to eradicate such thoughts."

He says further that one who has a firm faith in God (*upasana*) believes that when a sinful man chants the name of 'Swaminarayan', then even during his dying moments, he becomes pure, free from all sins and attains the highest abode of God - Akshardham (Vachanamrut, Gadhada I 56).

The Swaminarayan *mahamantra* was introduced by Sahajanand Swami, or Bhagwan Swaminarayan, on the thirteenth day after the passing away of Ramanand Swami. He called an assembly of sadhus and devotees and revealed the Swaminarayan mantra. The traditional 'Ram-Krishna Govind' mantra was replaced by Swaminarayan. In the Swaminarayan mantra, Swami means Gunatitanand Swami and Narayan refers to Sahajanand Swami. After this new mantra, Maharaj became popularly known as Swaminarayan.

An incident in *Aksharanand Swamini Vato* ('The Talks of Aksharanand Swami') describes the potency of the Swaminarayan mantra. It describes the story of Jehalo, a servant who tilled the land for Allaiya Khachar. Both were faithful disciples of Bhagwan Swaminarayan. On one occasion, Allaiya

Khachar, on returning from a trip, found that Jehalo had died. His body had been taken for cremation. Allaiya Khachar rushed to the cremation grounds and halted the lighting of the funeral pyre. He wanted the town's people to witness the power of the Swaminarayan mantra. He called to the dead man, "Jehalo! Jai Swaminarayan." To everyone's surprise Jehalo opened his eyes. He enquired why he had been called back from God's proximity in Akshardham. A few minutes later he said 'Jai Swaminarayan' to everyone and lay down. The funeral pyre was then lit to cremate the mortal body of Jehalo. The whole village was stunned by this miracle. The mere name of Swaminarayan had brought Jehalo back to life!

Gunatitanand Swami, the first successor and ideal disciple of Bhagwan Swaminarayan, explains that the Swaminarayan mantra is powerful enough to neutralize the poison of a black cobra. The incident of how Yogiji Maharaj was saved from the venom of a cobra bite bears testimony to the words of Gunatitanand Swami.

In his talks, Gunatitanand Swami prescribes chanting God's name as one of several means to realizing God. He says, "Prahlad was fiercely battling against God but he failed to vanquish him. The Lord then stopped him and told him that if he wanted to win him he would have to abandon his weapons and resort to chanting his name and remembering him mentally. Prahlad accepted God's proposal and six months later he won God's eternal blessings" (Swamini Vato 1.3).

Even today the efficacy of the Swaminarayan mantra is a reality. Once, a devotee, saddled with a heap of problems, came to Pramukh Swami Maharaj and emptied his woes. Swami blessed him and consoled him. "Chant the Swaminarayan mantra. Have faith in God and chant his holy name. The storm shall pass and you'll soon be faring through calm waters. You shall be happy." Later, the devotee said, "The gruelling events that led to my misery are yet to recede but I can say that chanting the name of Swaminarayan has brought untold peace to my heart."

Even though God's holy name chanted knowingly or unknowingly has its effect on the devotee, the effect is more pronounced when it is chanted consciously, correctly and with an awareness of its glory. Our ancient teachers have shown certain requisites for observing *nam-jap*. They are as follows:

1. Fix the hours for *nam-jap*. The most effective time is before dawn when *sattva* (goodness) is predominant.
2. Select a definite place. It is advantageous to sit in the same place each day.
3. Be seated in a steady pose because this helps to steady the mind and aids concentration.
4. Always sit facing north or east. This enhances the efficacy of *jap*.
5. Pronounce the mantra properly without any mistakes.
6. Keep a vigilant and alert attitude to check the mind from wandering or slipping into drowsiness.
7. Use a rosary as an aid to *jap*. Use the middle finger to rest the rosary and the thumb for rolling the beads. The index finger should not be used.
8. Whilst doing *jap* visualize the beautiful *murti* of Bhagwan Swaminarayan and the *guru parampara*. This will give thrust to this spiritual exercise.
9. Do not cross the main bead or crown of the rosary. Turn back when you reach the head.
10. Do not beg for any worldly objects while doing *nam-jap*.
11. Abstain from faultfinding while doing *nam-jap*.

13 SWAMINARAYAN MANTRA

Prof. Ramesh M. Dave

On the path of spirituality and mysticism, a mantra or mystic syllable is a must for various reasons. The Supreme Bhagwan Swaminarayan gave the Swaminarayan mantra on the thirteenth day after the demise of his Guru, Ramanand Swami. The Swaminarayan mantra has spiritual force and divine power. It has the power to manifest right knowledge, spiritual light, and divine bliss in the heart of an aspirant.

The mantra is composed of two words - 'Swami' and 'Narayan', which respectively signify Aksharbrahma Gunatitanand Swami and Purna Purushottam Sahajanand Swami. The conjunction of these two words imply the relationship between a devotee and his Supreme Lord. It suggests the *upasana* of Akshar and Purushottam, i.e., the ideal Devotee and the Supreme Master. The Swaminarayan mantra, when understood in this sense, suggests that an aspirant has to become like Aksharbrahma and worship the Supreme Parabrahma. In short, it explains the eternal and inseparable relationship between Akshar and Purushottam.

When recited loudly it emits a sound that is at once divine and *brahmanizing*. Its continuous loud recitation helps in concentration, meditation and attainment of the ecstatic bliss of the Divine. The mantra is the embodiment of God and his divine power. Therefore, when recited in chorus, rhythmically and melodiously with musical accompaniments, before the *murti* of God or in a mandir, it purges the mind of all impure thoughts and distractions. It creates a divine atmosphere around singers. Thus the Swaminarayan mantra is identical with the spirit of the Lord.

The effects and impact of this mantra are very subtle, sublime and divine. Its power of spiritual influence is incomprehensible. To a man of undivided devotion, its power is revealed by God at his sweet will, especially when he is pleased by mantra-recitation and showers his grace on a devotee. The strength of its power is now known to a scholar or a yogi. But it is also commonly experienced by a devotee. The experience of the divine power of mantra-recitation is the unfathomable bliss and presence of the Divine in the heart. Consequently, the devotee's interest and involvement in the world declines and he withdraws himself from the objects of enjoyment.

The Swaminarayan mantra liberates one from all sins, done consciously and unconsciously in this life and previous lives. It is the supreme mantra with the most subtle and purificatory effect.

Its recitation accomplishes all wishes. It yields good health, a peaceful life, material prosperity and worldly wisdom to a man of worldly desires. It helps in preserving health and curing illness. It helps in gaining peace of mind from fear, tensions and worries. It helps in resolving conflicts. It helps in overcoming obstacles and hardships in life. It helps in putting an end to pain, misery and suffering.

However, to a spiritual aspirant it helps in getting rid of his faults, vices and insufficiencies. Its recitation helps in concentration and meditation. It alone helps in disentangling oneself from the cycle of births and deaths.

When it is recited uninterruptedly, keeping God alone in view, its spiritual effects are great and indescribable. It dispels the darkness of ignorance and enlightens the soul by the light of spiritual wisdom. It fills the heart by the bliss of the Divine!

When it is recited by the instructions of a God-communion Sadhu (Pragat Brahmaswarup) its effects are all the more powerful. When it is recited incessantly, keeping the mind fixed on God, manifesting in the person of the God-communion Sadhu like Pramukh Swami Maharaj, then it *brahmanizes* the soul. It makes one a *jivanmukta* (liberated in the embodied state) and graces one with a place in the divine abode called Akshardham, in the service of the Supreme Bhagwan Swaminarayan, eternally.

It is the mantra recited by the most fortunate and spiritually pious aspirants.

It liberates even a sinner on his death-bed, if he happens to listen to it even once with reverence!

Its recitation liberates one from the influence of evil spirits. Its recitation drives away the ghosts, demons, witches and other evil spirits. They cannot harm the reciter of this mantra. Even the messengers of Yama (the god of death) cannot come near its reciter.

In conclusion, the Swaminarayan mantra relieves and redeems the aspirant from his mundane hassles and the cycle of births and death and bestows everlasting peace.

14 POWER OF PRAYER

Sadhu Amrutvijaydas

Very often, when all else fails, man turns to God and prays. But instead of using prayer as a spare wheel, if it is used as the primary force, it reaps rich rewards. Harnessing the power of prayer will energize all our activities. All we have to do is ask.

The Apollo 13 Story: April 1970

"Houston, we've had a problem." At 55 hours, 54 minutes and 53 seconds into the Apollo 13 mission, this heart-stopping outburst was relayed to Mission Control in Houston by the astronauts 200,000 miles away. It initiated an unbelievable flurry of activity. A coordinated operation to rescue the ailing spacecraft and its jeopardized crew began in earnest.

Having achieved its aim of landing a man on the moon, for NASA, this was considered a 'routine' trip to the moon. And it was, until oxygen tank number two aboard Apollo 13 exploded during a routine check procedure. It was then that technical expertize and divine inspiration worked hand-in-hand to ensure the safe return of the astronauts.

The explosion, which crippled the spacecraft, meant that not only was the moon landing called off, but that emergency measures to bring the craft and crew back to Earth had to be implemented.

No doubt, all the scientists involved in this great rescue, displayed exemplary teamwork and ingenuity. But there was an unseen force aiding their efforts. It was the divine force of prayer. Prayer has often succeeded, where other measures seem to fail. In the rescue of Apollo 13, this was also the case.

In an article entitled "What really happened to Apollo 13", Jerry Woodrill, who worked on the mission as the Alarm System Engineer, recognizes the prominent and indispensable part prayer played in the successful rescue of Apollo 13. In it, he says, "Many might regard the rescue as the 'spiritualizing' of a dramatic event for religion's sake. I would agree, had I not found a majority of evidence to the contrary."

He adds, "*The New York Times* reported special prayer services... Prayers were said at the Chicago Board of Trade and prayers for the Apollo 13 crew sounded at the Wailing Wall in Jerusalem." Even the United States government realized the necessity of prayer and so Jerry Woodrill writes, "The US Senate adopted a resolution urging prayers."

Finally, he says that his wife has a bracelet and medallion which was, "bought at the space centre exchange store shortly after the successful 1970 rescue. The large coin pictured praying hands with the words 'Apollo 13... And the whole world prayed'." This is a clear indication of how much NASA, the people with the most to lose, believed in the important contribution of prayer in their successful rescue.

The entire rescue operation was a perfect example of how effort combined with prayer leads to success.

Prayer

A prayer is a solemn request or thanksgiving to God. Prayer is instinctive to man and no one can do without it, whatever form it may take. To many, prayer is a last-ditch appeal to God to rescue them from desperate circumstances. But this need not be the case, since, through prayer one can establish a connecting link with God to help from beginning to end.

Surely, the secret of success lies in tapping the greatest,

inexhaustible reservoir of power conceivable. Therefore, direct prayer to God will ensure our success.

Preparing for Prayer

For prayer to be successful, certain prerequisites must be fulfilled, namely:

1. Faith in God. This is the root cause of success. We must realize the all-encompassing, all-pervasive power of God and have faith in his glory.
2. Surrender to God. If one has true faith, then one will automatically surrender one's all at the feet of God.
3. Love for God. Before we ask him for further favours, we must be grateful to him for what he has already given to us without our asking. We must love and respect his commands and sincerely observe them.
4. Purification. Purity of the body and *jiva* is the most important factor in winning the love and grace of God. To attain this purity, we must repent for our past mistakes, ask for forgiveness, atone for them and abstain from making fresh mistakes.

What People Pray For

Superbowl XXV. Only eight seconds of the match remain. The New York Giants are leading 20-19 against the Buffalo Bills. The Bills' kicker, Scott Norwood, is about to attempt a relatively easy field goal to win the match and the championship. As he prepares, the Giants' players are behind the upright, kneeling - their eyes and minds directed heavenwards - appealing in prayer to an even greater giant - God! Seconds later, their prayer is answered. The field goal is missed and the Giants win the Superbowl.

This is the sort of material gain people pray for. Though there is nothing wrong in it, it is when these prayers appear to go unanswered that people raise doubts in God. But, as William Shakespeare tells us, we fail to realize that whatever happens is for our benefit:

"We ignorant of ourselves,
Beg often our own harms, which the wise powers
Deny us for our good; so find we profit
By losing of our prayers."

All along, we pray for sensual pleasures and worldly gains, while we ignore life beyond the senses - the spiritual life.

It is this issue - prayer for spiritual gains - that is addressed by Bhagwan Swaminarayan in the Vachanamrut.

What Should We Pray For

Through our shortsightedness and narrow-mindedness, we ask for the riches of the world, but they fail to give us permanent happiness. So, we must realize our spiritual objective and pray for success in that direction - for it is this spiritual peace and happiness which is permanent.

As people grow older, their prayers to God change. As children, they pray for good grades, a bicycle and such other things. As adults they pray for a good job, a loving partner and a good home. But, all through life, prayers for spiritual progress must accompany these prayers for material gains.

Learning from Our Predecessors

After Prahlad had been rescued by Lord Nrusinh from the fury and torture of his father, Hiranyakashipu, he realized that this protection was just temporary. He knew that the real protection would be to save him from his spiritual enemies. Bhagwan Swaminarayan narrates Prahlad's ensuing prayer in Vachanamrut, Loya 3: "Prahlad said to Nrusinhji, 'Maharaj, I am not afraid of this terrifying form of yours. Moreover, I do not consider your protection of me as true protection. Rather, when you save me from my enemy's troops in the form of the *indriyas,* I shall consider that to be true protection.' Therefore, a devotee of God would not be elated if God were to protect him physically; and he would not be disappointed if he were not protected. Instead, he would remain carefree and continue to worship God."

After all, this is God's mission on Earth - to rescue people from materialistic temptations. To help us, Bhagwan Swaminarayan guides us in what to pray for by saying, "O Lord! It is the fault of the *indriyas* (senses) and *antahkaran* (mind). I am separate from them and they are my enemies. Please protect me from them" (Vachanamrut, Panchala 3).

Since our senses are our link with the outside world, it is important that they do not lead us away from God. Through prayer, and sincere observance of God's commands, our senses will not be drawn towards material temptations.

Bhagwan Swaminarayan emphasizes the importance of company while treading the spiritual path. He asks us to pray for protection against bad company. This bad company is of four types - one, Kudapanthi; two, Shaktipanthi; three, Shushka Vedanti and four, Nastik. By the company of Kudapanthis one disobeys the vow of celibacy; by the company of Shaktipanthis one eats meat and drinks alcohol and thus disobeys one's own dharma; by the company of Shushka Vedantis one negates the divine form of God, the *murtis* of his incarnations and his abode and leads one astray from devotion and faith in God; by the company of Nastiks one attributes everything to karma and eliminates the role of God and strays from the path prescribed by the scriptures (Vachanamrut, Gadhada I 48).

Thus, bearing in mind the nature and type of people likely to deflect us from our spiritual goal, we should steer clear of them and associate only with good company.

Besides external *kusang*, like bad company, we must also avoid *kusang* in the form of fault-finding. Bhagwan Swaminarayan knows of the fatal spiritual consequence resulting from such fault-finding. So he leads by example in Vachanamrut, Gadhada II 40. In this Vachanamrut, the *paramhansas* observe that Bhagwan Swaminarayan has performed one extra *dandvat* to his normal, routine number. When they enquire into the reason for this, Bhagwan Swaminarayan says, "Today, the following thought occurred to me: 'No other sin causes more misery to a person than when he somehow - knowingly or unknowingly - harms a devotee of God by thought, word or deed.' Thus, I offered one extra prostration to atone for any mistake that may have occurred knowingly or unknowingly harming some devotee of God by thought, word or deed."

Then he says that everyone should daily perform one extra *dandvat*, accompanied by a prayer asking for forgiveness from the sin of having insulted or pained any of God's devotees, knowingly or unknowingly, by body, mind or speech. Then, one must not take this as a licence to make further mistakes but must positively aim to avoid such mistakes.

All these prayers are for our spiritual progress. This is what Bhagwan Swaminarayan considers as real and permanent progress.

God Helps Those Who Help Themselves

Along with prayer comes effort. After all, what do we pray to God for? We pray for the success of our endeavours. Bhagwan Swaminarayan, highlighting the significance of personal effort, says that for one who is troubled by his own drawbacks, if he intensely and selflessly serves a great sadhu... God will shower his mercy upon him ... and he will be instantly relieved of his drawbacks (Vachanamrut, Gadhada II 7).

This is a clear example of how one's efforts earn the grace

of God and thus help one to fulfil one's aim. So the necessity of effort along with prayer is easily understood.

The Ultimate Objective

In many Vachanamruts - Gadhada I 23, Gadhada II 30, Gadhada II 45, Loya 7, Ahmedabad 2, Ahmedabad 3 and others - Bhagwan Swaminarayan defines our life's goal as: "To become *brahmarup* and worship Purushottam."

All the above prayers help us on this path. Even in Vachanamrut, Gadhada III 39, delivered just ten months before Bhagwan Swaminarayan returned to Akshardham, he tells us to pray for this goal. Addressing all of the *paramhansas* and *satsangis,* Shriji Maharaj said, "What is God's *maya*? *Maya* is nothing but the sense of I-ness towards the body and my-ness towards anything related to the body. These should be eradicated. Anyone who eradicates *maya* can be said to have transcended *maya*. In fact, it is the principle of all of the scriptures that one should eradicate *maya* and develop love for God. This principle must be understood - either today or some time in the future. Great devotees such as Hanuman, Narad, Prahlad have also asked from God, 'Protect us from *maya* in the form of I-ness and my-ness, and may we develop love for you. May we also have the company of the *Sant* who has transcended *maya* and has love for you; and may we develop affection and a sense of my-ness towards him as well.' Therefore, we too should do the same and ask for the same, as well as do *shravan, manan* and *nididhyas* on this principle."

So, we see, nowhere has Shriji Maharaj guided us towards materialistic pleasures. He knows their temporary nature. He wants to share with us the permanent and all-encompassing spiritual bliss he enjoys. So, he has guided us on how, through prayer, effort and the company of a Satpurush we can attain this happiness.

15 HUMILITY IN LIFE

Sadhu Jnanyagnadas

God Ordains, Be It Good or Bad

Meister Eckhart, a German mystic and Christian theologian, in a homely parable writes: "There was a learned man who desired that God show him a man who would teach him the truth. And once when he felt a very great longing, a divine voice said to him, 'Go to church, and there shalt thou find a man who shalt show thee the way to blessedness.' And he went thence, and found a poor man whose feet were torn and covered with dust and dirt, and all his clothes were hardly worth three farthings. And he greeted him, saying, 'May God give you a good day.'

'I have never had a bad day,' he answered.

'God give you good luck.'

'I have never had ill luck,' the poor man replied.

'May you be happy!'

'I have never been unhappy.'

'But why do you answer me thus? Pray explain this to me, for I cannot understand it.'

The poor man answered, 'You wished me good day. I have never had a bad day; for if I am hungry I praise God; if it freezes, hails, snows, rains, if the weather is fair or foul, still I praise God; whether I am wretched and despised, I praise God, and so I have never had an evil day.

'You wished that God would send me luck. But I have never had ill luck, for I know how to live with God, and I know that what he does is best; and what God gives me or ordains for me, be it good or ill, I take it cheerfully from God as the best that can be, and so I have never had ill luck.

'You wished that God make me happy. I was never unhappy; for my only desire is to live in God's will, and I have so entirely yielded my will to God's, that what God wills, I will.'

'But if God should will to cast you into hell,' said the learned man, 'What would you do then?'

'Cast me into hell? His goodness forbids! But if he did cast me into hell, I should have two arms to embrace him. One arm is true humility, that I should lay beneath him, and be thereby united to his holy humanity. And with the right arm of love, which is united with his holy divinity, I should so embrace him that he would have to go to hell with me. And I would rather be in hell and have God, then in heaven and not have God.'

"Then the learned man understood that true acceptance of everything with utter humility is the nearest way to God."

Simplicity and Humility

In the Vedas also, the devotees pray to God, "Even if you cast us into hell, do remain with us so that we can offer devotion."

Simplicity and utter humility are the two sovereign remedies on the path of devotion, whereas pride and hypocrisy are the two great obstacles.

God, himself, has ever remained modest, performing the lowest form of service and disregarding the insults hurled upon him.

Bhagwan Swaminarayan, during his stay in Loj at the ashram of Ramanand Swami, washed the clothes of the sadhus, brought water from the well, swept the floor, collected cow dung from the streets for fuel, performed every kind of *seva* in the most humble fashion.

Shri Krishna cleaned dishes during the Rajasuya Yagna performed by the Pandavs.

Durvasa humiliated Shri Krishna by spattering butter on his face and treating him and Rukmini as horses to pull his chariot. Shri Krishna, though an incarnation of God, acted like a humble servant.

Once, on entering Anand, Bhagwan Swaminarayan was pelted with stones, bricks, cow dung and garbage by some non-believers. He didn't retaliate nor think of cursing them. He even prevented his angered royal disciples, like Sura Khachar and Jiva Khachar, from fighting the mischiefmongers.

Nishkulanand Swami writes in the Bhaktachintamani, "How could a devotee even think of acquiring pride when God is ever humble."

Once, a sadhu struck Shastriji Maharaj with a stick so forcefully that it broke into two. Shastriji Maharaj calmly picked up the broken pieces and handed them back to the sadhu.

Once, Yogiji Maharaj was engrossed in performing his morning puja. A person put a banana skin on Yogiji Maharaj's head. Swami picked up the skin and put it aside without showing the slightest trace of annoyance.

Mulji Brahmachari was excommunicated by Bhagwan Swaminarayan for a minor mistake. The Brahmachari had realized the greatness of Shriji Maharaj. He knew that although he was not at fault the Lord had insulted and driven him away. And besides his excommunication, he was also forbidden to wear shoes and told not to eat sweet or oily foods. Inspite of the Lord's seeming injustice, Mulji remained unperturbed. He remained steadfast in his devotion to Bhagwan Swaminarayan. On having passed the tough test, Bhagwan Swaminarayan accepted him back into his service.

An uncultured man spat on Eknath while returning from his morning bath. Without a word of reproach, Eknath humbly went to the river Godavari and bathed again. This act was repeated a hundred and eight times. Eknath won over the man through humility. The man fell at his feet and asked for forgiveness. Eknath thanked him saying, "Thank you for giving me the chance to bathe in the sacred Godavari a hundred and eight times."

Annoyed with Socrates, his own wife poured a bucket of water on her husband. Laughing, Socrates thanked her, "I was feeling so hot from outside. You have cooled me down." His wife felt ashamed of her mean act.

Abraham Lincoln possessed a magnanimity rare in public figures. But Edwin Stanton had denounced him as a low, cunning clown. Yet Lincoln appointed him the Secretary of War for he found that he was the best man for the job. His colleagues complained that even as a cabinet member Stanton called the president a fool. Lincoln calmly replied, "I reckon it must be true, for Stanton is generally right." No wonder that a repentant Stanton, sobbing at the bedside of the assassinated president, declared, "Here lies the greatest ruler of men the world has ever seen."

Cultivating personal humility helps dissolve conflicts and miseries in life. It finally endows one with peace and happiness that transcend the realm of materialism.

16 PRAYER – WISHES TURNED GODWARDS

Sadhu Brahmaviharidas

Something strange occurs at the mandir in Ahmedabad during April and May; hundreds of school kids from the neighbourhood schools are seen climbing the mandir steps, jostling their way up to the main shrine. Every year this scene repeats itself. Why? Because it is Exam Time! The children come to pray for better results, and though they are rarely seen for the rest of the year, they appear in large numbers just before the exams. And this pattern is repeated at mandirs everywhere.

One may be tempted to brand such time-bound prayers as 'plastic' or 'hypocritical' where God is called upon in a 'use and throw' manner. However, from a broader viewpoint, it is the insecurity of possible failure that prods the youngsters to reach out for help from a higher force.

In reality, what makes the kids pray, often makes the elders pray.

On the surface the problems may differ; they may not be of passing exams or pining for toys and trips, but they may be of getting jobs or wanting a fatter pay packet. Whatever the case or condition, the basic fact remains undeniably true that most human prayers spring from a common feeling of insecurity, helplessness or hopelessness.

Prayer, a Last Resort?

When human strength sags and our confidence in ourselves and in things around us begins to betray us, we often turn to God. God is used like a spare wheel, never as the driving wheel.

In emergencies, and impossible situations God is contacted on a hotline for help; but not at other times. The tense moments of a hospital repeats and re-repeats itself countless times: The group of surgeons give a final heave, pull down their masks, remove their gloves, drop their heads in silence and say to the anxious relatives of a patient in a critical condition, "Just pray, we can do no more."

It was the same during the devastating earthquake that made Mexico City look like a cardboard city, tearing it apart from end to end. Thousands of residents were seen praying day and night for weeks following the catastrophe. God had been called upon to ease the misery!

The three year-long drought and famine that scarred the land and lives of people in Gujarat in 1986, 1987 and 1988 did much to revive the religious faith of millions. Prayers were resorted to as the last hope for rains; obviously, after all attempts at artificial rain and other human devices had failed miserably.

Though human prayers may remain self-centred, God is too compassionate to turn his back and ignore them. Though we may lack sincere faith in God, it is comforting to know, God has sincere faith in us. He helps us despite our follies in faith.

The Story of 'Gajendra Moksha'

The Puranic story of 'Gajendra Moksha' symbolically reveals the narrow nature of human beings compared to God's magnanimity.

In the early stages of the story, Gajendra, the elephant, dallies in a lake. Midway, his front foot is caught by a crocodile. A battle ensues. The mighty Gajendra works all his strength to go ashore but water is the homeground of the crocodile; its power is matchless and Gajendra's foot is caught in the vice-like jaws of the reptile. The scriptures say that the fight lasted a thousand years; neither warrior budging an inch either way. But then, Gajendra feels his strength fading and the crocodile swooshes across the water sensing victory. The water level rises furiously as the elephant begins to sink deeper and deeper. Just then, Gajendra sees a stray lotus flower floating in the lake. He picks it up, turns it skywards and offers it to God in the form of a prayer for help. Instantly, the all-merciful God realizes the plight of Gajendra, leaves his throne in the heavens above and rushes to the scene to liberate Gajendra. The story of 'Gajendra Moksha' (Liberation of the king of elephants) is startling in the sense that it draws a sharp, clear focus on human nature. Man, stubbornly, tries to solve all his problems without the help of God or prayer but sooner or later confronts a series of stalemates, where he exhausts himself; it is under such conditions that he turns to God. Realizing that nothing and no one in this world can come to help, like Gajendra, man turns his wishes towards God. He makes a plea for higher help. This means prayer.

Prayer, a Necessity for All

Victor Hugo has neatly embroidered this truth in silken words, "There are times in a man's life when regardless of the attitude of the body, the soul is on its knees in prayer." The most amazing of human achievers have admitted this use of prayer.

Mahatma Gandhi, the man who led India to freedom, confessed that he would have been a lunatic without prayer.

Lincoln, probably the most respected president of America, was seen many times quietly praying on the battlefield during the Civil War.

Dwight D. Eisenhower, America's hero of the Second World War and later president, declared, "Personal prayer, it seems to me, is one of the simplest necessities of life, as basic to the individual as suntans, food and water - and at times, of course, more so."

We also know the case of Arjun. He was intelligent, of unsurpassed wisdom, handsome, a great warrior and a person who had conquered sleep. Even he, the valiant Arjun was confused during the battle of Kurukshetra and finally surrendered himself at Shri Krishna's feet praying, "Guide me, O Lord!"

How Does a Prayer Help?

A not so distant example should suffice here. Dr Robert White (MD, PhD), a professor and co-chairman of neurosurgery at the Medical University in Cleveland, Ohio, and the Director of Neurosurgery at the Cleveland Metropolitan General Hospital was reputed as one of the top surgeons in the USA. It became a common phrase that Dr White never operated, 'his confidence did the job'. Such was the man's confidence in the operating theatre. Yet he disclosed in an interview published in *Readers' Digest,* October 1978 (UK Edition), "I pray a great deal, especially before and after surgery. I find prayer satisfying. I feel there are immense resources behind me when I pray, resources I need and want."

Charles Steinmetz, the mathematical wizard of America, seconds this view when he says, "I think the greatest discoveries will be made along spiritual lines. Some day people will learn that material things do not bring happiness and are of little use in making men and women powerful. Then the scientists of the world will turn their laboratories over to the study of God and prayer and the spiritual forces which as yet have been hardly scratched. When that day comes the world will see more advancement in one generation than it has seen in the last four."

Divine Prayers

In conclusion, we must consider that though all prayers reach God and are powerful enough to give us strength in our day to day duties, there are also those special prayers which have been said without a speck of selfishness. As humans we are likely to pray for our own progress and peace, for the benefit of our relatives and friends or for something centred on ourselves. We are likely to remain handcuffed to the pillar of self-centredness, but we can, nevertheless, still fix our vision on the great masters who pray - never for themselves but for the whole world. This is a prayer of divine proportions indeed.

After Pramukh Swami Maharaj was operated upon, in 1986, for a large but harmless tumour in the right upper thigh, he was shown a video recording of his own operation. Overall, the operation looked a painful experience and seeing it on the screen, Swamishri at once folded his hands and prayed, "O God! May no one else undergo such misery!"

Before or after the operation Swami only prayed to protect others from such pains, not himself. Such prayers are the finest forms of communication with God. Swamishri always says, "Every sincere prayer is heard and answered!" God not only hears and answers our prayers, but rather as John Masefield emotionally put it, "God warms his hands at a man's heart when he prays."

17 MENTAL IMAGERY, MANSI PUJA AND SUCCESS: I

Sadhu Mukundcharandas

The ancient rishis of India developed elaborate methods of offering devotion to God. Puja is one of them. The word is derived from the Sanskrit 'Puj' - to worship, to adore. Thus, puja is the act of worshipping God.

Puja is of two types: *pratyaksh* puja - with physical offerings, such as, fruits, flowers, incense, ornaments, rich garments, etc. and *mansi* puja - without any physical objects. In both forms, it is the *bhav* - deep veneration - of the devotee that is important. God accepts the *bhav* of the devotee and gives the fruits of devotion according to the *bhav*. Shri Krishna echoes this in the Gita (9-26):

Patram pushpam falam toyam yome bhaktyã prayachhati;
Tadaham bhaktyupahrutam ushnãmi prayatãtmanaha.

"I accept a leaf, a flower, a fruit or even water offered to me with a sincere heart and devotion."

In *mansi* puja, one imagines that one is offering devotion with material objects. *Mansi* puja is much harder than the *pratyaksh* form, so it is less practised. The fruits of both forms, nevertheless, remain the same. Therefore, allowance has been made for the devotee who may not be able to afford rich offerings and would yet like to express his devotion with the same intensity of feelings as one offering *pratyaksh* puja. In much the same words Bhagwan Swaminarayan has said this in Vachanamrut, Sarangpur 3. In fact, Shriji Maharaj attaches great importance to *mansi* puja and in Vachanamrut, Gadhada III 23, he has commanded the devotees thus, "One who is a devotee of

God should daily offer *mansi* puja."

Now, 200 years later we realize that Bhagwan Swaminarayan, or Shriji Maharaj, was far ahead of his time and what he had advocated then was not just hearsay or plain ritualism. Only in the past few years, has medical science started to unveil the great benefits derived from mental imaging.

Shriji Maharaj has minutely detailed the methods of performing *mansi* puja in different seasons in Vachanamrut, Gadhada III 23: "During the four months of summer, one should perform puja by first bathing God with cool, fragrant, pure water. One should then offer him a beautiful, washed, white *khes* to wear, which is thin and fine. After seating God on a beautiful seat, his whole body should be smeared with fragrant sandalwood from the Malay mountains, which has been collected in a bowl after forming it into a paste. Firstly, the sandalwood paste should be smeared on his forehead and closely observed; then his hands should be smeared and closely observed; then the paste should be smeared on his chest, stomach, thighs, calves, and other parts of his body. Those parts should also be observed. Then, beautiful kumkum should be applied on his holy feet as well as on the soles of his feet, and they too should then be observed. Thereafter, garlands of fragrant flowers such as *mogra, chameli, champa,* roses, etc., as well as various ornaments such as a cap, armlets, wristlets, etc., made of flowers should be offered. A fine cloth that is not too heavy and is as white as a *mogra* flower should be tied around his head; and a beautiful, white cloth which is fine and light, should be wrapped around his body."

After adorning such a royal attire who wouldn't like to hug the Lord? So, Shriji Maharaj complies to lovingly hugging the Lord as many times as one desires and savouring those moments in one's mind. He continues, "Then one should embrace God - once, or twice, or according to the degree of one's love. Thereafter, one should touch God's holy feet to one's own chest and head.

During that embrace, the sandalwood paste on God's body as well as parts from the garlands of flowers may stick to one's own body; and kumkum may also stick as a result of touching God's holy feet to one's own chest and head. All this should be visualized; i.e., one should feel, 'Sandalwood paste, kumkum and garlands consecrated by God have touched my body!' "

For the four winter months, Shriji Maharaj gives a superbly vivid account of *mansi* puja. He says, "During the four months of winter, one should perform puja by first bathing God with warm water and then offering him a white *khes* to wear. One should then seat God on a decorated cot with a velvet mattress that has been covered with a white bedsheet. One should offer a *surval,* offer a *dagli,* tie a rich orange *reto* of golden threads around his head, tie a rich *reto* around his waist, and place a rich *reto* over his shoulders. Then one should place various ornaments made of diamonds, pearls, gold and rubies on various parts of his body and adorn him with a pearl necklace as well. After offering these clothes and ornaments, the various parts of God's body should be closely observed. A kumkum *chandlo* should also be applied to God's forehead."

For the four monsoon months Shriji Maharaj says, "During the four months of monsoon, one should perform puja imagining that God has returned from some village, his white clothes having become completely drenched; or that he had gone to bathe with the *paramhansas* in a river and has returned from there drenched. After removing his wet clothes, he should be offered deep orange garments to wear; and his forehead should be smeared with yellow sandalwood paste mixed with saffron.

"In this manner, a devotee who offers puja in different ways according to the three different seasons increases his love for God, and his *jiva* benefits tremendously."

During the day, five *mansi* pujas can be offered. Just as one wakes up and after bathing and personal puja, one has breakfast, one should offer the same to God. The second *mansi* is at lunchtime, the third at tea time, the fourth at dinner in the evening and the final at night before one goes to bed. The offerings of food should be visualized in detail, using the senses of sight, smell, touch and taste. Again the food items should be those that are one's favourite and in *mansi* there is no limit as to the quantity and variety of items offered. For instance if one relishes the sweet item *jalebi,* instead of putting a few in a dish, why not imagine them in a large silver plate, layer upon layer of different colours, foot high, just like in a sweet mart! One could even offer a whole *annakut* in every *mansi.* There is no limit to the *bhav* of one's devotion. In the final *mansi* of the day, at bedtime, one could imagine that the Lord has adorned light and comfortable clothing, different from the clothes worn during the day. Obviously this depends on where one lives. If one lives on a higher altitude or in temperate zones, where it tends to get chilly at night, then one obviously imagines the Lord adorned in warm woollen clothing. If we ourselves usually drink milk, water, etc. before going to bed, then one offers the same to the Lord. One can then also imagine the bed frame to be made of sandalwood, so that all night the sweet fragrance pervades the mattress, quilt and pillows. The mattress can also be of air or water or just plain cotton. If the geographical region has mosquitoes then one can also imagine a large mosquito net around the whole bed. One then steps back and has darshan of the sleeping Lord.

Finally one offers prostrations and prayers to the Lord, for forgiveness for any mistakes made in the acts of devotion during the day and to bless and inspire one to offer more love and devotion towards the Lord.

Bhagwan Swaminarayan adds an extra dimension to *mansi* puja by teaching that the perfect master (the ideal devotee of God) is to be worshipped on par with God (Vachanamrut, Vartal 5).

It is interesting to note that *mansi* puja is really the same as the scientific phrase called mental imagery. In recent years, mental imagery has been successfully used by medical scientists in improving human health.

First, let us see a simple example of mental imagery to put it in perspective. Imagine holding a ripe juicy mango in your hand. Hold that image until you can smell the fresh scent of the mango. Then imagine taking a big bite and feel the juice stimulating the taste buds on your tongue and tickling the insides of your cheeks. Now try to forget the whole image. What remains! One's mouth is actually filled with saliva. This simple demonstration illustrates the power of imagination.

In a study conducted by Robert Kunzendorf, a psychologist in the USA, he attached electrodes to the eyes of 20 volunteers, five of whom were capable of producing vivid mental imagery, and had them look at coloured lights that were flashed in front of them. He discovered that each colour affected the retina differently. Green produced one electrical pattern, yellow another and so on. Kunzendorf flashed a coloured light at these people and asked them to imagine that it was another colour, they regularly reported seeing the other colour, and 25% per cent of the time their eye responded as though they were perceiving the imagined, and not the actual flashing colour.

Other scientists have shown that just imagining an object moving across the sky produces more eye movements than visualizing a stationary object.

In the late sixties a dental surgeon in Europe who loved sports combined yoga and mental visualization to improve the performance of athletes. Dr Raymond Abrezol taught them how to eliminate upsetting mental conditions that hampered their performance: nervousness before or during an event, lack of confidence, lack of concentration, fear of defeat, etc. He asked them to imagine running through their entire performance sequence in vivid detail. Physically, mind training improved precision of movement, economized energy usage and controlled posture. Psychologically, mind training improved concentration and attention and enhanced perception.

An example of this is Jack Nicklaus, the famous American golf champion who believes that his success is entirely due to practising concentration and visualization. He asserts that his golf game is only 10 per cent involved with the actual swing. Hitting specific shots is 50 per cent mental picture and 40 per cent actual set up. First, he tunes out the world and concentrates. He visualizes a mental film of the entire shot in his head, sharp and in focus. He sees the ball being hit, flying in the air, its path trajectory and shape, even its behaviour on landing. Only then does he physically prepare himself to make the kind of swing that will turn the previous images into reality.

This is a good example illustrating what Shriji Maharaj has said in the Vachanamrut that the senses behave under the influence and command of the mind. Bodybuilder Arnold Schwarzeneggar maintains that in weightlifting it's all "mind over matter. As long as the mind can envision the fact that you can do something, you can... I visualized myself being there already – having achieved the goal already."

In Russia, Olympic-level athletes receive 3-way training involving the athlete, the coach and the mind trainer. The latter helps develop the imaginative power of the athletes. They are trained to mentally run through vivid movies, like Nicklaus, and experience shows that such mental practice can be as effective as physical practice. In the East, such a combined mind-body approach has always been an integral part of oriental acrobatics and martial arts like Aikido and Kung Fu.

As we have seen, mental visualization thus greatly affects our physical abilities.

18 MANSI PUJA FOR FITNESS AND HEALTH: II

Sadhu Mukundcharandas

Mental visualization can help improve not only physical ability but can also produce creative genius. Nicola Tesla, one of the great but neglected scientists of this century, had trained his visualization faculty to such a degree that he could mentally construct an invention in detail. His mind was his laboratory. He felt that the trial and error method of experimentation that men like Edison used was wasteful and time-consuming. When Tesla was a child in Yugoslavia, his mother purposefully trained him in visualization, to play games in his mind. Later, he was able to rapidly learn 12 languages, develop a photographic memory and do maths instantly like an electronic calculator. His power of visualization was so precise that his skilled machinists said that if he were inventing a new turbine or some type of electrical equipment, he would produce every single measurement from his mind, including dimensions drawn to one ten-thousandth of an inch. It was this skill that led him to invent the A.C. system of power generation that won him the contract to harness Niagara Falls. He had 700 inventions to his credit.

Basically, the right half of the brain governs our artistic, musical, imaginative, innovative and visual abilities. The left side controls our scientific, logical, analytical, mathematical and verbal skills. Scientists believe that a person who uses both sides of his brain will be the most successful in either left or right brain professions. Einstein, for example, developed his theory of relativity while daydreaming about buildings flashing by when he was on a train. They appeared narrower than they were. He continued to muse on the problem and then, using analytical and logical left brain procedures developed the formula that changed the world. Later, he revealed that had he worked on this problem from a purely analytical and scientific point of view, he could not have envisioned the theory because it defied all the known laws of science. Because he also used his innovative and creative right brain abilities, he went beyond those laws. *Mansi* develops one's right brain abilities because it creates vivid pictures in one's mind. You actually involve your whole being, your senses and your feelings whilst offering *mansi* puja. This is corroborated by modern researchers. One in particular, Dr Owen Caskey, a psychologist in the USA says, "If you want to improve your life make a picture in your head of getting along with your spouse or of communicating with your boss. If you don't make pictures in your head, there's not going to be very much in life that's easy for you." Here, it is well to digress a little for the benefit of students who have problems in learning. Leading educators are introducing 'right brain strategy' to develop advanced learning techniques using mental exercises which induce states of mind especially conducive to accelerated learning. Their first requisite is a relaxed mind. Says Dr Caskey, "Relaxation skill is the most crucial element to improve learning ability. Anxiety interferes with learning. If you can rid an individual of anxiety, he is more likely to learn." This is achieved by visualization exercises, like the one mentioned earlier (p. 111) about the juicy mango. But *mansi* puja is in itself such an exercise and if it is practised regularly, it would be very easy for the student to get into a relaxed state of mind in preparation for studying. His personal involvement and interaction with God during *mansi* will be more subjective and fruitful than other abstract exercises. This method has two distinct advantages over others: (1) one does not become so deeply relaxed that one has trouble in concentrating and (2) it develops creativity and a powerful imagination easily. This is especially helpful to those students who complain of lack of imagination.

As far as health is concerned, *mansi* puja really does affect our body's chemical mechanisms to produce physiological changes. Researchers have begun to show how the images we produce in our mind influence our health. The first direct response of *mansi* puja on the body is profound relaxation. Generally our modern, urbanized living produces stress and some people are more prone to stress than others. As one psychologist has rightly observed, "The worst sources of stress are not in the newspaper headlines, but in our own minds!"

Physicians in the USA have devised their own relaxation and visualization techniques to help people suffering from depression, insomnia, asthma, high blood pressure, high cholesterol and even cancer. It is suggested that the images we produce may subtly change our emotions, creating either a positive or a negative effect on the immune system. J.K. Kiecolt Glaser and Hans Selye have documented the lowering of immunity in people suffering from depression and stress. A special type of cell in the blood, called T Cells, which fight infections, are less active during depression and periods of emotional stress. This enables illness to gain a foothold in the body. Overcoming stressful situations using positive mental imagery boosts one's immunity and thus improves one's physical health. *Mansi* puja is one form of positive mental imagery. If mental imagery can help people overcome disease, then it can also help healthy individuals keep their immune systems at peak level.

When we are disturbed and produce negative imagery, that is worry, the negative images in our mind induces the body to react in a detrimental way, leading to illness and disease, or even death. A classic example of this will help us understand the powerful effect of one's attitude towards an illness. In 1957, a cancer patient in the USA was given an experimental anti-cancer drug called Krebiozen. He believed it to be a powerful drug that would save him. His cancer literally disappeared! Then an article appeared in the news saying that Krebiozen was an ineffective anti-cancer drug. Unbelievable as it may seem, his cancer recurred. His doctor then told him that he was now giving him a super-refined version of Krebiozen which was really effective against cancer. Actually this time he was just given injections of water. Incredibly, his cancer went into remission for a second time. Some time later an article in the newspaper appeared which stated that the FDA was withdrawing the drug from the market. After reading this, the patient died within two days. Obviously the patient was horrified that he would have to die and the disturbed mind produced such negative images which led to harmful changes in his body, thus killing him.

Researchers have even begun to use mental imagery in treating terminal cancer patients. They have found that the size of their tumours can be reduced and sometimes even complete remission of the disease obtained. Dr Bernie Siegel, assistant clinical professor of surgery at the Yale Medical School, who has started teaching imagery to his cancer patients, was asked, "Has surviving cancer as much to do with our mental attitude as it does with the extent of the disease?" He replied, "Yes, absolutely."

Mind Rules the Body

Franz Alexander, MD, says, "The fact that the mind rules the body is, in spite of its neglect by biology and medicine, the most fundamental fact which we know about the process of life."

Norman Cousins narrates his experience with suspected tuberculosis in *Anatomy of an Illness*:

"My first experience in coping with a bleak medical diagnosis came at the age of ten, when I was sent to a tuberculosis sanitarium. I was terribly frail and underweight, and it seemed logical to suppose that I was in the grip of a serious malady. Later, it was discovered that the doctors had mistakenly interpreted normal calcification as TB markings. X-rays at that time were not yet a totally reliable basis for complex diagnosis. In any case, I spent six months at the sanitarium.

"What was most interesting to me about that early experience was that patients divided themselves into two groups: those who were confident they would beat back the disease and be able to resume normal lives, and those who resigned themselves to a prolonged and even fatal illness. Those of us who held to the optimistic view became good friends, involved ourselves in creative activities, and had little to do with the patients who had resigned themselves to the worst. When newcomers arrived at the hospital, we did our best to recruit them before the bleak brigade went to work.

"I couldn't help being impressed with the fact that the boys in my group had a far higher percentage of 'discharged as cured' outcomes than the kids in the other group. Even at the age of ten, I was being philosophically conditioned; I became aware of the power of the mind in overcoming disease. The lessons I learned about hope at that time played an important part in my complete recovery and in the feelings I have had since about the preciousness of life."

An exceptional example of the mind's profound capacity is of William Calderon, who recovered completely from the most dreaded disease of all, AIDS. In December 1982 he was diagnosed as having AIDS and told that he would probably live only six months. He became depressed and anxiety set in. Simultaneously, Kaposi's sarcoma, a type of cancer most associated with AIDS, appeared and began to infiltrate his body rapidly. A hairstylist by profession, Calderon was attending his salon when a regular customer noticed his despair. After revealing his story, Calderon was told by the customer that, "William, you don't have to die. You can get well." The customer then showed him how to meditate and perform mental imagery in line with the method Dr Simonton used. He began to have a positive attitude about life and people and then his tumours began to shrink. Two years later Calderon was re-examined and he showed no signs of AIDS. This is the first documented case of a complete recovery from AIDS and that, too, without the use of any drugs or conventional AIDS therapy.

In the final analysis it would seem that the more relaxed we are during our daily activities, i.e., free of stress, the fitter we become. Dr Herbert Benson, associate professor of medicine at Harvard Medical School, and president of Harvard's Mind-Body Medical Institute, has devised his own method of achieving relaxation. He advocates his method of focussing attention for 10 to 20 minutes once a day. Another such proponent, David Harp (MA), author of the new *Three Minute Meditator,* suggests mini-meditations, each one lasting from a few minutes to as little as 30 seconds, as often as you can during the day. Similar to *mansi,* it is interesting to note that the principles behind *mansi* puja advocated by Shriji Maharaj in 1829, are being verified and presented by the scientists of the current era as being beneficial not only to the physical body but also for attaining inner peace and tranquility.

19 THE SHADOW OF DEATH

Sadhu Brahmaviharidas

On 5 May 1993 a news agency in China solemnly filed a report that Li Ching Yu, the oldest man on earth, had died at 256!

People believed the Russians when they announced the death of Mislimov of Barzavu, in August 1973. They said he lived to enjoy the 100th birthday of his third wife and his grandchild.

Though we really do not know how close to truth these claims are, we still find them strikingly impressive, surprising and bewildering! The majority of humanity tends to marvel at life; yet overlooks the commonest and the most stunning part of it all - Death!

In the days of Shri Krishna, Yaksh bemused Yudhishthir with a similar question, "What is the greatest wonder of the world?" Yudhishthir unravelled, "Although, before his very eyes, man witnesses people dying and things perishing, he never, even once honestly feels that death shall befall him likewise."

Your Nursery Teacher Told You So!

Is it not absurd that we mechanically get into our daily routine sparing no thought or wilfully ignoring the most conspicuous feature of our life - Death? Since birth our eardrums have received the din of death, our eyes have seen its sieges and our mind has tolerated its tremors. Yet we forget!

On your zero birthday while you frolicked spritefully in your mother's arms, a birth certificate had been issued, but at the same time, the same people, set aside a similar piece of paper for the death certificate. Birth is an invitation to death. You may well recall the dramatic voice of your nursery teacher, "... and the b...i...g bad wolf died!" You cheered in a class-chorus as it meant a happy ending for the three little pigs. It was strongly suggestive that not only the baddies but even the goodies came to an inevitable end, whether unhappy or happy.

Now you're older and roaming the streets. It's Saturday. With a teenage gait and a stylish tilt you look up. Gosh! Colourful posters from the movie world arrest your eyes. They read 'Game of Death' and 'Death Race 2000'. Age comes harshly down and you find yourself in your early twenties, hung on a job. One evening, making full use of your cushioned sofa, you wearily turn on the TV. The box screens a few protestors waving "Death to..." The news terminates taking with it a few more years. A new horizon gives way. Crowded with dreams, you stand facing a small pit of fire or a church altar, holding a warm, delicate hand of your second half to be. Softly and shyly both of you whisper, "Till death do us part."

All this goes when death strikes.

Even the Strongest Proved Too Weak

At 33, death disposed of Alexander the Great with an ease of a spider gorging on a trapped fly. Napoleon, Stalin and Churchill were all great and sturdy but greater and sturdier still was death. The list is endless and it's here that the famous lines of a Gujarati poet, Narayandas, need framing:

As for a man, his days are numbered;
With dawn, as a bud of the field, he flourisheth.
With dusk, as a withered flower he falleth.

No Time for Goodbyes

When 900 people in Jonestown, Guyana, committed mass suicide in November 1978 the world was riddled by its suddenness and freakishness. Hardly anyone prophesied it or later believed it, but it was crystal clear. How inhumane was the instigator, the Rev. Jim Jones, is of little importance here as we are concerned with the unpredictability of Death.

Science Won't Help!

Many say science will curtail death and eventually eliminate it; as it has already increased our average lifespan from 30 in the 1900s to well over 60 in the 1990s. The question to ask is 'Will the space age scientist be able to devise a protective outfit to fight death?' The most logical answer is 'no'.

Today, the microscope has revealed the unseen world, the scalpel has discovered hidden regions and the telescope has found distant galaxies. Yet death has remained a mystery.

It's Coded Messages

So far, so good; we've closed in onto a few features of death.

(a) Death is predetermined; none can escape it.
(b) Death comes suddenly, unannounced.
(c) Death is too complex to be understood.
(d) Death is uninfluenced by scientific or worldly methods.

Birth brings joy; death brings gloom. We entered the world empty-handed and we'll have to leave it empty-handed. If our own body can't accompany us then what of our possessions? What use is expending a life for acquiring things which we are to leave behind? It would be like slogging day and night for 50 years at a factory and coming home without a dime! Vain and disheartening!

Before it's too late we must change things. We have to act fast because death may claim us anytime. Even now, at this very moment! But we can't understand it. We're in a fix! What do we do? Well, what does a child do when he's stuck with a sum? Simple! He runs to an experienced teacher. Our experienced sadhus and sages direct us to religion. Science remains mute on this topic, it offers nothing. Only religion offers us relief.

Steve McQueen, No. 1 Hollywood Star

His athletic physique, manly stride and a handsome squarish face topped with flaxen hair, hoisted him to the apex of Hollywood. For years, he remained the No. 1. Inwardly, a proud, rigid man disillusioned by success, Steve relentlessly despised God, until, at the age of 42, the doctors told him that he was a patient of terminal cancer. The horror of dying struck him. A dramatic metamorphosis followed. He found himself struggling to play a role he'd never played before. His film career was at stake, his dreams were dwindling, and he desperately needed aid. Past successes and publicity did poorly for his present state. At last, with a lacerated ego, he meekly turned to God. In 1979 a British newspaper reported, "A man who publicly scorned God began to privately pray for hours at an altar he specially installed at his place." In his own words, "I have touched God. He has given me more courage than I have ever had in my life." Though Steve never recovered physically, he died a different death. He had experienced that his entire life, though full of fame and wealth, was powerless when face to face with death. This understanding transformed him. He sought God during his final months and tried tirelessly in the limited time available. God indubitably assuaged the misery of his soul. He was fortunate enough to foresee death, we may not be so fortunate. We must act immediately! Opt for a resolution - a God-centred life, or a betterment, if we already are religious.

Overcoming Fear

In the Shrimad Bhagvat, King Parikshit, when informed

about his impending death in a week's time, became paralyzed with fear. At once he sought the succour of sage Shukdev and sought refuge in him. For a week he did without royal comforts, food and even water, focussing his senses on religious discourses. The knowledge of God elevated him, enabling him to transcend fear. He embraced death smilingly, fearlessly and went forth to become immortal. Through God he had vanquished the fear of death.

Both religious tales and God's words shed divine light which dispel this darkness. Bhagwan Swaminarayan says, "One who has devotion with exuberant love towards God will overcome fear of death and feel fulfilled" (Vachanamrut, Loya 2).

Does Death Call for a Party?

It has been bred in the very marrow of Indian Culture that death is not the inevitable, inescapable, tortuous ordeal. The Gita teaches, "The soul is never born nor dies; nor does it exist on coming into being. For it is unborn, eternal, everlasting and primeval; even though the body is slain, the soul is not."

With this knowledge, people realize themselves to be the soul; the soul never dies. No question of death lingers and the process becomes negligible. Moreover, Shri Krishna explains: "As a man discarding worn-out clothes, puts on new ones, likewise the embodied soul, casting off wornout bodies enters into others which are new."

Noteworthy historical events from the life of Bhagwan Swaminarayan up to this day confirm the statement.

A devotee in a vision was informed by the Lord that the elder of his two sons would expire in a month's time. And exactly a month later, the boy died. His relatives mourned and the village showed concern. But to their unthinkable horror, they saw the father distributing sugar crystals. He was celebrating his son's death and his entry into the abode of God.

Another month passed by and the Lord predicted his second son's death. It followed accordingly. People grieved at the two successive deaths in such a short interval. Yet, once again the father rejoicingly celebrated this inauspicious occasion. When the village folk irately questioned his behaviour, he clarified, "My sons were happy, but have become happier. They now sit in God's abode, eternally."

Jean de La Fontaine's saying demands some attention, "Death never takes the wise man by surprise he is always ready to go."

FESTIVALS

20 CHATURMAS: I

Sadhu Mukundcharandas

Mid-July to mid-November are the four most holy months in the Indian calendar. They are marked by austerities, devotion and celebration.

From Ashadh *sud* 11, Hindus engage themselves in a series of festivities. This day, which marks the beginning of the four holiest months in the Hindu Calendar, called Chaturmas, has an interesting story behind it. The Purans tell us that on Ashadh *sud* 11, Lord Vishnu descends into the Kshirsagar, the Ocean of Milk, for rest. On this day, Lord Vishnu also took the form of a dwarf called Vaman. He approached King Bali, who, although born into a family of demons, was a very righteous man. Lord Vishnu asked the king for a gift of land three strides in length. The guru of Bali, Shukracharya, and others warned the king against granting this gift, but the king did not listen. He took an oath to fulfil the wish of Lord Vaman. As the king took the oath Lord Vaman wilfully grew into a giant. In two strides he covered the earth and heavens. Bali realized at once that God in person had come to test him. He quickly offered his body, on which the Lord placed his foot, for the third promised stride. With devotion, Bali fulfilled the wishes of the Lord. The Lord regained Bali's wealth and kingdom for the gods, and Bali, by complying, won over the Lord's heart. Lord Vishnu promised to reside forever in Patal - the nether world of King Bali.

Lakshmiji, Lord Vishnu's consort, became unhappy when she heard of this. How could this be - she in the heaven of Vaikunth and her Lord in Patal. Distressed, she approached Shiva and Brahma, who on consoling her, promised that they would each spend four months of the year in Patal, in the Lord's stead thus freeing the Lord for eight months. And so, for four months of every year King Bali's tremendous sacrifice and devotion earns him the Lord's proximity.

During these four months the devout appease the Lord and remember him all the more because of his absence by taking vows to perform austerities, tell the rosary, perform prostrations, circumambulations, daily darshan at the mandir and spiritual reading. A story in the Purans tells us why it is necessary to enhance our spiritual endeavours during these months.

Once, in heaven, Indra, the king of the gods, and all the gods and goddesses were seated in an assembly. They were enjoying a dance performed by a beautiful damsel called Rambha. In perfect tune with the drums and rhythm Rambha danced, pleasing everyone. But towards the middle of the dance, the drum skin tore, and the dance had to be abandoned. A question now arose. Everyone wanted the dance to be completed, but from where would a skin for the drum be acquired that would give the necessary sound. Finally, the god of death, Yamaraja, pronounced that the skin should be from an animal or person who has never taken any vows or performed any austerities. The gods gave Yamaraja the responsibility for fixing the drum.

Yamaraja pondered as to whose skin could be used because everyone has performed at least a small austerity. After deep meditation he found an answer, "Subhadra, the sister of Shri Krishna," he said aloud. He sent his messengers with the necessary instructions. Now it so happened that in the assembly of the gods Naradji was also present. On hearing Yamaraja's decision he at once descended onto earth and told Shri Krishna about the assembly. The Lord at once approached his sister, Subhadra, and warned her. To say the least, Subhadra was dismayed and amazed. She, the sister of the Lord, and the wife of the famous and righteous Arjun was in such danger! She was born into a divine family, and was surrounded by people of high merit and religious standing, then why this punishment! It was unbelievable.

Shri Krishna advised her to perform the simple 'Gopadma' austerity. This entailed the sketching of a lotus the size of the hoof of a cow and then worshipping it with certain rituals. At once Subhadra performed the necessary rites. In the meantime, the messengers of Yamaraja arrived. But seeing Subhadra thus involved in service, they had to return empty-handed.

Subhadra was of high birth and herself a lady of much merit. Her brother was the Lord himself and her husband, Arjun, the favourite devotee of the Lord. Both loved and cared for her intensely. Even then, it was of the utmost necessity that she perform some austerity. If Subhadra was forced to observe certain sacred vows to free her from her sins then what of us mortals?

Chaturmas is a spiritual season for gaining knowledge, developing insights and strengthening faith. For four months, the entire atmosphere at home, the mandir and even work is surcharged with the light of the aspirants' spiritual endeavours.

The slightest acceptance of a vow opens the heart to God and his divinity. There is a constant expectancy. The devotee feels he is doing something concrete on the spiritual path and comes to appreciate once again the God-given fruits. He comes closer to God, understanding his ways and laws, and learns by firsthand experience the benefits of a spiritual life.

The Bhavishyottara Puran mentions the great advantages of performing austerities in Chaturmas. It says, "One who forgoes the tastes of the senses during Chaturmas comes nearer to God and is hence liberated from the cycle of births and deaths." Bhagwan Swaminarayan in his Shikshapatri has also instructed the devotees, "My devotees should take up extra vows during Chaturmas and those who are weak should take vows only during the month of Shravan."

We shall briefly see the importance of the festivals celebrated during these four months.

Guru Purnima

During these holy months we have the festival of Guru Purnima on Ashadh *sud* 15. For ultimate redemption the Upanishads point to a guru. The Kathopanishad says, "Arise and awake! Having approached the excellent and experienced, obtain knowledge from them." The first guru in Hinduism is Veda Vyas, who wrote the eighteen Purans, including the Shrimad Bhagvat Puran. His birthday is celebrated as guru Purnima. On this auspicious day Hindus all over India worship (*pujan*) their guru. 'Gu' in Sanskrit means one who removes darkness and 'ru' means to throw light, i.e., enlighten the aspirant. One who leads an aspirant from the darkness of ignorance into the light of spiritual enlightenment is called a guru. After having found a Gunatit Guru, through bowing or surrendering to him, followed by spiritual enquiry and service to him, the aspirant begins his march towards God-realization.

Hindola Utsav

Another festival that merits one with love and devotion for God is the Hindola Utsav (swing festival), celebrated for a month from Ashadh *vad* 2 to Shravan *vad* 2. This festival has its roots in the devotion of the *gopis* for Shri Krishna. In the natural gardens of Vrindavan they would, out of intense love, swing their Lord on swings made of creepers and overhanging vines. Today, devotees swing the Lord on decorative swings made of wood or silver. These are often decorated with exquisite and artistic designs made of materials such as flowers, vegetables, dry fruits, leaves, sweets, biscuits, fabric and many other items.

Installing God's *murti* in a swing is symbolic of installing him in one's heart. The gentle pulling of the swing symbolizes the aspirant's effort to entertain God and bring him closer to himself.

Shravan

Our holy personages hold 'Chaturmas' in great esteem, for they are the months when purity and righteousness fill the atmosphere. Of these four months, Shravan, is revered as the most holy. Each day of this month is filled with divinity. Even a small austerity or righteous deed performed knowingly or accidentally during this month yields great merits *(punya)*.

In the Purans it has been said, "Non-violence is the greatest dharma." Not only non-violence towards man but towards animals of all kinds. The enormity of such a definition of non-violence has not been bettered by any other religion other than the Hindu Faith. Nag Panchmi is one of the highlights of this ideal.

Nag Panchmi

Shravan *sud* 5 represents the day when the soil, heated during the summer, is cooled by the rains and creatures from below ground such as snakes *(nag)* come up to the surface. At this time no Hindu makes the mistake of killing any of these creatures and on the contrary he becomes merciful. Nag Panchmi marks the day when worship and *pujan* of the snake deity (Nag) is performed and milk is poured into snake pits.

Raksha Bandhan

On Shravan Purnima we see a confluence of three auspicious occasions. First, the Brahmins change their *janoi* (sacred thread). Second, devotees worship the Lord and third, sisters tie *raksha* (decorative bracelet made of sponge, cloth and paper) on the wrist of their brothers. Of these three festivals, Raksha Bandhan has gained wide popularity among the Indian masses.

Several stories relating to the origin of Raksha Bandhan are found in our scriptures. In the Vedas we find a mention of Sacchi, the wife of Indra, who, on tying a *raksha* on the defeated Indra, brought victory to the gods. In the epic battle of Mahabharat we find Kunti tying a *raksha* on Abhimanyu's hand, which thus earned him fame as a formidable warrior. We also have the story of Lakshmiji tying a *raksha* on Bali's hand and from then on a tradition of a sister (Lakshmiji) tying a *raksha* to her brother (Bali) was born.

The latter story may seem strange, for how could Lakshmiji, a goddess, ever have been a sister to Bali, a demon? To understand the answer let us look at how the brother-sister relationship materialized. When King Bali sacrificed everything to Lord Vishnu, the Lord was immensely pleased and promised him that he would stay with him forever. Consequently Lakshmiji spent many sad days, contemplating on how to bring back her Lord. After having decided to visit her Lord, Lakshmiji went to Patal. Bali was very happy to see Lakshmiji and welcomed her with admiration and respect. Lakshmiji tied a string on the hand of Bali and became his sister. Bali was all the more pleased and honoured for how could he, the sovereign of the demons have Lakshmiji, a goddess, as her sister! The new brother felt he should give a present to her new sister. But what could he give to a sister who had everything? Bali then promised Lakshmiji to grant her whatever she wanted. Lakshmiji asked for her Lord. Bali happily agreed to her wishes.

Even today, each year, the tradition of Raksha Bandhan reminds us of a true sister-brother relationship. It tellingly reminds our sisters to ask for the Lord; for one who has the Lord has indeed nothing more to desire.

Janmashtmi

More than 5000 years ago at 12 midnight Shri Krishna was

born in a jail to Vasudev and Devki. On his advent the chains that shackled his parents snapped, the jail doors opened and the sentries were numbed into deep sleep. The birth of the Lord liberates those fervent souls bound by the worldly fetters. Vasudev carried the newborn baby, fearing that Kans would kill his eighth child, like he had the previous seven. On reaching the banks of the stormy river Yamuna, Vasudev was troubled with the thought of crossing a rampaging river. He prayed to God and with bold faith stepped into the rough waters. Immediately the waters of the Yamuna parted. Vasudev took his child to safety and left him in the care of Nand and Yashoda. For centuries the story of Krishna's birth and his pastimes have been sung, re-enacted and celebrated, infusing devotion and peace in the hearts of millions.

Ganesh Chaturthi

Our holy books tell an interesting story about the birth of Ganesh - god of auspiciousness. Once, while Shivji was away from home, Parvati, his consort, created a child with her own powers. She called him Vinayak. The child was very obedient and followed his mother's wishes to the letter. On one occasion, his mother, wanting to have a bath, instructed Vinayak not to allow anyone through the door. While Vinayak was standing at the front door, Shivji arrived home. Neither was acquainted with the other. When Vinayak refused to let the Lord in, Shiva became furious. A fight ensued in which Shivji beheaded Vinayak. On seeing the tragic sight of her son, Parvati wept bitterly. Shivji, having been told that he had beheaded his own son, rejuvenated Vinayak by placing an elephant's head (the first animal that crossed his path) on to his body. Both Shiva and Parvati blessed their son saying, "Dear child, you shall be the first god to be worshiped in all meritorious deeds. Those who fail to worship you on auspicious occasions shall not be successful. We also pronounce you as the chief of our army - hence the name Ganapati, meaning, chief of all *ganas* (soldiers).

Ganapati is remembered as a god of profound intelligence as shown by his large elephant head, for his patience to listen to our innumerable scriptures through his large ears. His small elephant eyes endow him with the power of sharp insight and a powerful sense of detecting evil as associated with his snout. He also has an infinite capacity to contain the poison of hatred and evil in his large pot-belly.

The festival of Ganesh Chaturthi is celebrated with great pomp and festivity in the states of Maharashtra, Gujarat, Andhra Pradesh, Tamil Nadu and Karnataka. People install a *murti* of Ganapati on this day and offer worship for ten days before ceremoniously placing it in a river.

21 CHATURMAS: II

Sadhu Mukundcharandas

Vijaya Dashmi

The evil Mahishasur wreaked a reign of terror in the three realms and subdued the great kings and mighty gods to become the sole emperor of the three worlds. His tyranny, however, was short-lived. The kings, unable to bear the brunt of his evil rule, went to Brahma, Vishnu and Shiva and prayed for relief from terror. The three gods were annoyed by the wicked Mahishasur's doings. Out of their annoyance Shakti (a goddess) materialized. The gods equipped her with powerful weapons to vanquish Mahishasur. For nine days Shakti and Mahishasur were locked in a terrible combat. The tenth day saw the fall of Mahishasur and the triumph of good over evil leading to peace and happiness in the realms. Shakti was worshipped and lavished with honours and we now know and celebrate that triumph as Vijaya Dashmi. The nine-day Navratri festival commemorates the nine-day victorious struggle of Shakti over Mahishasur.

The significance of the battle between Shakti and Mahishasur has come to be identified today with the raging battle within us between the forces of good and evil, like pride, lust, jealousy, etc. Like the defeated kings, our mind, intellect and senses have succumbed to the overpowering forces of our animal nature. To regain our sovereignty, total refuge in God rewards us with a tremendous soul-strength (*atma-shakti*) to dethrone the evil forces altogether.

Vijaya Dashmi, popularly known as Dashera, is also remembered as the day when Shri Ram killed Ravan.

Ever since, many of our kings had commenced battles on

this day with strong hopes of victory over their enemies.

Today, the day is remembered and celebrated in many parts of India. In the north, huge effigies of Ravan are burnt. Displays in controlling and exercising horses are a highlight in some parts of the country. On this day, scholars worship the goddess Sharda and Sarasvati, and students consider this day auspicious for commencing their academic career. The *shami* tree, is also worshipped on this day. It is said that King Raghu (the dynasty in which Shri Ram was born) after completing a great *yagna* was giving away presents and donations to his guests. Kautsa, a disciple of Sage Vartantu, was one of several guests who had come to the king with the intention of receiving a large donation. When Kautsa saw the king respecting his guests by applying sandalwood paste contained in an ordinary earthenware vessel, he was disappointed. He felt he couldn't reveal his intentions to King Raghu, for the earthenware vessel the king was using reflected his poverty. And so Kautsa decided not to approach the king. The king noticed Kautsa leaving empty-handed. Immediately, he called Kautsa and asked the reason for his leaving empty-handed.

"Dear King," replied Kautsa "on seeing you, a mighty king, using a simple earthenware container, I felt I could not disclose my wish to you. Please do not be disappointed with me. I offer my sincerest regards and congratulations to you for, verily, there is none as charitable as you."

Kautsa then asked the king's permission to leave but King Raghu did not want him to go away empty-handed. He had pledged to fulfil the wishes of all his guests. He told Kautsa to stay and reveal the purpose of his coming. After repeated requests Kautsa eventually related his story to King Raghu: "I am a disciple of the noble Sage Vartantu," he began. "My preceptor has generously imparted to me the knowledge on fourteen different subjects. After completing my studies, I asked

Sage Vartantu as to what I could give him as guru *dakshina*. My guru replied, 'I have been satisfied by the excellent way you have received my knowledge. I take this satisfaction you have given me as your guru *dakshina*.'

"But I was not satisfied with my guru's words. So I asked him again. To my surprise he became annoyed and demanded, 'Go, bring me fourteen million gold coins.' And it was with this wish that I came to you, but seeing that you had none I was about to go elsewhere when you called me back."

"I shall fulfil your wish in a few days. Till then you shall be my honoured guest," replied King Raghu. Now having promised Kautsa, the king made plans to vanquish Kuber (god of wealth). When Kuber heard about the king's intention, he immediately rained gold coins in the night on a *shami* tree. This wise act of Kuber pacified the king and averted a terrible war. The king then called Kautsa and gave him the fourteen million gold coins.

Since King Raghu found the gold beneath the *shami* tree on Dashera, *shami* trees have been invariably worshipped on this day.

Sharad Punam

A popular belief among the Hindus is that Lakshmiji (consort of Vishnu) comes late at night on Sharad Punam seeking to lavish wealth upon those who are awake. Wherever she goes she asks, "Who is awake?"

Hence Sharad Purnima is also known as Kojagari Purnima.

Lakshmiji, as our spiritual commentators have said, is generous to those who are awake from within, who have the knowledge and experience of *atma*. Our Upanishads speak in the same spirit, "Arise and Awake."

One who rises from the slumber of ignorance and attachment

to material objects is indeed genuinely awakened.

The Sharad season is a season of breathless beauty and fragrance. On the night of Sharad Punam, the starry sky, forests perfumed with the smell of herbs and flowers and the cool air, are awash with the light of a full moon. People celebrate this night with a dish of sweetened milk and flattened rice grains. Sharad Punam is also remembered as the day on which Shri Krishna danced with the milkmaids of Gokul. It was on this most romantic of all nights that Shri Krishna decided to bless the milkmaids with the heights of divine joy. The Lord played his flute and captured the hearts of the milkmaids. When the flute player called, the milkmaids rushed to him. They would run leaving their husbands and children unattended, they would hurriedly go to him regardless of the shameful words people uttered about them and they would blindly run to him oblivious of their tender bodies. The call of the flute made them forget everything. Their profound love for Shri Krishna dissolved all bonds of attachment to village, tribe, husband, home and thoughts of shame. It was love that drove their souls to him on that night of the full moon. The Lord multiplied himself and danced with every milkmaid. The joyous and exalted stick dance commenced. It was a delightful occasion where the souls ecstatically danced with the Lord. As the night advanced, the milkmaids transcended all earthly feelings and became immersed in the Lord's divine love.

This blissful partnership with the Lord is possible for us if we become *atmarup* (the realization that one is *atma* and not the body) like the milkmaids. It is in this exalted state that one becomes eligible to offer supreme devotion to God.

And Sharad Punam is of paramount importance to the devotees of the Swaminarayan Sampraday because it marks the birthday of Aksharbrahma Gunatitanand Swami - the choicest devotee and eternal abode of Bhagwan Swaminarayan. Every year this festival is celebrated at Gondal in the presence of Pramukh Swami Maharaj. This festival honours Gunatitanand Swami for his qualities of dharma, *jnan, vairagya* and bhakti and as the choicest disciple of Bhagwan Swaminarayan. He is the gateway to eternal redemption. To experience supreme bliss one has to identify oneself with Akshar (Gunatitanand Swami) to worship Bhagwan Swaminarayan.

22 CHATURMAS: III

Sadhu Mukundcharandas

It may be noted that the English dates for each festival may vary each year because they are celebrated according to the lunar Indian calendar. The Diwali festival lasts for a period of five days.

Dhan Teras

The first festival is called Dhanteras which falls on the thirteenth day of the dark half of the month of Aso. On this day people worship goddess Lakshmi (Lakshmi *pujan*), the goddess of wealth, and their new account books.

The significance of this occasion is to remind and ensure that one's wealth is respected as a *devi* – a goddess – and spent for auspicious and charitable purposes. Wealth should be respected and not squandered to cause one's ruin or that of another.

Kali Chaudash

The second occasion is a day on which Hanumanji is specially worshipped. People normally serve Brahmins with special delicacies in honour of their deceased relatives. Prayers are also chanted to appease the gods and to ward off any evil influence. It was on this day that Shri Krishna killed the demon called Narak. The story of Shri Krishna's battle with him is found in the Shrimad Bhagvat. It describes how Narakasur, the king of Pragjyotishpur, unleashed a reign of terror on earth and in the heavens. He is believed to have conquered and plundered the earth and heavens. He carried away sixteen thousand daughters of the gods and imprisoned them in his mountain haunt. He also robbed Aditi, the mother of the gods, of her ornamental earrings. This last act was the final straw on the camel's back. The gods supplicated to Shri Krishna to come and destroy Narakasur. In reply to their earnest pleadings, Shri Krishna marched to the city of Pragjyotishpur. He scaled the mountainous region, waded through the red waters of a river and ripped open the wall protecting the mighty citadel. The Lord battled with the demon before finally plunging them into the nether regions (Patal). It was here that a fierce encounter raged between the Lord and Narakasur. The three worlds trembled when the demon hurled his powerful weapon called Shakti at the Lord. But the Lord remained unscathed. Narak flew into a frenzy and was about to deal his final blow when the Lord cut his head off with his powerful disc, the 'Sudarshan Chakra'. Narakasur had been destroyed. The Earth handed over the earrings of Aditi to the Lord. The Lord freed the damsels and at their wish accepted them as his wives. This day of victory is popularly known as 'Narak Chaturdashi'.

Diwali Day

This is the last day of the year in the Indian calendar. People invariably light their homes with lamps and enjoy a display of firecrackers. Beautiful *rangoli* decorations on doorsteps welcome guests. People visit and greet one another, sweets and gifts are exchanged.

Diwali marks the victory of good over evil and people express their joy by putting on fine clothes, decorating their houses and bursting crackers – each according to his means.

New Year's Day

The first day of the Indian year was the day when the citizens of Gokul during Shri Krishna's time, gathered their harvest and offered their thanks to Indra, the rain-god. Shri Krishna did not approve of this. He felt that instead of resorting to gods who would only reward them with worldly pleasures, it would be far better to take refuge in God and be blessed with the eternal bliss of the Supreme. The Lord convinced his father and elders of the village to stop worshipping Indra. By his wish everyone offered sweets and vegetables to a mountain called Govardhan. The villagers felt the Lord accepted their offerings through the mountain. When Indra came to know of this, he flew into a rage. He sent torrential rain over Gokul, sweeping away many homes and cattle. People felt they were left helpless before the wrath of Indra. This drastic turn of fate they attributed to their not having worshipped Indra. The Lord observed that the ignorant shepherds still placed their faith in Indra. They were unaware of the fact that the strength of the gods paled into insignificance when compared to the Ultimate Being. To convince them of this truth the Lord lifted Mt. Govardhan on the tip of his little finger. The villagers having no other shelter from the deluge immediately rushed underneath the mountain. And since then the custom of offering food to God began. It is now popularly known as the Annakut Festival.

Dev Diwali

The last day of Chaturmas is Kartik *sud* Ekadashi. This day, too, marks the good subduing evil forces. On this day the demon Jalandhar was destroyed by Shri Vishnu through blemishing the chastity of Vrunda, Jalandhar's wife. It was believed that the demon's invincibility was due to his wife's fidelity. When the Lord shattered her fidelity, Jalandhar died. The Lord married Vrunda. After her demise, she was reborn as a basil (tulsi) plant and hence the offering of basil leaves while worshipping Shri Vishnu. One this day, people light lamps to honour it as the day when Shri Vishnu married Vrunda and hence it is called Dev Diwali. Dev Diwali is also known as Prabhodini Ekadashi. On this day the Lord awakens from his slumber in Kshirsagar, the Ocean of Milk. This is the day when the Lord leaves, after having stayed for four months with Bali, to return to his abode. In front of the Lord are placed a variety of vegetables. From this day onwards, one can eat the vegetables that were abstained from during the four months.

On Dev Diwali, the four holy months of Chaturmas come to an end. In the Bhavishya Puran it has been said that one who sincerely fulfils and celebrates the four holy months is blessed with God's proximity.

23 RATH YATRA

Sadhu Mukundcharandas

Ashadh *sud* 2, (July) is Rath Yatra day. You may well wonder what Rath Yatra means. For Hindus it is a festive and meaningful occasion, where devotion to God is offered in a heart-warming manner.

"Rath" means chariot. "Yatra" means parade or procession. On this day, the *murti* of the deity is installed in a gorgeously decorated chariot and drawn by jubilant devotees through the open streets, so that people can have darshan.

Mahabharat Rath

In the epic, Mahabharat, before the battle, Shri Krishna puts a proposal to both Duryodhan and Arjun, who have come to seek his help. Duryodhan chooses the army of Krishna and Arjun takes Krishna on his side in spite of his pledge that he would remain weaponless. Krishna becomes the chariot driver *(sarthi)* of Arjun. Arjun is the *rathi* or owner of the chariot. The fighting has to be done by the *rathi* while the *sarthi* drives the chariot. The skill and expertize with which the *sarthi* manoeuvres the chariot through the enemy ranks enables the *rathi* to exercise his prowess. A good *rathi* but a poor *sarthi* invariably spells defeat or death for the *rathi*.

Even though the orders on how to fight and the battle arrangements came from other stalwarts called *maharathis*, the Pandavs were more than happy to have Krishna on their side, for they knew that Shri Krishna was not a mortal being and hence not a normal *sarthi* with human limitations.

On the eve of the battle, Duryodhan, leader of the Kauravs,

sends his chariot driver, Uluk, into the enemy camp. Uluk insults and humiliates Shri Krishna and the Pandavs, stoking rage and fury. The Pandavs are on the verge of pouncing upon Uluk but Shri Krishna pacifies them. He addresses the messenger, "Uluk! Suppose you ride your chariot beyond the three worlds *(trilok)* or take it and hide in the underworld (Patal), still, I can bring Arjun's chariot before you on the morrow."

The words of Shri Krishna reflect his adeptness in chariot driving and his spirit to lead the Pandavs to victory. No matter where the enemy goes, Shri Krishna is ready to take Arjun before them.

The climax of the Rath saga in the Mahabharat comes at the end of the battle, after countless warriors on both sides have been slaughtered on the battlefield. The Pandavs make their way into the eerie silence of the enemy ranks in Arjun's chariot, to pay respects to the dead. One by one they step off the chariot. Final, Shri Krishna says to Arjun, "You step off first and I'll follow." Now this seemed a little strange since during the battle days, Arjun and Shri Krishna had stepped off from the chariot many times without sequence. So why does Shri Krishna specifically instruct Arjun to step off before him? Seeing Arjun's questioning look, Shri Krishna assures him, "It is for your benefit." Arjun instantly obeys Shri Krishna and steps down. Shri Krishna follows him and the whole chariot then bursts into flames. The Pandavs just look on dumbfounded. "What has happened?" they question. "How is it that the great chariot, which had led them to victory, without any rhyme or reason has turned into a fireball?" Shri Krishna then explains, "Drona, Ashwatthama and other warriors among the Kauravs had shot their devastating weapons, like the Brahmastra, at the chariot. But because of me the chariot had stayed intact all the while. Today, with our task accomplished, I have abandoned it for good and hence you see it consumed by flames."

Similarly, God protects us, but as soon as he abandons us our life's chariot burns into cinders, i.e., our life becomes meaningless. When the *atma* leaves the material body - the chariot - the body becomes lifeless. It becomes useless. Glory be to the soul who lives a noble, charitable life. A life in tune with God's injunctions. It's worthy for such a soul's lifeless chariot (body) to be burnt on a funeral pyre.

Ramayan Rath

In the epic, Ramayan, a similar parallel is to be found. When Kumbhakaran, Indrajit and other evil elements have been killed, Ravan is angered. Brimming with fury and rage, armed to the teeth, he thunders into the battlefield on his chariot to kill Ram. Seeing this, Vibhishan becomes anxious for Ram's life. Ram then coolly explains to Vibhishan, "O friend! Behold my chariot through which I am always decidedly victorious. Courage and tenacity are its wheels, immutable truth and character are its flags; strength, discrimination, self-control and charity are its horses; forgiveness, mercy and equanimity are the reins and devotion to God is its *sarthi*."

Any man, who, according to Shri Ram, lives a noble life, with courage and tenacity, powered by the spirit of truth, discrimination, self-control and blessed with a generous heart abounding in forgiveness, charity and devotion to God, can fare undefeated through the stormy straits of life.

Ram adds further, "O friend! Whoever possesses such a chariot can never be defeated. With this chariot he can not only subdue minor temptations but transcend the trappings of this material world.

Shrimad Bhagvat Rath

The jewel in the crown of Bhakti scriptures is the priceless Shrimad Bhagvat.

The *rathi* of Shrimad Bhagvat is different from the battlefields in the above two epics. Here the *rathi* symbolizes love.

The story is that one early morning, while some *gopis* were going to milk cows and to fill water pots from the river Yamuna, they see a dazzling chariot on the outskirts of their village. They surmise that a kingly personality has come to visit Gokul. Slowly they learn that Akrur has come from Mathura to collect Krishna - their beloved. They become hysterical and forgetting their chores run straight for the chariot.

They surround it thinking all the while how to prevent their loved one from leaving. He is our life, our *pran* (life-force). How can we live without him? How will we experience bliss in his absence? What joy will there be without him?" And with these frantic thoughts they decide to stop the chariot by any means. Some plan to lie across its path, some resolve to hold the reins of the horses, some even decide to throw themselves in front of the chariot if it starts moving. The *gopis* were prepared to die rather than be separated from God. Such was their profound love for Shri Krishna. But as Krishna emerges from 'Nandbhavan' (father Nand's place), he glances at them just once and a path is created instantly for him - the *gopis* give way. What happened to all their brave plans? Shri Krishna climbs into the chariot. Not a word is exchanged and yet the message has been understood. The reins are pulled, the horses neigh, the wheels turn and soon the peacock feather of Shri Krishna recedes further and further until it is seen no more. The *gopis* are still standing there, speechless, watching their beloved depart. Why didn't they do anything?

It is said that when Shri Krishna glanced at the *gopis,* they saw in his eyes a profound desire to go. Immediately they gave up their resolves. Serving their master's wish was of paramount importance to them.

The chariot of the Shrimad Bhagvat portrays ideal devotion.

Devotion means following the wish, the will, the desire, the order of one's divine master. Whatever one may decide, however lovingly or with devotion, but to alter one's wish or completely overrule it and live to the Lord's wish qualifies a true devotee.

The Upanishad Rath

The profoundest and most practical, philosophical wisdom in the world is to be found in our Upanishads.

The story of the Upanishad Rath is found in Katha Upanishad (1.3.3-4).

After a three-day fast by the young, spirited Nachiketa at the doors of hell, Lord Yama is pleased and tells Nachiketa to ask for three boons. Nachiketa however has one supreme desire; to attain the knowledge of Brahma or 'Brahma Vidya'. Yama tempts him with worldly offerings but he remains resolute.

Yama becomes pleased. He begins to impart the supreme knowledge.

Atmãnam rathinam viddhi shariram rathameva tu,
Buddhim tu sãrthim viddhi manaha pragrahameva cha.
Indriyãni hayãnãhurvishayãnsteshu gocharãn,
Ãtmendriyamanoyuktam bhoktetyãhur manishinaha.

(Katha Upanishad 1.3.3-4)

"The *atma* is the *rathi,* the body is the *rath,* the intellect is the *sarthi,* the mind is the rein, the senses are the horses and the *vishays* (material objects) are the fields of pasture."

Herein lies the story of the sojourn of life *(jivan yatra)* for which we have been given the *rath* (the body).

The chariot, the wheels and the horses all symbolize motion or travel. The chariot is not to be kept stationary or in a 'garage' or on display in a museum. The sage of the Upanishad is telling us here to keep our body (chariot) active, always engaged in good deeds. If the horses are left to roam free they'll become unmanageable and wild, doing anything they please. But if they are harnessed together to a chariot with a driver they'll run with a single motive towards a specific goal. Similarly, the senses, if left to run free will create havoc for the *rathi,* e.g. 'feeding' on anything and everything without discrimination and if they are directed by a *sarthi* they'll be guided towards a fixed goal.

In the ninth verse, the sage elaborates further:

Vignãnasãrthir yastu manaha pragrahavãn naraha,
Sodhvanaha pãramãpnoti tad vishnoho paramam padam.

Meaning, the man whose *sarthi* (intellect) is knowledgeable, wise, alert and discriminative, whose reins (the mind) are in full control, only that man is able to traverse the path of *sansar* (material life), reaching the desired goal, that is, Bhagwan Vishnu's Supreme abode.

In this chariot, the *rathi* is *atma.* The horses, reins and drivers are the senses, mind and the intellect. The centre of attraction is *rathi* - the owner. The chauffeur will always drive with the best intentions of pleasing his boss. Similarly, the *sarthi* (intellect) drives with the best intentions for the boss *(atma)* and that is very necessary. He does not over-whip the horses, nor does he run them at a dead pace, but at a pace suited for the *rathi.* That is decided by the *sarthi.* The 'best intention' for the *rathi* is redemption *(moksha).* For that, the mind, the intellect and the senses work together to take the soul towards redemption.

By imbibing this concept of Rath Yatra given in the Upanishads our life's pilgrimage to eternity will proceed forward without hindrance.

Rath Yatra is a festival of accepting God's all-doership in life.

On 11 July 83 a Rath Yatra festival was celebrated in the presence of Pramukh Swami Maharaj at the Ahmedabad mandir. A small, beautiful chariot equipped to move was set up for the festival. On the previous night the chariot was tested and re-tested. It worked perfectly. The next morning after

Swami completed his morning prayers he came to perform *arti* of Harikrishna Maharaj seated in a small exquisite chariot. The chariot would not move due to a technical fault. The gadgetry somehow failed to operate. Later, in Swami's room someone said, "The chariot was in working order on the previous night and it failed at the last moment. I just don't understand why." Swami answered, "It is the wish of Maharaj. He probably wanted to give darshan in a motionless chariot." The words of Swamishri revealed the spirit of the Rath Yatra festival. After having handed the reins to God, it is his wish that prevails. He may give you joy or sorrow, wealth or poverty, fame or shame in spite of your sincerity and effort. Believing that he is the all-doer makes life happier and worth living.

SOCIAL

24 PANACEA FOR TODAY'S ILLS

Sadhu Atmaswarupdas

Introduction

Look at the today's papers. What do you find?

Wars! Terrible accidents! Riots! Crime is on the increase! A fresh orgy of mass murders! Mob rule threatens big cities!

War

In the first eight decades of the 20th century more than a 100 million became cannon-fodder at the hands of their fellow men.

Crime

There has been a cancerous growth of crime and violence. For instance, in the USA a burglary occurs every 10 seconds, a rape every 7 minutes and a murder every 24 minutes.

Drugs

A drug culture has emerged. It is made up of heroin addicts, shooting galleries, psychedelic lights and posters, rock music, underground newspapers, hippies, smuggling, drug pushers and the like. The drug problem is primarily a youth problem.

Moral Degeneration

Man has descended into an abyss of moral evil that defies imagination. Fraud and greed are triumphant everywhere. As Dr Einstein said, "There is no defence in science against the weapons which destroy civilization."

Juvenile Delinquency

Juveniles commit almost half of all serious crimes. In America, 15 is the peak age for crimes and violence! The key to a peaceful world lies with the care we take of youth, for they are the citizens of tomorrow.

Youths

Rebellion... The Generation Gap... Student Unrest... Juvenile Delinquency... Illegitimacy... Sexual Revolution... Pot... Escapism... these and many others are the social problems of today's youth.

Reasons

Why do children and youths go astray? Because they aren't brought up in the right way. We are failing our children. They are our future, our most precious resource, and yet are our most lawless citizens. We have never given them any spiritual training.

The world is in turmoil. The gravest problem scourging today's world is the 'Crisis of Character'. Crime stems from a lack of character.

The cause of all the violence is that raw human nature has been allowed to run rampant in society. So long as we are dominated by passions and desires, we will flout our neighbour, never leaving him in peace; and we will build institutions and societies which mirror our violent impulses, aggression and greed.

Education

Education, however, more than any other single factor, can mould the citizen of the future. But modern education has failed to provide solid goals and values that its youth can rally behind individually and nationally. It fails to teach students how to live. It commits the crime of developing the machine, instead of the man. The result is a mixed-up, unhappy and fearful world in chaos.

Remedy

Ours is a diseased humanity. The young people of the world show their utter contempt for the values of a society that has a materialistic slant to life through riots, demonstrations, etc. What society needs is a spiritual anchor. Man does not live by bread alone.

Religion

Religion is the life-giving water which quenches the fire of materialism that is burning the hearts of millions. It is meant to refine the nature of man. Some say religion has failed to do that. But it is really not so. In fact, religion has not been tried in its true sense. As C.C. Colton said, "Men wrangle for religion, write for it, fight for it, die for it, anything but LIVE for it."

Character

Undoubtedly, "The greatest, the highest and the noblest contribution that a man can make for the benefit and prosperity of this world is his pure and spotless character."

Today, the Swaminarayan Sampraday, founded by Bhagwan Swaminarayan two hundred years ago, is a dynamic force working miracles with the youth.

A Novel University

His Divine Holiness Yogiji Maharaj's impact on students is vividly borne out by the following incident.

In 1965, a mob of 2000 angry students of Sardar Patel University at Vallabh Vidyanagar in Gujarat, marched towards the Chemistry Department to burn it down as a show of protest for their grievances. At the head of the mob was a burning torch and the students were in a violent mood. However, to everyone's surprise, a dozen students halted the mob. One of them coolly suggested to the 2000-strong mob, "You may first burn us down before you proceed to burn the institution of education. It has been the source of education for thousands and will still educate thousands more for decades to come. What shall we gain by burning down the buildings?" These dozen youths held back the 2000 agitators. This seems incredible. Even the Head of the Chemistry Department could not imagine that there could be such bold and courageous students who would, at the risk of their own lives, make the mob see reason even in their frenzy. The mob dispersed.

The Head of the Chemistry Department subsequently called on those youths to find out in which 'university' their moral fibre had been moulded. Pat came the reply, "It is Yogiji Maharaj who has taught us this. We are followers of the Swaminarayan Sampraday which has always provided peaceful solutions to problems."

This has been made possible because Swamiji himself is an idol of selfless love.

Youth Power Sublimated

Pramukh Swami Maharaj has continued to inspire noble virtues in thousands of youths today. During a grand festival to mark the Birth Bicentenary of Bhagwan Swaminarayan in April 1981 in Ahmedabad, 10,000 youth volunteers were working round the clock to make the 37-day festival a grand success. Millions thronged to the festival. However, at that time, there were rampant anti-reservation riots with escalating violence going on in Ahmedabad and throughout Gujarat. The situation was out of hand, as even the Central Government arbitrators had failed to bring about a peaceful settlement. The Gujarat Government was ill-equipped to curb such riots. Curfews were the order of the day. However, the religious festival, held in the very heart of Ahmedabad City went on without any untoward incident. The youth volunteers, the fellow-students of the rioting students, were involved in an activity that transcended the worldly agitations and violence. In spite of the general atmosphere of looting, arson, and violence, these youths remained above the unrest and refused to be manipulated. Not only that but they also assisted for peace in Ahmedabad and Gujarat at large. Peace was soon restored in Gujarat.

Inspiring moral and spiritual values in children is the only panacea for our ills in society.

25 PARENT AND CHILD

Sadhu Anandswarupdas

Understanding children, encouraging them, and guiding them plays a significant role in moulding their character. Very often parental ignorance results in unwelcome consequences. How should parents react when their child spills a glass of milk? What should they say when their child comes home with a bad report card? 'Parent and Child' shows us how to deal with such problems.

Talking to children is an art. Children are seldom naïve in their communications. Their coded messages require deciphering.

On his first visit to school, while mother was still with him, John, age seven, looked at the paintings on the notice board and inquired, "Who drew these ugly pictures?" The embarrassed mother told him, "It's not nice to call the pictures ugly when they are so pretty." The teacher, who understood the meaning of the question, smiled and said, "In this school you don't have to paint pretty pictures." A big smile appeared on John's face, he had the answer to his hidden question, "What happens to the boy who doesn't paint so well?"

An interested observer listening to a conversation between a parent and child will note how little each listens to the other.

To reach out to children and to reduce parental frustration, we need a new mode of relating to children. It is based on respect and skill.

Abhinandan, aged ten, came home in an angry mood. His

class outing had been ruined by rain. Mother decided to use a new approach.

Mother: You seem very disappointed.

Abhinandan: Yes.

Mother: You wanted very much to go on this outing?

Abhinandan: I sure did.

Mother: You had everything ready and then the rain came.

Abhinandan: Yes, that's right.

There was a moment of silence and then Abhinandan said, "Oh, well, there will be other days." His anger seemed to have vanished.

What is so special about this approach, and what are its helpful components?

When a child is buffeted by strong emotions, he will not listen to anyone. He will not accept advice or consolation or constructive criticism. He only wants his feelings to be understood.

When a child makes a statement about himself, it is often desirable to respond, neither with an agreement nor disagreement, but with details that convey to the child an understanding beyond his expectation.

Shreya came home with a failing report card. He said to his father that he was not good at mathematics. His father thought that it would be of little help to tell him that he was pretty lousy with figures. Nor would it be helpful to dispute his opinion or to offer him cheap advice such as, "Try harder and you will do better in maths." Such words would only hurt his self-respect and the instant lesson would erode his confidence. His father said in earnestness, "Mathematics is not an easy subject. Some of the problems must be very hard to figure out." Shreya almost sighed with relief. His inner reaction was, "I must live up to my father's faith in me."

We find that parents have a tendency to pamper their children with flattery. To understand this, consider the function of a mirror. A mirror merely reflects an image as it is, without adding flattery or faults.

The function of an emotional mirror is to reflect feelings as they are, without distortion.

To a child who has such feelings, these statements conveyed in a loving tone are most helpful. They show him clearly what his feelings are. Clarity of image, whether in a looking glass or in an emotional mirror, provides opportunity for self-initiated grooming and change.

It is a widely held belief that praise builds up a child's confidence and makes him feel secure. In actuality, praise may and often does result in tension and misbehaviour, especially when it's inept. Peter had behaved like an angel throughout the journey from London to Dundee. Mother thought that he deserved some praise. She turned to him and said, "You are such a good boy Peter. You behaved so well. I'm proud of you."

A minute later the sky fell on them. Peter pulled out an ashtray and spilled its contents all over them. The ashes, the cigarette butts and the smoke came like atomic fallout.

Mother was terribly upset because all this happened just after she had praised him so sincerely. She wondered, "Isn't praise good for children anymore."

Weeks later Peter himself revealed the cause of the explosion. All the way home he had been wondering how he could get rid of his younger brother, who was snuggled up between mother and father in the front seat of the car. Just then mother had congratulated him on his goodness. The praise made him feel guilty and he wanted desperately to show that he did not deserve it. He looked around, saw the ashtray, and the rest followed.

The single most important rule is that praise should deal

only with the child's effort and accomplishments, not with his character and personality.

Sanket, aged ten, accidentally spilt a glass of milk on the table.

Mother: You are old enough to know how to hold a glass. How many times have I told you to be careful!

Father: He can't help it; he's clumsy. He always was and he always will be.

Sanket spilt 50 paise worth of milk, but the caustic comments that followed may cost much more in terms of loss of confidence. Mother could have handled the situation calmly by saying, "I see the milk is spilt. Here is another glass of milk, and here is a sponge." Sanket would surely have looked up at her in relief and disbelief and would have cleaned up the mess.

When things go wrong it is not the right moment to teach an offender about his personality but it is best to deal only with the event, not the person.

When a child is repeatedly told by his parents or teachers that he is stupid he comes to believe it. He starts thinking of himself as such. He then gives up intellectual efforts, feeling that his escape from ridicule lies in avoiding contest and competition. His safety hinges on not trying.

Thus it can be seen that the intellectual progress and the character development of a child depend to a large degree on the common sense of his parents to accurately judge a situation and then take the necessary action.

26 TACKLING YOUR TEENAGER

Sadhu Anandswarupdas

The methods suggested below are not merely techniques, but interpersonal skills, helpful only when used with empathy and genuineness. They are effective when applied selectively and appropriately.
There are no hard and fast rules to bring up your teenager successfully but there are always good suggestions, which should be administered with discretion and thought regarding various conditions, attitudes, personalities, time and space. Teenagers are, unlike machines, complex and unique individuals, for whom no perfect manual has ever been written.

The No-Answer, Answer-Unvoiced Advice

Adults usually react to their teenager's problems or statements either by approving or by disapproving. The most helpful response however is often non-judgmental. A non-evaluative response contains neither praise nor criticism. Instead it identifies feelings, recognizes wishes and acknowledges opinions.

An example will clarify this point. Nilay, aged 15, is a gifted public speaker but he speaks poorly at recitals, and when it comes to the actual day of his speech he cries and complains of nervousness. His parents tell him, "You've nothing to worry about," and use coaxing such as "the audience doesn't know when you make a mistake," or "you're behaving very childish, dear." The parent in actual fact is denying the son's feelings.

Every time Nilay spoke, it was never a total success. There

were places where he forgot, stumbled and even stopped. Many a time he would weep and call himself a failure.

When this happened his father would make the mistake of minimizing the poor speech and insist that he had spoken well, but he knew he was lying and Nilay was aware of it.

It was quite a while before Nilay was scheduled to speak again, but when the day arrived so did the normal tension and tears. But this time his parents chose to react differently. When Nilay said he was not prepared to speak and that the parents should announce that he was not well and therefore could not speak today, they just listened carefully. Then the mother finally spoke, "I know it's frightful to get out there and speak to all those people. You must feel they are judging each word you say. Of course you feel nervous." Nilay could not believe what he heard. He said brightly, "You understand how I feel, I never thought you really did."

When Nilay got up to speak he spoke much better. Though he did make a few mistakes he held a very different attitude to them, and he even smiled over to his parents whilst speaking. A smile of success.

Let's look at another situation.

Parva, age 17, was interviewed for a summer job, but was turned down. He came home disappointed and depressed. However, his father, a skilled parent, tackled the situation very effectively. He realized that what his son needed was not straightforward advice, but a listening ear. That ear would do all the necessary advising.

Father: You really wanted that job, didn't you?

Parva: I sure did.

Father: And you had prepared so well for it too.

Parva: Yeh. A lot of good that did for me.

Father: What a disappointment.

Parva: It sure is, Dad.

Father: Looking forward to a job and having it slip away just when you need it is tough.

Parva: Yeh. I know.

A few moments of silence, then Parva said, "It's not the end of the world, I'll find another job."

Many unskilled parents would have tackled the situation differently. They would have immediately responded with one of the six responses below.

1. By pity: "O how awful! I am so sorry. My heart breaks. You were unlucky and other people have all the luck. I am so sad for you."
2. By criticism: "The trouble with you is you don't know what to say, and when to say it. You always blunder. You lack poise and you fidget too much. You rush everything and are never patient enough."
3. By reasoning: "What did you expect? To get the first job you wanted? Life is not easy. You may have to go even ten times, before anyone hires you."
4. By comparison: "Take me for instance. When I was your age and I went looking for my first job, I polished my shoes, got a haircut, wore fresh clothes and carried *The Times* with me wherever I went. See, I knew how to get instant respect."
5. By cliché: "Rome was not built in a day, dear. You've got a long way to go. Don't get depressed so quickly, laugh and cheer up."
6. By minimizing the situation: "That's nothing. There's no reason to be sad about it. I don't see why you are so depressed about it? Jobs come and go. It's not even worth bothering about."

Notice how Parva's father didn't offer any concrete advice. He just listened, adding a comment here and there, helping Parva clear his thoughts. If Parva had been confronted with any of the six responses it is likely he would never approach his father again for any sort of help, feeling his parent failed to understand him and his problems.

Avoid Preaching in Chapters

When teenagers ask questions all they usually want is a straight 'Yes', 'No', 'Good' or 'Bad' for an answer. Some parents have the habit of lecturing. Says Palash, age 17, "My father never converses, all he does is make speeches. He goes too deeply into the simplest of matters. I ask a short question, I get a long answer. Now I avoid him. I do wish he could talk in sentences and not chapters."

Says Mahesh, age 17, "Father never knows when to stop talking. He goes on and on. He can talk at length without even knowing that he has lost his audience. Even when I'm dead bored he never realizes it. He talks but he doesn't communicate."

Do Not Be Too Understanding!

When teenagers are troubled by conflicts they feel unique. They do not want instant understanding. In fact, to them their emotions seem new, personal, and private. It makes them feel very grown up. And when they are told, "I know exactly how you feel. I remember, at your age I felt the same," they feel insulted. It distresses them to be so transparent, so naïve, so simple; especially when they feel complex, mysterious, and inscrutable. However, to sense exactly when your teen needs understanding is a very difficult and delicate task. You cannot be expected to deal with every situation perfectly, but knowing the theory will always contribute to a better approach to the needs of your teenager.

Try Not to Invite Dependence

Adolescence is a time when dependency causes hostility.

Parents who refuse to let go and who foster dependence are, in actual fact, inviting unavoidable resentment. Teenagers crave independence. The more self sufficient the parents make them feel the less hostile they become. A wise parent makes himself increasingly dispensable to his teenagers. He sympathetically watches the drama of growth, but resists the desire to intervene too often. Of course, this does not mean you are to let your teenagers be free to do as they please. But whenever it is possible allow the teenagers to make their own choice and to use their own powers. Lace your language with words that encourage independence.

"What do you think is best for the family?"

"Do you feel that God will be pleased with this particular decision?"

"Why don't you think it over and then we'll decide together."

To inspire confidence in your teenager they should be made to feel their thoughts and suggestions are of importance. Give them opportunities to use their creativity, and make their own decisions. One devotee in Ahmedabad after moving house allowed his two teenagers to make their own choices about furnishing, painting and decorating their new rooms. Their happiness knew no bounds. Even in the mandir they would share their experiences with the sadhus. Finally, when the rooms were complete their faces reflected an inner warmth of satisfaction and confidence, and of course, a warm love for their parents.

One parent told the story, "My 16-year-old told me how he was planning to work out his problems with a schoolteacher. He wanted to know what I thought of his plan. I said, 'I have faith in your ability to make the right decision.' My son seemed satisfied. In a considerate voice he said, 'Thank you.' "

Asking Others to Advise: Don't Label Them in Their Presence

It is a frequent experience with the sadhus that a parent will introduce his teenager and add, "Swamiji, he's lazy and he failed his exams," or "He talks back to his mother," or "He's always glued to the TV and plays too much cricket!" Imagine the feelings of the teenager! He tries to make a good impression before someone new, and before he gets off the mark, he is slandered there on the spot. This can be very painful for the teenager; it instigates him to even hate his parents. Can they help it? Parents often treat teenagers as if they are deaf. They talk about them in their presence as if they are deaf or mere objects. If parents feels that they should ask someone to try and help explain something to their teenager it is important not to do it in the child's presence.

Don't Hurry to Correct Facts

A teenager often responds to correction with obstinacy. He becomes unreachable and unteachable, determined not to be influenced by anyone or forced into anything.

As one teenager said, "There is a certain satisfaction in being in the wrong that a goody-goody will never know."

Another teenager reacted, "My father is a natural born improver. It hurts him to see me doing things my own way. He always has a better way - his own. His corrections are tattooed in my memory with needles of hate. I dislike my father's advice. I am determined to make my own mistakes."

A bitter-tongued parent cannot teach respect for facts. Truth for its own sake can be a deadly weapon in family relations. Truth without compassion can destroy love. Some parents try too hard to prove exactly how, where, and why they have been right. This approach cannot but bring bitterness and disappointment. When attitudes are hostile, facts are unconvincing.

Avoid Cliches and Preaching

Says fifteen-year-old May, "I can't talk to my mother. She becomes overconcerned. Instead of helping me, she starts suffering. Her eyes fill with tears and her face says, 'Oh, poor thing. It hurts me more than it hurts you.' How would you like to be helped by a doctor who is so sympathetic that he faints at the sight of blood? That's my mother."

To be helpful, we need to learn empathy - an ability to respond genuinely to a child's moods and feelings without being infected by them. We need to help teenagers with their anger, fear, and confusion, without ourselves becoming angry, fearful, and confused.

27 DOUBLE STANDARDS

Sadhu Atmaswarupdas

Hindu religion talks of the feelings of 'I-ness' and 'Mine-ness' as *maya*. It is this ignorance that obstructs one's path to God-realization and happiness in life. One should recognize it as it manifests in various forms in our lives in this age of self-centredness. L.N. Hales writes briefly on 'I'.

"I hate the chap who tries to beat the traffic lights;
But if he happens to be me – well, that's all right.
I loathe the car that in a jam, twists in and out;
But If I'm sitting at the wheel I slyly grin.
At drivers who lean on their horns, I rave and shout;
But when some fool gets in my way,
I always honk him out.
I grow indignant at the chance another takes,
But I drive 60 miles an hour and trust my brakes.
I wonder, is it possible they cannot ever see,
that traffic laws were made for them and
not at all for me?"

'I am the measure of all things' is the predominant spirit behind our behaviour.

Similarly, our attachment to things we call 'mine' manifests itself in life.

- This is a strange world. If you threw an occasional party, you are being graceful.
- If your neighbour does, he is trying to show off his aristocracy.
- If your son elopes with a girl, well, boys will be boys.
- If your neighbour's son does it, shame on him.

- If you run for election, you are seeking to serve the nation.
- If your neighbour is a candidate, politics is the last refuge of a scoundrel.
- If you get promotion, it was something long overdue.
- If your neighbour gets a rise, it is the reward of consistent sycophancy.
- If your son is studious, he is widening his horizons.
- If your neighbour's son burns the midnight oil, he is a bookworm.
- If you build a big house, it is to accommodate your large circle of friends and relatives.
- If your neighbour does it, it is a vulgar display of opulence.
- If you go abroad often, it is because travel enriches your outlook.
- If your neighbour does it, he probably has a connection with smugglers.

One could go on talking and feeling in this manner for hours on end. Such an attitude or standard would thin one's personality and fatten the 'I' and 'Mine', thus weighing one down with discomfort and hostility. Let us step out from the circle of self-centredness and live a benevolent, peaceful and holier life.

28 GOSSIP

Sadhu Vivekjivandas

In a small town in Norfolk, England, two neighbours were enjoying a savoury conversation. Their talk centred around the young couple living on the opposite side of their street.

"I swear there's something wrong between them," said Mrs. Smith.

"You now I'd felt the same thing the other day when I saw the young man storm out angrily," revealed Mrs. Stevenson.

"And just this morning I heard the young lady cry."

"O that wretch of a man!" snapped Mrs. Stevenson.

"You know Mrs. Stevenson, I think that husband of hers is..."

Their conversation went on for a full hour.

* * *

A selection for the annual drama was made in Tom's College. Every year he got the plum part but this year Peter was selected for the lead role. Tom was disappointed and angry. On his way home from college he lashed out bitterly about his teacher's choice and Peter's incompetence for the role. His high voltage monologue didn't stop till he took the turning home.

* * *

In a prestigious office block in Mumbai, one of the junior clerks was listening with interest to his colleague's account of their boss' latest scandal:

"And then do you know what happened next?"

"No, tell me!"

"Well, just between you and me, he..."

* * *

It topples governments, wrecks marriages, ruins careers, busts reputations, causes heartaches, nightmares, indigestion, spawns suspicion, generates grief and makes innocent people cry in their pillows. Even its name hisses. It's called gossip. Office gossip. Shop gossip. Party gossip. College gossip. Satsang gossip. It makes headlines and causes headaches.

Millions of people the world over maim or murder the reputation and character of their neighbours, friends, relatives and superiors through the devilish habit of gossiping. Gossip accuses people. It charges others with wrong, branding them with faults and follies. Gossipers are like lynch mobs that charge, convict and condemn all without a trial.

They reject authority, wreck unity and friendship and destroy peace of mind. And in all this they find pleasure that clamps them for hours.

In our world of fragile relationships gossiping has become a popular sport. You don't pay anything – all you need to spare is, TIME!; and you know how much you have when the subject is GOSSIP! Yogiji Maharaj used to say that a man gets more taste out of gossip then he does from a sumptuous feast. A gossiper lives on a diet of others' faults and scandals.

Gossip Addicts

People gossip due to several (all of them wrong) reasons.

1. Inferiority in power, popularity and talent breeds gossip. Such people gossip about others and pull them down. They try to enhance their worth by resurrecting their egos on the ruins of others. The gossiper experiences a temporary feeling of value, which quickly crumbles, leaving him feeling more miserable than ever. He or she desires to gossip again to experience another high.
2. Frustration produces gossipers too. When you don't get the things you desire or when you are dissatisfied with

your life you hunger and thirst for satisfaction. So what do you do? Well some people eat or sleep, desperately trying to drown their frustrations. Others talk, talk, talk and devour their friends and neighbours away. After gossiping they feel better - but for a little while only!

3. Idleness promotes gossip. People who are idle with their hands are active with their tongues. When you have nothing to do or you want to do nothing you slip into gossiping. Those little free minutes between schedules or those enormous hours spent in travelling are often spent in utter waste when you've gossiped all the way. And when you have no companions you gossip with yourself, shuffling files in your mind branding and accusing someone of some wrong.
4. Verbal clashes and difference of opinions string up people for gossip. You've probably echoed bitter words about someone you had a row with.
5. Contrasting or revolting habits make fertile ground for gossip. When you dislike another's habits or traditions you are inclined to gossip. If you don't like the way others talk or look, the way they walk or eat, you make them the topic of your gossip.

In Satsang

In the chronicles of Satsang we find many examples of devotees who have spiritually erred or fallen due to gossiping.

Allaiya Khachar was initially wedded with profuse love and devotion to Bhagwan Swaminarayan, but later rejected him and preached that he was not God but a mere Brahmin from the east. Allaiya poisoned the minds of the two thousand aspirants he had brought into the Satsang-fold with doubts about Shriji Maharaj's divinity. He gossiped because his pride was hurt.

Jiva Khachar, out of jealousy for Dada Khachar, developed

a burning hatred for Bhagwan Swaminarayan. He, too, gossiped bitterly about him and severed his ties with him.

Another incident which headlines the feelings of Bhagwan Swaminarayan on this subject was the victory of Muktanand Swami in a debate against the Vedantins in Vadodara. When news of this reached Shriji Maharaj in Gadhada, he was extremely happy. The news also spread to the sadhus and devotees in Gadhada. When two sadhus, Nirvikalpanand and Haryanand, heard of this, they turned green with envy. They went up to Maharaj and out of pride dismissed Swami's victory as a trifle matter. "Maharaj," they said, "Muktanand Swami's victory against the Vedantins was like the victory of a mighty lion over a meek fox. It was not a great feat by Muktanand Swami. If you had sent us we too would have won the debate." Maharaj was hurt by their jealousy and disrespect for Muktanand Swami - a senior and most revered sadhu.

In the time of Gunatitanand Swami, one Jala Bhagat, in spite of his love for Swami, had no faith in him. After hearing Swami's sermons he would often go to Amarsinh, the ignorant doorkeeper, and ask him about the truth of Swamiji's sermons. The doorkeeper would stamp them as big lies and thus begin his gossip.

Any talk in Satsang that defames, accuses, or destroys a devotee's character is gossip. Once you form a habit of gossiping you will eventually pin the blame on the guru and thus spell your spiritual ruin.

The Cure for Gossip

There is a remedy for this harmful habit if we adopt the following measures:

1. Don't Listen to Gossip

Gossiping would stop instantly if people stop listening.

When someone digs up some fault or scandal try to leave as tactfully and gently as possible, "I have to make a phone call," "I'm expecting some guests at home," "I have to rush for my next appointment." And if you have the boldness to tell him that you are not interested then do so.

Listening to gossip makes you an accomplice. Yogiji Maharaj disapproved of worthless, negative conversation. Once a sadhu, who had travelled by train with two devotees, was asked by Yogiji Maharaj what he did on the way. The sadhu replied that a devotee had gossiped all through the journey. "And you listened to him?" Yogiji Maharaj enquired. "I had no other place to go to and I couldn't tell him to stop," the sadhu replied. Yogiji Maharaj told him to fast even though he had no desire to listen to the devotee's gossip.

Don't listen to gossip. Accept only good things into your mind - things that help you and others in a positive way.

But what if the gossip you hear is true! Then convey it to the responsible authorities but don't spread it.

2. Remain Silent

When you don't have a way out or the courage to tell the gossiper to stop then don't respond. Try to divert the conversation to some other topic and if this fails, remain silent and don't respond.

3. Knowing There's No Way to Erase the Sin of Gossip

Your attitude changes when you realize that there is no atonement for the sin of gossip. There's a story about a woman in Chicago who ruined the reputation of several people through her habit of gossiping. After some time when she realized her sin she went to confess and ask for atonement. The priest told her to buy a turkey and remove its feathers on her way home. She did as the priest had instructed and returned the next day.

The priest told her that she had accomplished only half the atonement.

"And what more do I have to do to complete my atonement?" she asked.

"Now go and gather all the feathers," the priest replied.

"But that's impossible!" she exclaimed.

"Likewise, Madam, it's impossible to correct your sin of gossiping."

4. Speak to Edify

Speak virtuous words. Praise the works of God, his devotees, your colleagues, friends and neighbours. Say what is good in others and encourage others to do their best. Dr Samuel Johnson, an 18th century literary genius and a compiler of the first English dictionary said, "The habit of looking on the best side is worth more than £1000 a year."

Use your tongue to bring life - not death.

29 FEAR!

Sadhu Brahmaviharidas

No human being ever born has escaped the sensation of fear. From childhood to old age, the objects of fear change and vary but gradually he overcomes some of them, and new ones, more terrifying, replace them. Fear is a companion of life, one of the strongest emotions of man that both saves him and in many cases destroys him.

It began as a joke...

In South India, at Mannipal Medical College a class was in progress. The professor was dissecting a human body while a group of students stared on. Inside the dissection room there were more than twenty tables, each with a dead body. One student challenged a friend, "I bet you can't come into the chamber at midnight, dead on the stroke."

"Of course I can. I'm not scared."

"Then come tonight and touch all these corpses, one after another."

The challenge was taken. The class ended. Everyone dispersed. The same night, a few minutes before twelve, the challenged student faced the entrance of the dissecting room.

He wore a bold face but a mild sensation of fear worked its way up his nerves as he entered. He was alone. It was dark and silence was growing heavier. Pushing open the doors, he began his challenge.

One, two, three, four,... one after another, he touched the bodies as he nervously moved on...

He wasn't afraid... or was he?

This wasn't the first time he was touching dead bodies.

But unfortunately, it would be his last!

The moment he touched the eight cadaver, the body rose. It came alive!

An intense fear shocked him as he collapsed with an unfinished breath. He died instantly.

What had happened was that the challenger friend, just for a joke, had removed the corpse from the eighth table and slept naked in mimicry. But he arose at the touch, it terrorized his friend to the extent of effecting his death!

This is a true incident, reported in the *Times of India* in the year 1971. Though such dramatic incidents are rare, the curse of fear, with its multi-faceted figure still shadows the world.

Different Types of Fears

Triskaidekaphobia	fear of number 13
Pantaphobia	everything/anything
Claustrophobia	confined spaces
Acrophobia	heights
Agoraphobia	open spaces
Bibliophobia	books
Ailurophobia	cats
Ergophobia	work
Brontophobia	thunder
Pyrophobia	fire
Mysophobia	germs
Belonephobia	sharp objects
Plurophobia	multitude
Xenophobia	strange people

Fear has invaded virtually every facet of our life. An atmosphere of fear puts strain on normal life.

J.B., a man of 35 was on his routine jog around the park at 6.30 am. Suddenly another man brushed against him and overtook him with greater speed. At once, J.B. checked his pockets, suspecting that the man might have been a pickpocket.

And yes, his wallet was missing!

No questions asked; the man produced the wallet, and J.B. proudly returned home, victorious over a mugger.

But when he sat down for breakfast, to his disbelief, he saw his wallet on the table. He had forgotten it there. Then, whose did he have in his pocket?

Flushed with embarrassment, he searched the wallet for the telephone number of its rightful owner. He rang up to apologise.

"Well, I'm very sorry... but I thought you were a mugger and stole my wallet by colliding into me... But..."

And at the conclusion of his apology he inquired,

"But why on earth did you give me your wallet without resistance!"

The reply came, "Well, I thought you were the mugger!"

Both men were innocent. Neither was a criminal. Yet fear and distrust had distorted their minds. Fear, however little, promotes chaos in life and in society.

Chemistry of Fear

Fear is commonly regarded with scorn and fearlessness extolled as a desirable attribute.

But, in fact, if man was without a sense of fear his survival would be jeopardized, since he wouldn't have the mechanism which would warn him of danger and heighten the powers of the body and mind to make an immediate escape. This fear-reaction is normal fear. It is really an ally of man that helps the preservation of his species.

There's a true story of four G.I.s who were ambushed on a very narrow road in Vietnam. They leaped into a ditch. Fully aware of their exposed position, suddenly, with common mind they jumped back to the road and rushed to the jeep. They could not turn it around for lack of space to manouvre. Desperate with fear, each man took a wheel and together lifted the jeep, turned it around quickly, jumped in and at full speed, through crossfire, headed to safety. Back at camp, the same four together could not lift the jeep off the ground from one wheel!

Their amazing strength surfaced at the time of crisis. Fear, in a sense of urgency, brought it out!

During such spurts of fear, the face pales as the blood is diverted from the skin to the internal organs. The heart beats faster and a lot of energy is released. The eyes open wide to see better and the mouth opens up for mouth breathing which is less noisy than nose breathing. This is to sharpen hearing, the skin perspires freely and some animals tend to make their appearance more terrifying to the opponent, (cats fluff and rise on their toes, reptiles and amphibians swell the body or neck). In short, the body prepares for fight or flight!

A subtle aspect of normal fear helps to improve quality of life. It promotes progress. A headmaster is afraid of the educational authorities, so he trains the students well. The students fear to fail the exam, so they study hard and maintain a standard. A doctor doesn't desire a bad reputation, so he researches and saves many lives.

Yet, all these activities would be much safer if done out of love for the result, than the fear of a superior authority! The above fears could easily mutate into abnormal fears. With the case of the four G.I.s, a permanent scar on the memory of the frightful ambush could lead to imaginary fear and nightmares!

Abnormal Fear

Another name for abnormal fear is 'phobia.' It is a chronic fear causing such symptoms as nervousness, dizziness, panic, inability to concentrate, insomnia – even heart attacks.

Phobias are psychological fears. They have no objective reality. Even when there's nothing to be frightened of, the victims feel horrified. Thus, phobias are peculiar, private, irrational and unnatural fears that display stupidity in a mild or intense form.

What paralysis is to the body, phobia is to the mind. It undermines your mind and health, destroys your personality and explains why millions of people who have it accomplish little and enjoy little!

One woman showed her agoraphobia (fear of open spaces) by growing frustrated, faint and wobbly should she leave a bus at an open place. Justifying, she said, "The buildings are like giant tombstones falling on me." Thus she leaves at an earlier stop where many companions get off together.

Exact opposites are plurophobics who fear crowds and claustrophobics who does not go into lifts or narrow corridors for fear of confined spaces.

On average one person in every ten in the world suffers from a phobia. Famous names appear on our list.

Newton was fearful of water. Mozart ran away at the sound of a trumpet or hunting horn. Schopanhauer trembled at the sight of a razor. Carlyle never dared to set foot in a ship; although a keen critic of heroes and heroic deeds, he was afraid of an ordinary shopkeeper. Edgar Allan Poe, Schumann and Chopin were all afraid of the dark. Maupassant had a fear and horror of doors. Erasmus was horrified by fish, and Frederick the Great had an aversion for all new clothing or new uniforms. It is on record that Caesar's whole body trembled during a thunder. He fled to the deepest cellar in the palace and covered his head with thick fur. John Bunyan feared the sight of bells and King James had a neurotic fear of swords.

Conquest of Fear

Fear arises when one feels inferior to the surroundings

and is individually incapable of overcoming it. Dr Adler, a psychiatrist, demonstrated that the feeling of insecurity and inferiority is universal and native to the human being, so that by his very constitution he is in need of reserve power, not his own to help him to manage life. The man of faith in God feels supported by all the resources of the universe. He never feels lonely or deserted. The famed psychologist William James supports, "A religion which gives the sense of an infinite power behind the finite individual and infinite goodness, tends to itself to remove all fear, to produce a fearlessness so far as the religion is really believed" (*Varieties of Religious Experiences*).

Another noted psychologist of London, Dr Hadfield reconfirms, "I have attempted to cure nervous patients with suggestions of quietness and confidence but without success until I linked those suggestions on to the faith and the power of God."

Thus, many past and recent psychologists agree that religion shows a way to the elimination of all normal and abnormal fears. Faith in God has freed many from the shackles of fear.

When total, wholesome trust is placed, one becomes as unfearing as Arjun of the Mahabharat. During the eighteen-day ravaging war, Bhishma, the dauntless warrior vowed to kill Arjun. Bhishma seemed supreme in warfare and invincible in combat. Everyone feared that Arjun was sure to die. At night time, all the Pandavs – the brothers of Arjun – were gathered in a tent, fretting and worrying. Krishna, entered and was surprised not to find Arjun there. Searching Arjun out, he found him fast asleep in his tent. He shook him once, twice, thrice saying, "Wake up! Don't you know Bhishma has vowed to kill you tomorrow?"

"Yes" came a sleepy reply.

"Then aren't you scared for your life? How can you sleep when such danger awaits you?"

"Because you are awake my Lord!"

The Lord broke into an assuring smile. Arjun was convinced that his fate lay not in the hands of Bhishma but in the hands of the Lord. The Lord was awake, watching over him, protecting him. So there was nothing to fear!

Fearlessness Is a 3-letter word

Fearlessness is a 3-letter word - GOD.

Today, a living testament of such fearlessness is Pramukh Swami Maharaj. Swamishri is a powerhouse of courage and confidence. People confide in him, inquire from him, put faith in him and hold him dearer than their souls. Hundreds of thousands of people have risen above everyday fears; for his union with Bhagwan Swaminarayan is unshakable and his ways are unique. Swami speaks to those who have THE FEAR:

...Of Public Speaking

He speaks of Gunatitanand Swami. He was no scholar in Sanskrit. And yet Bhagwan Swaminarayan asked him to go to Memdavad and face an assembly of scholastic giants in a debate. Gunatitanand Swami never once feared the thought of failure. He boldly went, spoke with faith and conviction and emerged victorious.

...Of Failing Exams

Swamishri often quotes Yogiji Maharaj, "Study regularly, four hours a day if in school and eight hours if at college; then you will be confident in any exam. Fear comes due to lack of preparation. So prepare extensively and pray fervently."

...Of Superstitions

Recently, a devotee, Ramesh Darji, was tormented by black magic. At home, in a small village in Khedbrahma, Sabarkantha, Ramesh went to sit on the bed and it collapsed. A thundering crack tore the room wall before his eyes. The sound filled the neighbourhood. And many relatives advised Ramesh to give up faith in God and surrender unto the evil spirits. Ramesh remained staunch and undeterred. A week later he came face to face with the sorcerer who was surprised to see him alive after he had tried his most vicious spell! Ramesh's faith in Bhagwan Swaminarayan became diamond-like. Superstitions and sorcery are mere wind when one remains close to Swamishri.

...Of Progeny

Swamishri insists we instil in our children the right character in their young, green years. Only then, will they never turn against us and turn sour in life! Sweeten our children's character to ensure success.

...Of Death

In the words of Bhagwan Swaminarayan, spoken in Vachanamrut, Loya 2, "In my mind, I feel that there are four types of devotees of God who no longer fear death and who feel completely fulfilled. These four types are: first, one who has faith; second, one with *jnan;* third, one with courage; and fourth, one with affection. These four types of devotees do not fear death, and they feel fulfilled while still alive.

"One who has faith has established absolute faith in the words of God and his *Sant*. Therefore, by the strength of his faith in God, he does not harbour any fear of death. Also, he believes, 'I have attained the manifest form of Purushottam Bhagwan, and thus I am fulfilled.' "

An old lady of the village Ghandala was so sincere in her faith that Bhagwan Swaminarayan revealed her date of death. She was overjoyed and literally prepared for the event. She could picture herself in heaven, eternally free. Her husband disbelieved her as she looked too healthy to die. But she did die as predicted. She embraced death cheerfully – faith was the secret of her fearlessness.

...Of Responsibility

Swamishri was asked if he had any worries due to the responsibility of being the master (guru) of the BAPS Swaminarayan Sampraday. Swamishri replied, "The master is Bhagwan Swaminarayan. I am a servant, just here to manage and carry out his commands."

Swamishri never feels the pressure of being the head of the Sampraday, for he knows Bhagwan Swaminarayan is the head. He tackles all problems according to the wish of Bhagwan Swaminarayan and hence he feels no pressure whatsoever.

Cancel out fear with faith. For there is no force in this world more powerful than faith especially when it is faith in depth, faith that is real, bona fide. Faith is no palliative; it's a cure – the only sure cure for fear.

As this saying maintains,

"Fear knocked on the door; Faith answered it and nothing was there!"

30 ADVICE ABOUT INTERNET

Translation: Sadhu Vivekjivandas

On 10 August 2000, during the Kishore-Kishori Shibir at Perry, Georgia, USA, a question-answer session on internet use was held with Pramukh Swami Maharaj. The focussed, practical and penetrating answers by Swamishri provide clear and ethical guidelines to all netizens.

Q: For what purpose should we use the internet?

A: Science has advanced tremendously today. Before using anything we should exercise the power of discrimination (*vivek buddhi*) as prescribed by our shastras. Such discrimination develops through the company of good people, the realized Sadhu and God.

The internet is both good and bad. With relation to business and academic studies, it is very lucrative. But in logging to academic sites, one is also influenced by its dark side. At present you should have only two priorities – studies and satsang.

Many are overconfident about themselves, thinking that nothing will happen by looking at such things. But even the great have fallen. There are examples of people who were greater than us, from our Sampraday and others, who have succumbed to such obstacles.

Ekalshrungi rishi was a recluse who was not even aware of the distinction between man and woman. From childhood his father had taken such care to seclude him. He was a person of strong mind yet he fell. Similarly, you may feel nothing will happen to you but these are enticing matters. A click of the button, then a brief glance, and you feel like seeing a little more. And then you go deeper and get drowned in it. If you do not exercise discrimination, you will lose everything. You will decline in your studies and then ruin your life. New research and more discoveries will continue to be made. First came the telephone, then TV, video and now the internet. And tomorrow morning something else will arrive and it will be faster! The element of 'speed' is demonic.

There are glamorous and pornographic videos published by people who want to earn money. They are not concerned whether your thoughts become corrupted, society gets spoilt and the country devastated. The authorities get taxes from them so they are not willing to stop them. There is only one means to stop it - personal understanding. To realize it yourself. When you realize that drugs, *gutka* and other addictions are poisonous, then you will be able to stay away from them.

The only reason for such evils in life is the lack of discrimination in daily living. If you mentally resolve that you don't want to use them then you will never succumb to liquor, gutka, etc. Otherwise these are demonic things that are so alluring that one gets enticed. Within, lies one's desires, so on contact with such things there is obviously a greater attraction. So no matter how strong you may be but you will lapse. Therefore, if you are vigilant then you won't have problems. Be cautious and don't ever see and use the bad things on the website. The internet looks good but it is like slow poison. As you experience it more and more you spoil your life. Spread this message so that others may be saved. To save a drowning person is our duty.

Q: Should we chat on the internet?

A: You can chat on what is necessary but not on unnecessary things. There is no objection to chatting on academic or business matters. If you want to know about religion then you can chat. There is no objection to chatting about things that enhance your character, culture, faith in religion and God, and make your life good and philanthropic. But there is no benefit in chatting about things that spoil your life, family and society. This means that you should not chat and listen to bad things.

Q: How much time should we spend on the internet?

A: Today, we see that people get so carried away on the internet that they spend hours on end watching it. The youths are greatly affected by it.

You should use it for a little while. Once you get the answer to your question, you should shut it off. There's no need to extend any further. And if it is related to your studies, satsang and business then work on it, but otherwise don't waste your time.

Give all your attention when it is related to your studies. Second, spend time for devotion and satsang for it will mould your life and help control your mind. You will reap its benefits in future. You will not be affected by bad influence. And with the remaining time serve your mother and father, do the household chores – respect your parents and please them by obeying their wishes. And there is nothing wrong in playing sports.

In brief, spend the amount of time necessary but don't waste it. If you spend a little more time in good things then there's no objection. If you spend 15 minutes extra in matters related to study or mandir then its OK. But you should not spend even a single minute in looking at bad things.

31 ON MARRIAGE

Translation: Sadhu Vivekjivandas

During a youth camp on 30 September, 2000 in Orlando, USA, Pramukh Swami Maharaj discoursed on the marriage institution. Swamishri describes the institution's past and present condition and points out its prevailing weaknesses and solutions.

Today, more and more people suffer from despair and anxiety. Another generic attribute is that everyone wants to do things in his own independent way. Where there is a need for restraint, one talks of freedom and permissiveness. One asks, 'Why should we have discipline? Let people do whatever they want.' Such are the changes in attitudes.

Formally, people had less wealth and splendour. They lived in simplicity but were happy, whereas, today, people have so much but are unhappy.

If man exercises restraint then life will become conducive to happier living. During the ancient *gurukul* system of education, students had to compulsorily study till 25 years. Their first lesson was in discipline. They obeyed the guru's command and studied what he taught. When they went home, they obeyed their parents and the parents loved their children. When a son got married, his wife was treated by his parents as their own daughter and the son was treated likewise by his in-laws. But today these sentiments have waned and we consequently face problems.

The element of self-control in people is absent. An elephant becomes useful when it is controlled with an *ankush*. One may feel why should there be such pressure? But it is not pressure, it is a means of control. A horse is bridled so that it does not run riot and create havoc. An ox is pierced with a ring through its nose to control it during farming. Similarly, to help us live a proper, meaningful life, the great sages and seers have prescribed a moral code of conduct in the scriptures. With the intention to promote all-round happiness, they pondered deeply and with great foresight. But we don't like it! We don't want any restrictions or rules that bind. We don't want anyone to have any control over us. It is because of such attitudes that we create problems for ourselves. And the consequences are frustrations and an array of difficulties.

What is the meaning of Satsang? To keep the company of those who are true and good. With the company of good people one is inspired by wholesome thoughts and able to maintain one's integrity. And conversely, bad company shatters one's morality and the social and family structure. The family structure was once beautiful. The entire family lived happily together with the grandfather and there were no problems. Whereas today, no one wants his grandfather, his father and mother. And the father does not want his son; the husband his wife. This is the tragic situation we have today. And the reason is people have given up moral restraints and discipline. So instead of progress we have downfall! We have endeavoured to become modern but lost our culture in the process.

We want to realize Ekantik Dharma (dharma, *jnan, vairagya* and bhakti) and for this we must abide by and preserve our moral restraints. The climate of permissiveness in society is not good, and you know it because you have the element of discrimination through Satsang. But because of the social environment you live in, sometimes such questions regarding the need for discipline arise in your mind too.

It all hinges on controlling one's mind and disciplining one's senses. And to do this one has to renounce bad company.

Bad company (*kusang*) means that which leads you astray from morality – and you should beware of *kusang*. It could be the things you see, eat, a conversation or the company you keep. And once you have identified it, you should refrain from associating and thinking about it. You should renounce it even if it means losing monetary benefits or mundane success and fame. But people take that little benefit and sacrifice their morality. There is no need for this! Whatever one achieves immorally will be the source of pain and misery. And that is why Bhagwan Swaminarayan has advocated shunning bad company and things that come in the way of dharma. If we have faith then God will assist us.

Previously in our culture, the village Brahmin (priest) performed all the rituals. He was the deciding person who saw and arranged marriages. And the parents of the boy and girl would accept it and have them married. Even though the decided couple had not seen each other, their parents not having seen the prospective bride or groom, still the marriage worked. Questions and differences must have cropped up, but the newly married couple had a resolve to share the joys and sorrows together and live together till the end. Whereas today, a minor difference immediately results in separation and break up. But one should at least make an effort to understand and tolerate each other. But no! Even after having children, one files for divorce.

Then the tradition of the village Brahmin deciding the marriage faded and parents or an aunt or sister would see the match and decide the marriage. Then after marriage, they (wife and husband) would never think that because their parents had decided it hasn't worked so they should break up. Whatever had been decided would do. They would live together till the end, even if it meant living in misery or pain. There was no thought to the beauty or education of a girl. Since the elders had decided, the couple accepted.

And today, we find that the girl and boy search for their

own partner. They choose and decide regardless of their parents and relatives. They stay for two months, four and six months and still end up divorcing. Even though they decide by themselves still they break up.

Formally, the family structure was united. The father figure managed all the social affairs. Whatever he did, the son, daughter, daughter-in-law agreed. Whereas today, there is a lack of unity in the family. Every member earns his or her money. When the son turns eighteen and starts earning, he then independently manages his own affairs. The wife too earns. Whereas before there was one bank balance in the family. Today we find 'This is my money and that is yours. You pay your own share of the electric bill.' Ironically, the wife and husband 'share' to such an extent! Where lies the love between them! Even in matters of food provisions the same sentiments. How can such a marriage survive? This then shows that people's minds are different! As long as your minds are not one then you are not united. 'You pay half the rent and I the other half. My wages and your wages! I will spend my money in whatever way I wish and not the way you want!' But this is not Hinduism. If you decide to live according to norms, then no matter where you are, you will not have problems.

How can you have different bills when the husband, wife and parents live together? Why should the menu be different? Everyone should sit together, eat together, talk together, respect and love each other.

Because of the prevailing air of independence and freedom we are losing our cultural roots and values. People succumb to the enticing social climate. But no matter what, one should follow one's true values, cultivate greater faith in dharma, God and his commands. The more one preserves spiritual values in life, the more one's mind will be fortified, the better one's thoughts, the more peace and progress one will attain.

32 GREEK CONCEPT OF HAPPINESS

Paresh D. Bhatt

Virtue and happiness go hand in hand according to Socrates. His disciple, Plato, maintained that the goal of man is a virtuous life. To acquire virtue man should have knowledge and should know how to apply it. It is true that not all people have the same intellectual level. The total knowledge of the philosophers exceeds the knowledge of the soldier whose total knowledge, in turn, exceeds that of the artisans. Every person should apply his own knowledge. Virtue consisted, therefore, in application of one's own knowledge. But the proposition that knowledge is virtue implies that there is an objective good to be known and that it can be known by rational and logical investigation rather than by intuition, guesswork or luck.

The good or objectively real, whatever everybody thinks about it, ought to be realized not because man wants it but because it is good. The virtuous life is not determined by man himself but is fixed. This 'highest good' is the supreme and ultimate purpose of the universe and occupies the central position in the realm of ideas. Man's soul finds itself in that strange intermediary position of being a member of two worlds, i.e., the material world of sense perception and the spiritual world of ideal reality, but the soul is actually supersensible and belongs to the spiritual world of eternal ideals. Plato reasoned that the soul, being eternal, had a pre-existence in the ideal world where it learned about the eternal ideals. The individual now living in the sensory world, barred from the ideal world, can recollect the great ideal in faint reminiscences.

In the realm of ideas, the concept of the ultimate occupied

a central position and Plato maintained that knowledge of the ultimate good was necessary in order to become good.

In contrast, according to Aristotle, good can be known on the basis of experience of human behaviour and desires. In order to discover the good man aims at, we have to look at man's daily activities and examine his behaviour. We would discover that man has a hierarchy of purpose. He deduces that from these multiple purposes there has to exist a higher good or purpose, which must be self-sufficient, final and attainable by man. The highest good man desires for or aims at is happiness. The question as to what the happiness or highest good man is aiming at, Aristotle's answer is that, that each man is endowed with reason. Man's potential, he maintains, should be realized, for it is in its realization that man's highest good is found. In other words, man's happiness lies not only in possessing knowledge but also in its application. Aristotle also finds room for secondary elements, i.e., pleasure and presence of certain external items.

A concept fundamental to Aristotle's ethical philosophy states that God and Nature create nothing in vain, that everything in this universe has been created to achieve a purpose and has been designed to perform the given function or type of activity for which it was fashioned. In the case of man the goal of actions is happiness. The function of man's highest nature, his rational soul, is to live a well-ordered life in which every phase of man responds to his rational dictates; in the sense that his lower nature behaves in conforming to reason. This virtue comprises essentially of use of one's ability to act purposefully in conforming to one's intellectual insight. Virtue means application of intelligence to practical situations and concrete action.

Plato and his disciple, Aristotle, felt that the State should aim at the moral elevation of the people. That which corresponds with man's characteristic function is moral. Plato and Aristotle regarded this as the disposition to effectively realize reason as a characteristic function. According to them the purpose of the State is the elevation of his realization or in other words the State exists to assist man in the realization of his characteristic human function. The State should endure that every person is so situated as to afford him an opportunity to effectively realize his characteristic function.

According to Plato, even as an individual's happiness depends upon his virtuous achievement, the good or happiness of society is contingent upon its realization of ideal justice. The ideal State is one in which every individual functions in his best according to his natural abilities. The fact that each person contributes his talent to the State by working at tasks for which he is best suited, helps to bring about harmony within society. And such harmony is regarded by Plato as identical with justice.

For Aristotle, the basic function of the State is to extricate man from the crude natural condition in which he finds himself in and to guide him into the civilized culture of an ethical and intellectual life and accomplishment wrought through the finer arts. Thus the goal of the state is good living, a life of happiness based upon virtue. Outside of the State, the perfected moral life is an impossibility in as much as man is a political or social animal by nature. In order for man to realize himself, he must activate his social nature, an exercise that requires an existence within some society. As a complement to man's needs, the State must also be considered the instrument whereby man may attain his goal; consequently, the purpose of the State is that of ethical training for the benefit of its citizens. Just as the highest virtue for the individual is intellectual activity, so the highest duty of society is that of achieving and making the proper use of a state of peace. Man's natural condition is not one of belligerency, as the Spartans taught, but one of peace. Aristotle, commenting on the failure of Spartans which he attributed to its military education and bellicose way of life, said that the Spartans, geared for war and not for peace in times of peace rusted like sword in a scabbard.

PERSONALITY DEVELOPMENT

33 CHARACTER: THE HOME OF HAPPINESS

Sadhu Paramtattvadas

After years of warring between the Netherlands and France, the Dutch emerged triumphant. King Louis XIV of France, naturally upset, reprimanded his ministers for their defeat. Colbert, one of King Louis' leading advisors, retorted politely, "Sire! The measure of a nation lies not in its length and breadth, but in the character of its people."

The nineteenth century American poet and essayist Ralph Waldo Emerson echoes this truth, "The true test of a civilization is not the census, not the size of cities, nor the crops - but the kind of men the country turns out."

A similar sentiment in different words is spelled out in, "When wealth is lost, nothing is lost. When health is lost, something is lost. But when character is lost, everything is lost."

What Is Character?

We see that many have realized the importance of a good personal character - but people seem divided when it comes to defining 'good' or 'bad' behaviour. Some have taken good behaviour to mean helping the needy, donating money and other such benevolent acts. Many only go as far as outer appearances - manners, etiquette, hygiene, etc. A few stop at purely physical acts, such as, going on a pilgrimage, performing rites and rituals, etc.

True, all these qualities can be part of a good character - but it doesn't end there.

So then what is Character? Is it invisible, indescribable?

No. Look in the *Oxford Dictionary* and you'll find 'character' defined as: - n. *the collective qualities of characteristics, especially mental and moral, that distinguish a person or thing; moral strength.*

However, the concise but revealing definition by Dwight L. Mody goes a long way in helping us understand what character really is. He says, "Character is what you are in the dark," i.e., what/who you are when you are alone!

People may try their best to appear 'goody-goody' in public view, but on closer inspection, their private lives can be a totally different story. Alphonso Karr believes:

"Every man has three characters:
one that he exhibits;
one that he has;
and one that he thinks he has.

In the end though, we cannot afford to forget that at least one person will always know what we are really like - our innerself!"

The Predominance of Character

There is a beautiful verse in the great Hindu epic scripture, the Mahabharat, that brings character into true light.

Shilam pradhãnam lokesmin shilam sarvam pratishthitam.

It means: Character is predominant in this world. It is the upholder of all.

Once, Lord Indra arrived unexpectedly at the palace of Bhakta Prahlad. Prahlad greeted Lord Indra with appropriate respect. Indra was pleased with the royal reception. When Indra was ready to leave, Prahlad did not forget the Indra replied, rather shrewdly, "Character!"

Prahlad was taken aback for a moment or two, but bound by his promise, he agreed. "Very well," Prahlad said in return. But at precisely that moment, Prahlad witnessed a strange sight. He saw the personified forms of Dharma (Righteousness), Vartan (Moral Conduct), Bal (Power) and Lakshmiji (Prosperity) begin to leave. "Where are you all going?" Prahlad asked hurriedly.

Lakshmiji answered, "Without a doubt - Righteousness, Truth, Conduct, Power and I (Prosperity) are all dependent upon Character. Therefore, we must follow Character." Character is the home of all virtues.

Keeping and Losing Character

Nowadays it seems harder than ever to be good - and even harder to stay good. With ever increasing doses of violence, corruption, seduction, etc. being force-fed to us from all sides - be it by a TV commercial, an ad in a magazine, a film or a billboard - it requires an extra, concerted effort to stay aloof from bad influences, to stay clean. A mere splash of bad conduct can leave a lingering stain and spoil an otherwise pristine character. We all know how a blotch of tomato ketchup stands out loud on a gleaming white T-shirt. But as explained by the Japanese proverb: "The reputation of a thousand years may be determined by the conduct of a single hour." A bad impression is harder to shake off than it is to earn a good one.

Thomas Paine's observation rings louder than ever, "Character is easier kept than recovered."

Our Capital

Of all our 'personal' belongings - money, property, health, fame, beauty, knowledge, talent, etc. - character alone is our true, lasting and indispensable asset. It is born from our day-to-day or rather, moment-to-moment actions and inclinations.

"Character is the result of our conduct," says Aristotle.

With our pure conduct as our capital, it seems we have the purchasing power to acquire anything.

In the Mahabharat we find, "With character one shuns all vices and attains righteousness, prosperity and salvation."

Bhagwan Swaminarayan explains in his Shikshapatri that

if our actions are in line with the scriptures, then happiness is ours too.

"He who abides by the codes prescribed in the scriptures will find happiness here (on earth) and hereafter (in heaven)" (Shikshapatri 8).

Pramukh Swami's Mission

Once, Pramukh Swami Maharaj was in the southern Gujarat village of Karcheliya. After visiting 50-60 homes in the dusty, sticky summer afternoon, Swamishri arrived, dripping with perspiration, at the house of Chhaganbhai. Even Swamiji's upper cloth was wet with sweat.

A devotee there told Swamiji about a miraculous laminated photo. "Bapa," he said, "water constantly trickles out of this *murti* of yours!"

Not the least bit amazed, Swamishri took his right index finger, wiped his brow, and commented, "Chhaganbhai, that water won't do anyone any good. This water (sweat) will!"

It has been Swamishri's ever untiring efforts of going to the people - meeting, talking, listening, counselling, consoling, inspiring and elevating. That is, his hard work has cleansed the characters of thousands across the world. This is his one and only life mission to see one and all happy by making their lives better.

Once, Swamiji was asked for a formula that would help all towards a better life. Spontaneously Swamiji replied, "Develop a good character yourself and help develop a character-rich society." Says Charning, too, "The great hope of society is the individual character."

Swamiji often explains, "We believe not in converting people from their religion, but rather transforming their lives for the better. Not brainwashing - but rather washing brains, washing hearts."

Swamishri's mission can be said to be nothing less than the mission of God. As Alexander Pope has said, "An honest man is the noblest work of God." Clearly, this reveals Swamiji as God's 'Character Envoy'.

Finally, let us share the sentiments of a spiritual leader of the Ramanuj Sampraday, the respected South Indian saint Pujya Chinna Jeer Swami. On December 1995, in his address to the assembly at the Amrut Mahotsav festival in Mumbai, he said, "Not only does Pramukh Swami Maharaj turn outer wastelands into wonderlands (referring to the spectacular 70-acre 'Swaminarayan Nagar' township that was once nothing but bog-land), but he does it with people, too. I see him as a great sculptor of society, and his every sadhu, every devotee, every volunteer, as pieces of his art, his masterpieces!"

34 TEAMWORK

Sadhu Chaitanyamurtidas

There is unrest in the forest, there is trouble among the trees; for the maples want more sunlight and the oaks ignore their pleas.

Once upon a time in a forest, the maples and the oaks had a small problem. The maples believed in growing horizontally because they believed that breadth was more important than height. And so they grew wide and fat. But this prevented the oaks from expanding. The oaks, on the other hand, believed in vertical expansion; they believed height was more important than breadth. And so they grew tall and lofty. But this blocked most of the sunlight for the maples. And so, a fierce battle started in the forest - the maples growing fat and the oaks growing tall. The maples made their case to the oaks that they were not getting enough sunlight, but the oaks simply closed their ears and ignored all their pleas. The battle grew in intensity until eventually a war broke out and in the end the oaks were killed due to lack of space and the maples perished due to lack of sunlight. The forest which was once lush green turned into a dry, lifeless desert.

This story was once related to a class of elementary school students and they were asked to come up with ideas on how the tragedy of the maples and the oaks could have been averted. Some of the solutions they came up with were truly ingenious.

One boy answered, "Why could they not just have compromised: On Mondays, Wednesdays and Fridays the maples could have held their breath so the oaks could get more room and on Tuesdays, Thursdays and Saturdays, the oaks could have bent down a bit to allow the sunlight to reach the maples. This way, on Sundays, they could have got together and really enjoyed each others' friendship."

Another boy came up with a mathematical solution, "What if they both agreed to arrange themselves in alternating rows - one row of maples and then a row of oaks and so on. That way the maples would have been free to grow along their row and the oaks free to expand along their row. And if they aligned themselves east-west, along the path of the sun, both would have been guaranteed enough sunlight throughout the year and both could have lived happily and in harmony in the forest."

This was just a test of creativity, but of all the solutions given by the children of that class, the common factor was teamwork. Both the maples and the oaks had to work together as a whole, as a team, for one common purpose - survival.

Boxes

The story of the maples and the oaks is just an example, but in reality, when we have to perform any task teamwork is absolutely essential.

Because, when one person is working alone, there are no complications - he can do the job the way he likes. But, as the number of people involved in a project increases, the complexity of successfully completing the task grows exponentially.

Suppose a box is to be moved from one point to another. When one man has to do it, any way is the right way - he can either push it or pull it - both are equally correct. There is no wrong way for one man. But when two people have to move the box, the advantage is that there are three right ways but there are also three wrong ways. If one man pushes from one side and the other pushes from the other side the box will not move. If one pulls on one side and the other also pulls from the opposite side, the box will not move. If one pulls and the other pushes from the same side, the box will not move. If the box is to be moved both have to work together as a team in a coordinated manner. Both have to push or pull from the same side or if they are on opposite sides, one has to pull and the other has to push. Group work increases the necessity of teamwork.

Variables

We have all learned in mathematics that the complexity of an equation increases exponentially as the number of variables increases. In the same way, when performing a task, the complexity of the job increases exponentially as the number of individuals increases. It becomes more and more important that they work in a coordinated manner. If the individual members do not work together in harmony, the task cannot be performed successfully, no matter how capable each individual member is.

That's why people often joke that one Indian is equal to two Japanese. Now if this is the case, then logic tells us that two Indians should be equal to four Japanese, and three Indians should be equal to six Japanese and so on. But what happens in reality is that one Indian is equal to two Japanese, but two Indians are equal to only one Japanese. Why? Because one Indian works fine alone, but when two Indians get together they usually end up fighting for supremacy. They cancel each other out and the single Japanese comes out ahead.

This is just a joke about Indians, but in reality, it can be applied to any group of people that don't work together as a team. Group work increases the necessity of teamwork.

On the other hand, if the members can manage to overcome individual differences and work together as a team; if there is harmony among all; if all are working together in sync – then the members as a whole can do much, much more than the individual could do alone. It thus follows from the universal concept that the whole is always greater than the sum of the parts.

No single part of a plane can fly on its own. Throw up the wing of an aircraft and it will tumble down to the ground. Throw up the tail, or the fuselage, or even the engine and each will fall to the ground. But now, assemble all the parts into one specific shape – the shape of an airplane – let them work together as a team and the same parts which fall when on their own, can fly through the sky.

No single part of a large ship can float on its own. Throw the nuts and bolts of a ship into water and they will sink. Throw the hull, or the propeller, or the rudder and they too will sink. But assemble all the parts into the shape of a ship and let them work together and the same parts, which would normally sink, will float on water. The whole is always greater than the sum of the parts.

Pujya Yogiji Maharaj often told a story of a flock of doves in the jungle. Once some doves were happily feeding on some seeds when all of a sudden a bird-catcher's net fell on them and trapped them. Immediately, all the doves started screaming and flapping their wings in confusion.

But then one Superintendent dove, as Yogiji Maharaj called it, got up and told the others, Listen! If we flap our wings like this randomly, we won't be able to lift the net. Let's become one and flap together with synchronicity. When they did this they were able to lift the net. They all descended on a distant tree and the net remained stuck on the branches and all the doves escaped. No single dove on its own was capable of lifting the net. But when they worked together as a team they accomplished what was impossible for any individual dove to achieve. The whole is always greater than the sum of the parts.

That is why teamwork is so very important when we want to successfully complete a job or project. But, of course, teamwork doesn't come on its own. Teamwork isn't a product which can be forced from people like eggs from a chicken under floodlights. In order to bring harmony and grace to the project, each individual has to contribute and sacrifice something.

In general, the recipe for teamwork consists of three main ingredients: a goal, a role, and a toll.

1. There has to be a common goal among the members.
2. The members of the team have to play their role.
3. The members have to pay a toll - something to be sacrificed.

1. Common Goal

First, and most importantly, there has to be a common goal. Even though the members of the team have different views, even though they come from different backgrounds, even if they have different ambitions, this common goal is the glue which unites all the members of the team.

Dry cement on its own is extremely powdery. Step on it and it will get crushed. Blow on it and it will be dispersed.

But add water to the same powdery cement and it can create buildings which can withstand winds of over 100 mph. In the same way, a common goal does to a group of people what water does to cement - it focuses everyone's energies in one direction, towards one goal.

Trees

Trees on their own are known to fight over resources. If you look under any typical tree, the roots generally reach half as deep and twice as wide as the tree we see above the ground. But, when the roots of two trees touch, a long battle for dominance starts - each wants exclusive rights to the water and minerals in the soil.

That is, unless there is a particular type of fungus - the Mycorrhiza fungus - on the scene. An Oregon State University scientist has found that the fungus not only reduces competition but, on the contrary, it inspires the trees to act as a team. Whether the trees are of the same species or of different species, the presence of this fungus helps create an entire underground network for the trees.

The individual trees abandon their selfish nature and, with the aid of the fungus, start acting as a community. If one tree has access to water, another to nutrients, a third to sunlight, the trees begin sharing resources through this common fungal linkage between them.

In the same way, a common goal does to people what the fungus does to trees – it acts as a link to bind individual members of a team. In Satsang we may have different viewpoints, different opinions, different likes and dislikes, different natures, different methods but if we realize that we all represent One God, if we realize that we all represent One Guru, One Sanstha and One Goal, our differences will become secondary and we will be able to unite together as a team.

Our common beliefs and goals act as a glue to bind us all together into a team.

2. Each Must Play a Role

But a common goal is not enough. Every member of a football team has a common goal – they all want to win the game. But that doesn't necessarily mean they will be able to work together.

Something more is needed – and that something has to do with the individual player's role. If the team is to be successful, each member has to play his role properly.

Football team: quarterback, running back, defense, kicker.

In an American football team, the quarterback has to concentrate on playing the role of the quarterback. He can't say to himself, "I'm sick of just throwing the ball all the time."

The running back has to concentrate on playing the role of

the running back. He can't say to himself "I'm sick of running all the time; I want to throw the ball as well."

If the team is to be successful, the defence has to play defence. The punter has to punt, the kicker has to kick and the linesmen have to block. Each must concentrate on playing his role to perfection.

Second Violin

But of course the problem is that everyone wants the limelight. Everyone wants to be the man who gets all the glory.

Once, a conductor of a famous symphony orchestra was asked what he thought was the most difficult instrument to play. He answered immediately that without a doubt it is the second violin. He said, "I can find plenty of people to play the first violin because they are always noticed, but it is difficult to find people to play the supporting, background role of the second violin. Everyone wants to be in the limelight."

But, if we think about it, each part of the team, no matter how small, is just as important as any other part. The small gears of a watch are just as important as the big gears.

King Is Not Always the Award-Winner

In a play there are many roles; someone has to play the king, someone the queen, some the soldiers, and some even have to play the minor role of the servants. But, the award doesn't always go to the king - which is the most glamorous role. The award for best acting may be given to the servant - which seems to be a background role. Whoever plays his role best will win the award.

In a successful team, each member must play his role, no matter how minor it may seem.

In the same way, if a Satsang centre is to work harmoniously, the president must play the role of the president properly, the

Yuvak Mandal must play the role of the Yuvak Mandal and the Bal Mandal must be ready to play the role of that Bal Mandal. We can't have the case of 'too many chiefs and not enough Indians.'

If a festival is to be successful, the Stage Programme Department has to concentrate on playing its role, but so must the Cleaning Department.

If a family is to work in harmony, the father must faithfully play the role of the father, the mother must be a mother, and the child must also be ready to play the role of the child.

In order to build a team, each member must concentrate on playing his/her role to perfection. This is the second requirement.

3. Sacrifice

And lastly, in addition to having a common goal and playing one's role properly, teamwork's most important ingredient is: sacrifice. Each individual member has to be ready to give up something for the good of the whole. In a successful team, the goal is greater than the individual.

Air Florida

In January 1982, an Air Florida plane took off from Washington Airport. But in just a few seconds, it struck a bridge over the Potomac river and immediately crashed into the river throwing all of the passengers into the icy, cold water. When the National Guard Rescue helicopters came to the scene only six survivors were clinging to the tail section of the plane.

The rescue men lowered a rope and ring from the helicopter. One of the male survivors immediately helped another fellow passenger to the ring and signalled to the rescue squad. The helicopter returned to the river bank to drop off the rescued survivor. Four more times the helicopter returned to get another survivor and each time that man gave the ring to someone else. And when the helicopter returned the fifth time, the man could not be found - he had drowned in the waters. At some moment in his heroic act, the man must have realized that he could not possibly survive if he continued to give the ring to others. But still each time he gave the rescue ring to the others. He sacrificed his own life for the good of others. We don't have to die for others, but maybe we can sacrifice some of our likes and dislikes for the sake of the whole team. Maybe we can learn to tolerate others' faults and drawbacks for the sake of the team. Maybe we can be more kind and helpful to others. If we can do this much we will be able to make a successful team.

Conclusion

So, as we have seen, the recipe for teamwork consists of three main ingredients:

1. A common goal
2. Playing our role properly
3. Sacrifice

When a group or a team works with these three qualities, there is practically no limit to what it can accomplish. Yogiji Maharaj used to say, *"Apde whole Bombay rangi nakhie, jo tran vastu hoy to - samp, suhradaybhav and ekta."* - We can 'colour' all of Bombay if we desire, provided we have three qualities - Harmony, Friendship and Unity.

Coming together is a beginning, staying together is progress, but working together is teamwork.

35 COOPERATION

Sadhu Vivekjivandas

Cooperation rather than competition brings out the best in us. This has been borne out by studies. We live in an age of interdependence and thus the need for others should become the focus for a happier and fruitful life.

In the early 1900s, a young athlete named James Rector of Hot Springs, Arkansas, was a track star at the University of Virginia. When he was chosen in 1908 to compete at the Olympic Games in London, he was the odds-on favourite to win the 100-metre dash.

Rector used the crouch stance perfected by US athletes, in which the runner was poised to dash off at firing of the starter's gun. A week before the Games, the coach of the South African team approached him. "We have a great runner, Reggie Walker," he told him. "I shouldn't ask this but he'll be competing against you in the 100 metres. But when I see how you Americans save time with your crouch - well, someone ought to teach him."

Rector hesitated only a moment, "Bring Walker here. I'll coach him."

Next morning, Rector coached his rival again and again in the sprinter's start. The Olympic record book reveals how well Walker learned. He beat Rector and went on to fame. Rector came second. The records are still there for anyone who cares to read them. But the story is silent on Rector's sense of cooperation and fair play. Throughout his life, Rector was hailed as the true champion by all who knew the story of how he lost the race.

James Rector, though he lost, turned out to be one up in the game of life. He had imbibed the spirit of cooperation and sportsmanship. His story stands as a glowing example of humanism in an age where our lives are cluttered with competition and self-centredness. We find people frantically competing for success, fame and adulation. Potbellied barons of industry vying with each other and nations bent on producing new breeds of devastating arsenals for superiority. In fact competitive practices have infiltrated all areas and levels of human life. The alarming signal on this subject is that competitive attitudes fuel our fragile, explosive attitudes. We become bent upon catapulting to the top at the cost of fowling another's nest.

The competitive spirit has overwhelmed our lives to such a degree that we have forgotten how to have recreation or fun without some contest that pits one against another. The losers are devalued or scoffed at. Playing an innocent indoor game for fun can turn aggressive when competition comes into play. Millions of people hold the view that competition motivates people, it brings out hidden talents and potential in people and it also fires a man with enthusiasm and a spirit to work.

But does competition really bring out the best in us? Do we perform better when we rival with others than when we work together for mutual benefit? Do we retain our peace of mind or level of happiness once we enter this hassle?

Recent studies in America provide growing evidence that cooperation outpaces the results of competitive attitudes. Cooperation promotes teamwork and harmony. It enables people to view others as friends and not as adversaries by creating a congenial atmosphere that allows room for encouragement and healthy criticism. A climate of cooperation makes one less self-centred by widening one's field of awareness to the needs of others. It exposes one to a gamut of human outlooks, problems and solutions.

Cooperation destroys walls of suspicion and distrust. It fosters unity and dissolves partisanship. It stimulates an 'us' or 'we' mentality and breaks the 'I' or 'them' attitude. By contrast, ego-building competitive attitudes build barriers of envy and hatred.

Cooperation promotes more cooperation. Competition encourages more competition. Cooperative situations are more satisfying and enjoyable whereas competitive situations make one tense and highly strung.

The next time you find yourself either vying or cooperating with someone at work or at college or with a devotee in Satsang, just compare how you feel and react.

The noble have always left a stamp of their loftiness through acts of humanism. They have refrained from restricting their happiness through shallow acts of selfishness and personal gain. Charles Darwin, the famous naturalist toiled on *The Origin of Species* for twenty years before he got it ready for publication. When he was about to make his theory public a strange and exciting coincidence took place. Unaware of the fact that Darwin was ready with a thesis on the subject, his friend, Alfred Russel Wallace (in Malaya), sent him an original paper on the same subject with a request to introduce him to the world as the originator of a new theory on evolution.

It was a bitter trial of character indeed! A lesser man would have succumbed to the temptation of removing such an obstacle by means fair or foul. But Darwin, a noble man, decided to recommend his friend's thesis at the cost of abandoning his own. He said, "I would burn my whole book rather than behave in a paltry spirit." Finally it was decided that it would be introduced as a joint work by the two friends.

When Wallace came to know the actual situation, he went one better than Darwin by admitting that the credit for discovering 'The Origin of Species' belonged to none other than Darwin.

The story of Chaitanya Mahaprabhu's action in throwing his superb commentary on Nyay (logic) into a river for the sake of promoting his friend Raghunath's commentary called *Dadhiti*, is another eloquent example of selflessness. This clearly proves that lack of selflessness invariably promotes a competitive spirit.

The task of cooperation becomes stiffer when the individual you deal with seethes with envy and hatred. An interesting narration in the Shrimad Bhagvat illustrates how two conflicting forces joined in cooperation to accomplish an otherwise impossible feat. The holy scripture tells us of the incessant conflicts and skirmishes between the gods and the demons. The story goes that when the gods were fighting a losing battle and had lost the potency to revive their dead, they sought Brahma's assistance. They beseeched him to help them out of their tragic predicament. Brahma counselled them to approach the Lord himself. The gods went to the Lord entreating for help. The Lord acknowledged their prayers, stipulating that they would need to seek the help and cooperation of the demons. And so the stupendous churning of the ocean began. The two sworn foes joined hands in friendship and went about the mighty task. With the towering Mt. Mandara as the churning staff and Vasuki, the gargantuan serpent, as the rope, the gods were rewarded with a pot of elixir (*amrut*). Cooperation made the task, otherwise impossible, feasible.

In Vachanamrut, Gadhada I 4 Bhagwan Swaminarayan illustrates a telling incident of how Naradji won the pleasure of Bhagwan Narayan. The story in the words of Bhagwan Swaminarayan is as follows, "Once, both Naradji and Tumbaru went to Vaikunth for the darshan of Lakshmi and Narayan. There, Tumbaru sang before them. As a result, both Lakshmi and Narayan were pleased and rewarded him with their clothes and ornaments. Seeing this, Naradji became jealous of Tumbaru, and thought, 'I shall also learn to sing like Tumbaru and please God.'

"Then, Naradji learned the art of singing and sang before God. But God commented, 'You do not know how to sing like Tumbaru.' Thereafter, Naradji performed austerities to please Shiva and received his blessings to master the art of singing. However, when he sang before God again, God was still not pleased. In this way, Naradji continued for seven *manvantars* (i.e., 2,147,040,000 human years). Despite this, God would not be pleased with his singing.

"Finally, Naradji learned to sing from Tumbaru himself and then sang before Shri Krishna Bhagwan in Dwarika. Only then was Shri Krishna Bhagwan pleased, and only then did he reward Naradji with his own clothes and ornaments. Thereafter, Naradji abandoned his jealousy towards Tumbaru."

Cooperating with another is as important as seeking cooperation from another. Naradji found it difficult to seek cooperation from Tumbaru because he himself was bound by envy. Eventually, when he went to Tumbaru in all humility and sought his tutelage, the Lord showed his pleasure.

Aksharbrahma Gunatitanand Swami emphasizes the indispensability of unity or cooperation for spiritual progress. In his talks, Swamini Vato, chapter 3, no. 58 he says, "When unrighteousness prevails among the gods, humans or the sages, they are robbed of the happiness they possess. This unrighteousness is born out of conflicts and division of minds. But if harmony (which springs through cooperation) prevails, unrighteousness fails to devastate our lives.

"Once Bhagwan Swaminarayan talked of a king who ordered a quiverful of arrows. He then summoned his mightiest warrior to break the arrows in the quiver. But he failed. The king took out a single arrow from the quiver and called the weakest of his men and told him to break the arrow. The man effortlessly snapped it in two. The king then gathered his men and said, 'If you remain bound together like the arrows in the quiver you shall remain invincible to the onslaughts of the enemy and the kingdom shall flourish and remain intact.'

"Similarly, O sadhus, *parshads* and *brahmacharis*, if you remain united and live with a cooperative spirit your inner enemies (of ego, lust, greed, jealousy) shall fail to vanquish you. And if you fail to abide by this principle, your slightest inner failing (i.e., base instincts) will toss you out from the Satsang-fold."

His Holiness Yogiji Maharaj was an ardent promoter of cooperation. He drummed the words, '*Samp, Suhradbhav* and *Ekta*' (harmony, friendship and unity) into the Satsang-fold. He often depicted with meticulous detail an anecdote about a flock of birds trapped in a hunter's net. Their sudden confinement caused panic. Each flapped its wings to escape but their uncombined efforts were in vain. The leader of the flock called for cooperation. The birds flapped their wings in unison and lifted the entire net, thus freeing themselves from confinement.

His Holiness Pramukh Swami Maharaj while speaking on this subject, relates the story of four poor brothers who resolved to rid themselves of their penury through appeasing Varun, the sea god. And with the motive of acquiring wealth they started worshipping Varun. Eating only once a day, the four brothers shared their duties in a spirit of cooperation. While one begged cereals and flour the other brought wood and the third fetched water from a well and the fourth cooked the food. Months passed by and Varun was pleased by their unity and spirit of mutual cooperation. Varun decided to test them before rewarding them with riches. So, in the guise of a Brahmin, he approached the brother begging for flour and said, "You are toiling away while your brothers speak ill of you!" "That's impossible," defended the brother. The 'Brahmin' made further efforts in arousing the suspicion of the brother but failed. He tried the same strategy with the other three brothers and failed each time. Pleased by their unity and mutual friendship, Varun lavished riches on the four brothers. Varun was happy that the wealth endowed to the four would not divide their minds and thus disturb the amity existing between them.

How to Cooperate

1. Meet those whom you are concerned with on a regular basis.
2. Learn to forgive the faults and mistakes of others.
3. Have a regular exposure to Satsang.

Cooperation is the cradle of many virtues and conditions. Out of it springs friendship, love, reverence, a binding unity, peace, happiness and many many more virtues. Though cooperation requires you to spare time, forfeit your rate of progress, fame and even riches, it will, like, James Rector, Charles Darwin, Naradji and the four brothers immortalize you into monuments of humanism. It will make you happy in the Satsang-fold and propel you towards God-realization.

36 EMPTY YOUR CUP

Sadhu Vivekjivandas

"Do you realize you will have to unlearn all that you have learnt and start from square one?" asked Bruce Lee to a person wanting to learn the martial arts.

The man responded, "No."

Bruce smiled and placed his hand lightly on his shoulder. "Let me tell you a story my *sifu* (master) told me. It is about a Japanese Zen master who received a university professor wanting to know about Zen. The professor ceaselessly talked about himself and his opinions. The master perceived that the professor was not so much interested in learning about Zen as he was in impressing him with his own opinions and knowledge. The master listened patiently and finally suggested they have tea. The master poured his visitor's cup full and then kept on pouring. The professor watched the cup overflowing until he could no longer restrain himself, 'The cup is overfull, no more will go in,' he said.

" 'Like this cup,' the master said, 'You are full of your opinions and speculations. How can I show you Zen unless you first empty your cup?' "

"Bruce studied the man's face. "You understand the point?"

"Yes. You want me to empty my mind of the arrogance of the knowledge I have so that I can learn."

After the 16th century the martial arts in the Orient came to be appreciated for its potential for self-development. It is more than a physical contest between two opponents who inflict damage to one another. Fundamentally they are avenues through which one can achieve spiritual and mental tranquility. This emphasis came to light after the 16th century. The martial arts were not merely seen as a combat-to-the-death means but as a tremendous exercise for inner development. Thus, the art of sword fighting, *kenjutsu,* became transformed into *ken-do* – 'the way of the sword'. Soon, other martial arts were given the ending *do,* which means 'the way'. In other words, 'the way to enlightenment, self-realization and understanding'. This Zen element (Zen is a Japanese sect of Mahayana Buddhism that aims at enlightenment by direct intuition through meditation), i.e., the enlightenment aspect, is found in various degrees in aikido, judo, karate-do, tae-kwan-do, hapkido, jeet-kune-do, etc.

The Zen in martial arts dilutes the role of intellect and emphasizes intuitive action for self-development. Its final aim is to free the individual from anger, illusion and false passion.

The practice hall where you learn and better the art is called a dojo. It is here that you learn more about yourself – your fears, anxieties, reactions and habits. It is a world where a partner teaches you who you really are and your reactions to various situations. The conflicts that take place in the dojo helps you handle conflicts that take place outside in the world. The disciplines you learn in the dojo carries over to daily life. Each dojo is presided over by a *sifu* or *sensei* – a master.

In the realm of religion an individual is taught how to free himself from animal instincts. He masters the art of spiritual combat from his guru. The dojo he goes to is the mandir. Here, he learns more about himself, his passions and habits. He comes to recognize his inner conflicts and the means to root them out through satsang.

The path to spiritual freedom requires him to relegate his intellect and promote sound faith. Moral disciplines help to reinforce his character; introspection gives a clear picture of his conflicts and satsang, i.e., association with his guru, frees him from the influence of all passions and conflicts. It is the *sensei* or guru who drills him for mental tranquility.

To the conflicts raging in Arjun's mind on the battlefield of Kurukshetra, Shri Krishna tells him to empty his cup and seek his refuge alone. He says:

Sarvadharmãnparityajya mãmekam sharanam vraja.

"Renounce all your duties and take refuge in me, alone" (Bhagavad Gita 18.66).

Manmanã bhava madhbhakto madhyãji mãm namaskuru.

"Fix your mind on me, be devoted to me, sacrifice to me, prostrate thyself to me" (Bhagavad Gita 18.65).

Mãmev ye prapadhyante mãyãmetãn taranti te.

"Those who come at my feet transcend the three *gunas* (i.e., *sattvagun, rajogun* and *tamogun*)" (Bhagavad Gita 7.14).

A man approached a guru for knowledge.

"How long will it take?" he enquired.

"One month," the guru replied.

"But I already know the following things." The man started rattling off a list of what he knew.

"Then it will take one year!" the Guru replied calmly.

"But you said only a month a minute ago!"

"Young man, after having told me what you know I will first have to empty your cup before imparting the redeeming knowledge."

As long as we are 'full' we perceive things through our own attitudes and beliefs. This hampers us from receiving the guru's knowledge.

Socrates, the great father of philosophy, believed and preached, "There is one thing I know, that I know nothing." It was with this maxim that Socrates scaled the heights of wisdom.

Yogiji Maharaj cited an anecdote about a Brahmin who was invited to a neighbouring village for lunch. He took a bag of grams to munch on the way. He finished eating them before reaching the village. The grams made him thirsty. So he drank lots of water. This made his stomach full. When he arrived at the village and sat down for lunch, he managed to eat only five sweetballs whereas his friends had completed fifteen and were still asking for more. "What's the matter with you?" one of them asked. "You've only eaten five!" said another.

"O it was those damn grams I ate! If only I hadn't eaten them I wouldn't have been thirsty and bloated," the Brahmin lamented.

Yogiji Maharaj explained the moral of the story, saying, "Like the sad Brahmin who failed to eat his share of sweetballs because of the grams, we, too, come to the mandir filled with worldly thoughts. This renders us helpless in having our hearty share of the spiritual food of God's wisdom. Whenever we attend a spiritual discourse sit with an empty, clear mind."

Try emptying your cup and you'll learn tremendously. You'll find room for improvement in the academic, social and spiritual aspects of your life.

The principle rule to learning and imbibing is humility and emptying oneself of all airs.

37 PAUSE!

Sadhu Vivekjivandas

A split second pause in the midst of action was the secret of Bruce Lee's success. He said, "Many martial artists attack with the force of a storm without observing the effects of their attack on their opponents. When I attack I always try to pause, stop the action, to study my opponent and his reactions before going into action again. I include pause and silence along with activity, thus allowing myself time to sense my own internal processes as well as my opponent's."

The Japanese have moon-viewing parties at which no conversation is allowed. They merely sit in the elegant surroundings and watch the moon rise, and nurture their appreciative abilities.

In the United States many top managers spend a quiet hour in introspection each day, free from appointments or phone calls. This has resulted in increased production and fewer problems.

In our hectic schedules we never plan for empty slots for doing nothing. This concept of doing nothing is also an activity and exercise. For example the pause in a piece of music or in a beat is not lack of music, it is an integral part of the composition. Meaningful pauses enable one to take stock of oneself. They also allow room for appreciating people and the good things they do.

Pauses play a crucial and guiding role in one's life. They may, on the surface, seem to be a waste of time because you see no immediate results. But in the long run you realize the benefits of daily reflection. Thoreau's solitary reflections on the shore of Waldon Pond, Massachusetts, unveiled many hazy and hidden truths of life. He built a small home with his own hands and lived in it for two years. The purpose of his retreat was to investigate whether he could live life on the basic necessities, namely, food, shelter, clothing and fuel. He writes after his experiment, "... most of the luxuries and many of the so-called comforts of life, are not only indispensable, but are positive hindrances to the elevation of mankind."

We all need to adopt pauses in everyday life to reassess our groundings in domestic and spiritual matters. Without proper introspection one can never gauge one's successes or failures.

A distinguished explorer spent a couple of years with the natives of the Upper Amazon. He once embarked upon a further exploration of the Amazon jungle. He was very eager to chart new terrains and thus urged the natives carrying the supplies to hurry. For the first two days they complied with the explorer's commands. They took the minimum rest, getting up immediately each time the explorer told them to. But on the third day the exhausted natives took an unscheduled rest. The explorer got irritated and ordered them to start walking. The chief explained they were spent and couldn't move further until their souls had caught up with their bodies.

In our over-indulgent schedules of work and entertainment we forget our spiritual identity. We become tired of life and need a pause to reclaim our lost soul.

Each day, Schopenhauer, the German philosopher, retreated to a nearby garden and pondered about his true identity. He would begin by asking himself, "Who am I?" One evening the gardener came to lock the gates and saw Schopenhauer. He shouted to him, "Who are you? It's time to leave." Schopenhauer replied, "I am trying to find out who I really am."

Bhagwan Swaminarayan explains how trivial we become due to our extroverted tendencies. He says, "The soul that resides in one's body has an inclination of seeing things without. It perceives beauty and ugliness, youth, old age and many other physical aspects of life but it never sees its own self. Such a person is the most ignorant among the ignorant."

In the Katha Upanishad the Lord of Death in a dialogue with Nachiketa says, "God created the senses with outgoing tendencies; therefore man beholds the external universe and not the internal self *(atma)*...

"Our ears can detect and listen to even a distant noise. In fact all our sense organs gallop outward toward their objects.

"But some wise men with eyes averted, i.e., senses turned away from sensual objects, desirous of immortality, see the *atma* within" (2.1.1).

This state of introspection is the pause we have been referring to. Like Bruce Lee, who evaluated the impact of his every attack, we need to analyse the effect and worth of our daily actions. The man who sharpens knives or tools always stops to see whether the instrument has been sharpened enough. Similarly, daily pauses enable us to see whether we are straying or overdoing anything in life.

Gunatitanand Swami draws our attention to the importance of introspection and evaluation in our lives. He says, "The European takes the shelter of his bungalow to ponder and unburden himself of his problems and frustrations. Similarly, we must spare time for introspection from our routine work" (Swamini Vato 2.182).

An incident from the lives of Mulji and Krishnaji (devotees of Bhagwan Swaminarayan) echo the importance of pausing before taking a major decision. Mulji and Krishnaji had a burning desire to join the monastic order of Bhagwan Swaminarayan. But a firm refusal from their parents hampered their dream from materializing. After several years of striving they left home for Gadhada, where the Lord resided. They requested Bhagwan Swaminarayan to initiate them into the monastic order. Bhagwan Swaminarayan cautioned them, "The monastic life is a bed of thorns. You'll have to bear the burning heat and biting cold, the brunt of insults and persecutions from sadhus (outside the fold). Are you both ready to swallow all this? Go and ask this to your self."

A pause was offered to the two devotees. The Lord wanted them to find out whether they were really equipped for the rigours of ascetic life. Mulji and Krishnaji examined their minds and returned radiant and victorious. They returned with a determined resolve to embrace the ascetic path. The Lord initiated them both; appointing one of them as the head of the Ahmedabad mandir and assigning the other to stay at the Junagadh mandir.

Govindram and Mayaram Bhatt were brothers and devoted disciples of Bhagwan Swaminarayan. They, too, realized the importance of reflection. Once, they decided to set up a small shop in Mangrol - their home town. They started discussing about how they could start and what things they could sell. The subject dragged on throughout the whole night. When the cock heralded the break of dawn the two of them paused and looked at each other in surprise. A single thought crossed both their minds. Mayaram suggested they shelve the idea of starting a shop. Govindram agreed instantly. The reason was simple. Both inferred, at the end of their uncompleted marathon discussion, that if the initial planning stage took them the entire night then they wouldn't have any time to spare for prayers and worship once the shop was booming! Both brothers made no compromises in sacrificing their prospective material gains.

Gunatitanand Swami says, "We should always think about why we have come (into this Satsang) and what we are doing." Only through daily reflection do we get a clear picture of our purpose and actions.

The quiet hour adopted by top managers, the moon

watching party (for appreciating), the pauses we have in music, the retreat of Thoreau (for truth), the search for the self by Schopenhauer, the moment of final decision for Mulji and Krishnaji and the two brothers who decided to refrain from starting a business - all these illustrate the importance of pause or daily reflection in our lives.

38 CONQUER HASTE!

Sadhu Vivekjivandas

A disciple was having tea with his Zen master when the postman delivered a letter from the master's family in Korea. Knowing that the master had been eagerly anticipating the letter, the disciple paused in his conversation to allow his master to read the letter. Imagine his surprise when the master put aside the letter and carried on with the conversation.

The following day the disciple praised the self-control of the master, saying that he would have read the letter at once.

"I did what I would have done had I been alone," the master said. "I put the letter aside until I had conquered haste. Then, when I set my hand to the letter, I opened it as though it were something precious." This allowed him to open the envelope slowly and carefully.

The disciple enquired what such patience led to.

"Those who are patient in small things in life and control themselves will one day have the same mastery in great and important things," replied the master.

Like so many things we may not have pondered about the significance of patience or how haste spoils the things we do. You'll probably be surprised when you sit down to jot what damage you do to yourself and others by being hasty.

A commuter was boarding a departing train during the heavy morning rush hours in Mumbai. He managed to land his feet in the packed compartment but a little movement from inside threw him off balance. He slipped and his left foot got caught between the moving train and the platform. He was dragged along like a rag doll with the train. The scene was horrifying. The emergency chain was pulled. The train came to a halt. The man, still conscious, was lifted from the gap. His foot was mangled and soaking in blood. His left leg was later amputated.

A few seconds of haste cost him his leg and a lot more!

Squeezing through the closing doors of a train, alighting from a moving bus or hurriedly crossing a busy road or putting your foot on the accelerator when the light is amber (advancing to red) are some common aspects of haste. You've probably escaped without any harm till now, but what of the day when you don't! The commuter, instead of waiting for the next train that would have been empty, lost a leg, spent six months at home and ruined a brilliant career. Haste never pays! A Chinese wisdom quote says:

"One moment of patience may ward off great disaster,
One moment of impatience may ruin a whole life."

A student, poor in patience, finds it torturing to sit through the long classes each day. He hurriedly completes his daily assignments feeling satisfied with what little he has understood. In exams many start scribbling their answers at the word 'go', spending little or no time in understanding the questions. The loss is invariably great!

At work you become feverishly hasty when you fail to meet your boss's or client's deadline. And to get things done briskly you breathe down the neck of your juniors. You are easily given to verbal eruptions at the slightest flaw or further delay. Haste distorts your character. You part from your normal self, thereby losing courtesy, understanding, calmness, foresight and discrimination between right and wrong.

In any avenue of life (including satsang) we find haste makes one vulnerable to forming false opinions about others. The haste impulse is so strong that one passes judgement without knowing the 'why' and 'what' of the situation. One becomes highly sensitive! Waiting for a friend who is late; or when everyone's in the car and you're waiting for your brother; when a player fails to turn up for your team; or you have to wait for your food - these are some situations where you react bitterly. You bark out the nastiest of things.

A hasty person rushes into his work without proper preparation or planning. He simply does not know the lesson of exploring the assignment from different angles before rushing headlong into it. He thus fails to score high on the success sheet.

A person loses patience when he experiences a financial loss. He then becomes prone to doing something foolish which he regrets later. The opportunity for riches, fame and status drastically changes the mental chemistry of a man. To see that he gets it first he does the vilest and silliest of things. The affinity for worldly things distorts his outlook and actions.

In times of insult and praise you lose your composure and get agitated. Insult prods you to react explosively and praise makes room for arrogance. Either way one incurs damage to oneself.

Bhagwan Swaminarayan emphasizes in the Shikshapatri that one should not take hasty decisions on mundane matters, and neither should one, out of moral lapses, hastily punish oneself or another by cutting a hand or any part of the body.

To foster patience you need to ponder on the monuments of patience around you. The apple tree or mango tree in your garden did not flourish and bear fruit within a day of planting. Your grown up child is a testament to your patient nurturing and care. Greatness, too, does not come instantly.

An aspirant went to a guru for *moksha*. He prostrated before the master and asked him how long it would take him to realize God. The guru looked at the aspirant and murmured, "Ten years!"

The aspirant breathed with impatience, "Ten years!"

The guru then calmly murmured, "It'll take twenty years!"

The aspirant was irritated. "But you just said ten a minute ago!" He was losing his patience.

The guru was quick to observe this and replied, "It will take thirty years!"

The aspirant fumed and left.

The more the haste the more the time required to impart and assimilate.

Once, someone asked Pramukh Swami Maharaj that in this age of 'instantness' he should bestow him with instant happiness. Swamiji replied back brilliantly, saying, "People who have invented or discovered 'instant' objects have put in years of patient intelligence and labour. For God's happiness one must patiently engage in spiritual efforts."

Patience and effort go towards making a man great; towards making him divine. Bhagwan Swaminarayan says, "One cannot, out of haste, cultivate equanimity towards the good and bad or glamorous and ugly objects of the world. Only through patient effort can this ideal be attained. It is like a rope that gradually grooves the stone of a well while drawing water. And that is why one should not become hasty and indignant while persevering to attain equanimity for one's *moksha*."

39 LIVING IN THE PRESENT

Sadhu Vivekjivandas

On a Monday, during a lecture at a college in Wyoming, Arizona, a physics professor, with a hundred students before him, suddenly burst out, "I have only one student present in this lecture of mine!" The sudden outburst caught the fullest attention of all the students.

"Why Sir, we are a hundred!" exclaimed an intrepid backbencher.

The professor explained, "Out of the entire class only Peter has been paying attention to what I've been saying. The rest of you have been mentally wandering in and out of this lecture hall."

We are all given to walking out (mentally) during conversations and satsang assemblies. Probably, in the last fifteen minutes you've stretched to places far and wide and to things way out of your reach. To make your mind stable doing one thing at a time is quite tough. Real tough! For students, mental wandering distracts concentration and dilutes academic performance.

Joe Hyams was learning Hapkido from Master Han. Once, he sandwiched his practice session between business appointments. His performance at the dojo (practice hall) that day was absolutely poor. In spite of him knowing the Hapkido motions, he performed poorly. Simply because he kept on glancing at the clock after each motion.

"Your mind is elsewhere," said Master Han.

Joe admitted that he was thinking about his next appointment. The master bowed to Joe, signalling the end of the lesson. On his way out Joe found Han waiting at the doorway.

"You must learn to live in the present," preached Han. "Not in the future or the past. Zen teaches that life must be seized at the moment. By living in the present you are fully aware of yourself and your environment. Your energy is not dissipated and is always available. By thinking about things other than what you are engaged in distracts you from the present."

The majority of us fall in the same bracket - split between the things we've done and the things we are going to do. We leave the present unattended, hence problems and miseries grow, and life eventually breaks down.

Yogiji Maharaj narrated a telling anecdote of Shekh Challi. The story describes how a rich man promised Shekh Challi (a poor man) some money if he would carry a pot of ghee for him. Shekh Challi agreed. He placed the pot on his head and followed his master. On the way Shekh Challi pondered as to what he would do with his wages. "I shall buy a goat with the money. Then, I'll start a small milk business. And with the profits I'll purchase a cow. With the money I get from the milk, I'll buy more cows. In no time I'll have a booming dairy business. Then, I'll have enough money to afford a nice home, get married and have kids. And when I will be relaxing at home my son will come to call me for dinner. But I shall refuse."

At this point Shekh Challi shook his head in refusal with the result that the pot of ghee fell to the ground and broke, spilling the ghee on the ground. The master fumed with anger, "You've spilt my ghee you simpleton!"

"But... you've only lost a pot of ghee and... I've lost a home, a wife and kids," replied Shekh Challi.

We all pay the penalty, like Shekh Challi, of leaping into the future at the cost of the present. The habit of being fully conscious of the present adds tremendously to the efficiency and quality of the work we do. But, as soon as we temporarily divorce ourselves from our present action we get entangled in a web of thoughts.

Shouldn't we anchor ourselves firmly to what we are doing! Concentration is a principal factor in boosting efficiency and quality of work. A tightrope walker performs his act with single-minded concentration. He never allows his mind to be swayed by the cheering crowds or with thoughts of his wife and kids.

Jack Dempsey was an aggressive and determined American boxer. He said, "I have had my lips smashed, my eyes cut, my ribs cracked but I never felt any of these blows. I kept on saying, 'Nobody is going to stop me, nobody can really hurt me.' " In his most challenging fight he knocked his opponent flat in four minutes and earned $100,000. When he fought he said he never heard the roars of the crowd.

Immunizing yourself from deflections and concentrating entirely on the present is what goes to making a champion.

The epic Mahabharat describes the 'Swayamvar' (competition for the hand in marriage) of Draupadi - the daughter of King Drupad. Kings and princes from all lands travelled to Kampilyanagar, the capital of King Drupad's kingdom. The contest for the hand of Draupadi required the participants to stand on a pair of scales, with one foot on each pan, and pierce the eye of a fish, revolving on a pole above, by looking at it from its reflection in the pool of water below. Many kings and princes failed the balancing act on the scales and fell in the pool of water. And those who succeeded in standing still failed to hit the target. Arjun, however, stepped confidently onto the scales and with singular concentration pierced the eye of the fish and won the hand of Draupadi.

To those aspiring for success and efficiency the lesson of Arjun's concentration provides immense inspiration. While he mentally blanked out the entire courtyard and all stray thoughts the kings were probably split by pride or passion for Draupadi, or by thoughts of riches and fame. A man can never think soberly when intoxicated with pride, passions, thoughts of fame, riches, hastiness, etc.

Our daily performances in the academic sphere, business or satsang world are foiled by such elements. The lesser we have of these the more our mind does not stray from the object of action. The process of eradicating these hurdles altogether requires spiritual efforts – prayers, disciplining of body and *sant samagam*. Temporarily, however, the prescription of arousing an interest in what we do will help us avoid distractions. Once we make whatever we do into an interest we'll find that intelligence, effort, disciplining of body and mind come easy to us. The frequency of slipping in and out will decrease. This will help us to live in the present.

40 A LEAP TO EXCELLENCE

Sadhu Vivekjivandas

Sometimes we persist with things we have no talent for. Having plunged into it headlong we think we'll finally become a superstar! And when we don't, the situation becomes sore and discomforting. Many of us have gone through this before we find a field that finally suits us and allows us our talent to show. Till then the ride is rough, bumpy and unpleasant. For personal growth and utility value, you must find where your capabilities lie and what your limitations are.

Once the martial artist, Bruce Lee, was having breakfast with one of his students. The student, in his mid-forties, was down-hearted after an unsatisfying practice performance. He felt he was too old and his body too stiff to achieve any real ability in jeet-kune-do.

"You will never learn anything new unless you are ready to accept yourself with your limitations," Bruce answered. "You must accept the fact that you are capable in some directions and limited in others, and you must develop your capabilities."

The student argued that ten years before he could easily kick over his head.

Bruce smiled, "That was ten years ago," he said gently. "You are older today and your body has changed. Everyone has physical limitations to overcome."

The student replied that he (Bruce) was born with the natural ability of a martial artist.

Bruce laughed. "I am going to tell you something very few people know. I became a martial artist in spite of my limitations.

My right leg is almost an inch shorter than my left. That fact dictated the best stance for me - my left foot leading. Then I found that because the right leg was shorter, I had an advantage with certain kicks.

"And I wear contact lenses. Since childhood I have been nearsighted, which meant that when I wasn't wearing glasses, I had difficulty seeing an opponent when he wasn't up close. I initially studied 'wing-chun' because it is an ideal technique for close-in fighting.

"I accepted my limitations and made the best of what I had. And that's what you must learn to do. Perfect your kicks at waist level and they will be so formidable you'll never need to kick higher.

"Instead of trying to do everything well, do those things, which you are capable of. What you lack in flexibility and agility (through age) you must make up with knowledge and constant practice."

First, draw a line between the things you can and cannot do. Then focus your efforts on developing the things you are capable of doing. As you grow in skill and talent your limitations will shrink.

If you are a college student and you have a bad memory, don't despair. Accept the fact and put more effort into it.

Edison had a very poor memory - especially in his youth. At school he forgot everything he was taught, and he was always at the bottom of his class. He drove his teachers to despair. They declared he was retarded. He attended school for only three months, after that his mother taught him at home. Later in life Edison developed a remarkable memory for scientific data.

A little effort and proper guidance can draw you away from the frustration of your inabilities or oddities. We all have some talent in one thing or another. Finding it and developing it will definitely help to build a positive image of yourself.

Socrates was ugly yet his wisdom more than compensated for his poor looks.

Charles Steinmetz was born with a crooked leg and arched backbone that gave him a grotesque hump. During his childhood, children shunned him because of his clumsy body and inability to participate successfully in many activities. Using the greatest asset blessed upon him, Charles ignored his physical disabilities about which he realized he could do nothing and worked to excel his mind. At the age of five he could conjugate Latin verbs. At seven he learned Greek and a little Hebrew. At eight he had a good understanding of algebra and geometry. When he went to college, he excelled at studies. He graduated with honours. He had saved money so he could rent a dress suit for the convocation. But the college authorities posted a notice on the bulletin board excusing Charles from the ceremony.

Later, he went to America. Several companies denied him a job because of his awkward appearance. Eventually, General Electric employed him as a draughtsman for $12 a week. There, in addition to his regular duties, he spent long hours in electrical research. After some time the chairman of the board of General Electric Company recognized his rare genius. He said, "Here is our entire plant. Do anything you want with it. Dream all day, if you wish. We'll pay you for dreaming."

Charles worked long hours. During his lifetime he patented more than 200 electrical inventions and wrote many books and papers on problems of electrical theory and engineering.

Developing one's mind overshadows one's physical frailties. The lustre of knowledge leaves a dazzling impression upon those who come to hear you.

Stephen Hawking is one of the world's greatest theoretical physicists. He is the Lucasian professor of mathematics at Cambridge, a seat once occupied by Sir Isaac Newton. Since his early 20s, he has suffered from Amyotrophic Lateral Sclerosis (ALS), a progressive deterioration of the central nervous system that usually causes death within three to four years. Hawking's illness has advanced more slowly, and now seems almost to have stabilized. Still, it has robbed him of virtually all movement. He has no control over most of his muscles, cannot dress or eat by himself and needs round-the-clock nursing care. In 1985 Hawking nearly suffocated during a bout of pneumonia. He was given a tracheotomy that enabled him to breathe. The operation saved his life but silenced his voice. Now he 'speaks' only by using the slight voluntary movement left in his hands and fingers to operate his wheelchair's built-in-computer and voice synthesizer.

While ALS has made Hawking a virtual prisoner in his own body, his intellect roams freely from the infinitesimal to the infinite, from the subatomic realm to the far reaches of the universe. In the course of these mental expeditions, Hawking has conceived startling new theories about black holes and the tumultuous events that immediately followed the Big Bang from which scientists believe the universe came into being. Through his prodigious intelligence he has won the admiration and respect of students, professors and residents of Cambridge.

He says, "One of my friends bet a bag of sweets that I would never come to anything."

Kip Thorne, a Caltech physicist, says, "I would rank him besides Einstein, as the best in our field."

Rocky Kolb, a physicist at Fermilab in Illinois says, "In general relativity and early cosmology, Hawking is the hero."

Developing one's better capabilities eclipses one's shortcomings. In spite of a poor or medium academic record, excelling in a sport or whatever can put you in the spotlight of public admiration. The same applies if you are poor in sports but intelligent in academic matters. By developing your advantages you soar to success and shadow your incapabilities or shortcomings.

But when one enters into the subject of spiritualism one finds an enlightened soul supercedes all. Having realized one's soul and God, one transcends all limitations and discrepancies. One's joy becomes limitless. In fact one becomes a dispenser of joy to others. King Janak initially ridiculed the ugly and clumsy Sage Ashtavakra (an enlightened soul mentioned in the Shrimad Bhagvat), but later revered him for his profound spirituality. Where the intelligent sages had failed, Ashtavakra succeeded in satisfactorily answering the king's queries.

In the time of Bhagwan Swaminarayan, a devotee called Nath Bhakta was physically frail and poor. He could barely count to ten and yet Swaminarayan stamped him as intelligent compared to the minister (*diwan*) in the court of Vadodara who brilliantly ruled three large states for his master. In Vachanamrut, Gadhada I 50 Bhagwan Swaminarayan says that intelligent are those who, in spite of having little worldly intelligence, are engaged in seeking their salvation. And those proficient in worldly matters or in scriptural learning are feebleminded if they don't endeavour for redemption.

On the surface this may seem unacceptable. But the man striving for redemption is in fact endeavouring for eternal happiness whereas the efforts of the worldly intelligent are directed towards temporary happiness. From the two different rewards - one temporary and the other eternal - one can easily deduce the more intelligent of the two.

Essentially, the martial arts concentrate on attaining enlightenment or self-realization rather than mere physical excellence. A true *sifu* (master) sees karate, kung-fu, aikido, etc. as avenues to spiritual serenity and mental tranquility.

41 SMASH THAT BAD HABIT!

Sadhu Anandswarupdas

Believe it or not! A poker game ran for 5 months!

The London *Sunday Times* newspaper, dated 5 June 1983, reported this game played in Las Vegas in 1949, between a Mr. Moss and a Greek. The game lasted 5 tense months, with breaks for rest every four to five days. Finally, the Greek lost a staggering sum of two million dollars. Despite his drastic loss he came back to gamble the very next day. The poor man could not help it. He was a compulsive gambler. The habit of gambling had become his life.

Bad habits can range from stuttering, squinting and nervous twitches to dangerous driving, smoking and drug abuse. They can tarnish us socially, overburden us with guilt and, in the more serious cases, harm us physically, and even cost us our lives.

Nature has already supplied man with knowledge and instinct far greater than any beast in the forest or water. In spite of these endowments, why does man fail to attain his goals? The answer is simple: his habits set him adrift. Therefore, in truth, the only dividing line between those who fail and succeed lies in the difference of their habits. So, the first law of success, which precedes all others is to form good habits and stick to them. But can this difficult feat be accomplished? Yes!

Positive Thoughts

Make it a point to think positively, and you will gradually build your future on positive habits. You must substitute a positive thought for every negative thought you hold in your mind. Inspect these thoughts you have built in your consciousness, and if they reflect fear, worry, hate and failure, replace them with carefully chosen opposite thoughts of a positive nature. If you feel poor, you must think of wealth to come. If you feel incompetent, you must remember past successes.

A positive thought is to appreciate and like everything around you. We must like the sun for it warms our homes, yet we must like the rain also for it quenches our thirst. We must like the light for it shows us the way, yet we must like the darkness also for its shows us the stars. We must welcome happiness because it enlarges our hearts, yet we must endure sadness for it opens our souls. We must acknowledge rewards for they are our due, yet we must welcome obstacles for they are our challenge.

The technique to master such positive principles and make them part of us is to keep them constantly in mind and practice them religiously until they are transformed into good habits.

Good habits work for us, even when we're not at our best. Unlike conscious actions, they don't depend on how we feel or how busy we are. Habits are always more reliable than memory.

During an entire period of 20 years at his post, a lighthouse keeper had been accustomed to a gun going off and making a loud bang every hour, day and night. This was the procedure used for warning ships.

One night, due to a minor fault, the gun failed to trigger off and make a bang. The old keeper had been fast asleep and when the gun failed to go off, he jumped in bed, "What was that?" he roared with alarm.

Exceptions

Another essential factor is: Never allow an exception to occur till the new habit is securely rooted deeply in your life. Each lapse is like letting a carefully wound up ball of string to the ground. A single slip undoes more than a great many turns wound up again. So one must learn to proceed firmly before one can afford any exceptions. Exceptions weaken the habit.

To seize the first possible opportunity to act and execute every resolution is the best course. Sometimes one may think it is like the insurance a man pays on his house. The premium he pays does him no good at the time and may never bring a return. But if there is a fire, his having paid the money will be his saviour. Therefore, one who has daily insured himself to a habit of fociussed attention, energetic willingness and self-denial is one who will stand like a rock when everything shakes around him.

By constantly repeating an act at every possible opportunity, we reinforce and invigorate the habit.

A young man was very eager to learn Sanskrit. But due to poor memory he could not force himself to learn the strange new words. He went to his guru who gave him a gourd full of sesame seeds. He was told to say a word and take one seed out of the gourd. He was to continue in this manner until the gourd was empty before he started on a new word.

The young man came home and did as prescribed. It was a tedious procedure but he persisted. A few years later, he became a renowned scholar. Repetition made him into a scholar.

The key to every door of success is good habits. It remains for us to enquire, not tomorrow, nor today but right now about the type of habits we have. Discard all bad ones.

Think positively and act immediately.

42 YOGIJI MAHARAJ'S SPIRIT OF SERVICE

Ram Murthy

Introduction

Yogiji Maharaj was an embodiment of service. No matter how trifling it may appear to the world, it was the heart-throb of life for him. It ranged from washing the clothes of sadhus to preparing food for devotees at all sorts of odd hours. Nothing would put him off. He considered it an honour and a privilege to serve others.

Essence of Greatness

Once, Yogiji Maharaj was travelling by train to Bochasan. At every station devotees flocked to his compartment to greet him and receive his blessings. A young man who was travelling in a first class compartment was curious to know the qualities which made him such a respected figure. He came to Yogiji Maharaj and offered his respects. Yogiji Maharaj asked him, "Who are you?"

The youth replied, "I am a resident of Palanpur and native to Kolkata where we have a tea business. I am going to London for higher studies." After introducing himself, the young man said, "Everybody is attracted towards you. What makes you such a charismatic personality?"

The youth thought Swamiji would rattle off a list of qualities of head and heart which made him so popular. Imagine his surprise when Yogiji Maharaj replied, "I acquired this quality by scrubbing utensils and through the grace of my guru Shastriji Maharaj."

It is but proper to credit one's greatness to the grace of one's guru. But what has cleaning of utensils got to do with acquisition of greatness? It will come as a surprise to those who are not familiar with Yogiji Maharaj's life. Cleaning utensils may appear to be an ordinary thing for others, but it had great meaning for his philosophy of life. The simple action (of cleaning utensils) typified *seva* dharma or service which is essential for spiritual elevation.

Role Models of Service

Yogiji Maharaj constantly kept in view the lives of Shriji Maharaj, Gunatitanand Swami, Bhagatji Maharaj, Shastriji Maharaj and other senior sadhus and devotees as examples of service whose model had to be followed. He would say, "Parvatbhai agreed to become a servant of Dada Khachar. Rajabhai ploughed Parvatbhai's fields. Muktanand Swami drove the plough of Mulubha. Gunatitanand Swami was passing through the district of Bhal with a group of 30 sadhus. It started raining and the sadhus' footwear became wet and covered in mud. Gunatitanand Swami collected them and wrapped them into two bundles. He placed the luggage, weighing 40 kg, on his head and walked 7½ miles. Shastriji Maharaj walked 90 miles to get *mesub* (a kind of sweet) for Bhagatji Maharaj. He trekked from Dholera to Navda in pouring rain in chest-deep water and reached Gadhada. If he had written a letter would not a sweetmeat dealer have delivered the sweet? But he said, 'I have to get it so that he (the guru) can eat it.' This is total dedication. If we understand that our guru has walked 90 miles then would we feel any discomfort in walking?

"Shriji Maharaj used to wash the *kaupins* of sadhus. Muktanand Swami would render service and used to visit the neighbouring places of Loj to beg for alms. Maharaj would make chapattis for sadhus.

"Once the Mahant of Tarnetar Mandir came to Junagadh for Gunatitanand Swami's darshan. Swami was engaged in sweeping the mandir courtyard. The Mahant, not knowing that he was talking to Gunatitanand Swami, asked him where he could find the Mahant. 'Go to the assembly hall. He will come there,' said Gunatitanand Swami. Imagine the surprise of the Tarnetar Mahant when Gunatitanand Swami washed his hands and feet and came to receive the visitor.

"The Mahant of Tarnetar asked, 'Were you not the one who was sweeping the courtyard just now?'

" 'Yes, in our scheme of things he who serves is great.' "

A Night Call

It was late at night. In Sarangpur Mandir, all the sadhus and devotees were fast asleep. Suddenly Shastriji Maharaj, who was sleeping on a cot, woke up. He found a group of about 75 devotees before him.

"Welcome," said Shastriji Maharaj, sitting up on the bed. "Where have you come from?"

"Our bus which was bound for Kariyani broke down. We would like to spend the night here."

"Good. Make yourselves at home. This is your mandir. Have you eaten?"

"No, but why give you trouble at this odd hour?"

Shastriji Maharaj smiled, "What trouble do we sadhus have? This is a service which we would perform gladly." Then Shastriji Maharaj thought, "Who will be prepared to cook food for 75 devotees at this hour. Most of the sadhus have retired after a tiring day's work." Then he suddenly remembered Yogiji Maharaj. A beaming Shastriji Maharaj searched for Yogiji Maharaj's sleeping place. When he approached, Bhagvatswarupdas was awakened by a faint noise and asked, "Who's that?"

"I am looking for Yogi Swami to prepare food for some

newly arrived devotees."

Bhagvatswarupdas recognized Shastriji Maharaj's voice and said, "Merciful guru, he was telling beads till 1.00 a.m. and slept thereafter. He gets up at 3.00 a.m. and does not sleep during the day. It is good if he is allowed to sleep undisturbed for some time."

"But Bhagvatswarup Swami, barring Yogi who will do what I say now?" There was a tinge of softness in his tone. He said, "Only Yogi will save my face. Let me wake him."

"What if the devotees are fed in the morning?" Bhagvatswarupdas suggested.

Yogiji Maharaj was a light sleeper. When so much talk was going on it was not possible for him to still lie sleeping. He got up and stood before Shastriji Maharaj with folded hands. The guru was overjoyed when he saw his disciple and said, "Yogi. Come. You have to cook food."

"I am ready, Swami..." And Yogiji Maharaj happily got up for another round of service. He prepared food and served the devotees. When he finished at 3.00 a.m. his joy was unabated.

Joy in Service

Younger people were the special charge of Yogiji Maharaj. He would mix with them freely and do things in such a manner that they would be inspired to follow his example. Once he was visiting East Africa. He went inside the bathroom at the mandir in Dar-es-Salaam. On seeing a pile of clothes belonging to some youths he locked the bathroom and happily started washing them. It was only when he came out that everyone realized that Swami had washed the youths' clothes.

In a matter-of-fact manner he recounted his experiences in the field of *seva* to a night assembly on 3 June 1959. He told the young men among the audience, "I have served 40 *sadgurus*. When I was serving at Sarangpur Mandir devotees would come from Navagam, Mojidad, etc. They had to leave early in the morning so I had to prepare food packets for them. I would get up at 2.30 a.m., prepare 100 to 150 *rotla*. Normally provisions from the store were issued in the morning. But I would collect *gor* and pickles the previous day so that I would not have to wake up the storekeeper early. By 4.00 a.m. I would prepare packets of 10 or 15 *rotla* with *gor* and tie them in cloth. Today if you ask me I can prepare food for 50 people, serve them all and still would not get tired one bit." When he gave this talk Yogiji Maharaj was around 70 years old.

On another occasion he said, "How can one get such a beneficial opportunity of serving food! I have been serving food for 40 years. I have never eaten first. I ate *dal* or whatever that was left after serving others. And then would have my meal at night. You will be immensely blessed if you serve food."

Glory of Service

Once, Yogiji Maharaj went with some sadhus and devotees to bathe at Narayan Ghat in Ahmedabad. At that time Kothari Babubhai was changing his dhoti after bathing. Yogiji Maharaj got hold of the wet dhoti lying down and said, "Let me wash your clothes." Babubhai was taken aback by the offer. He took hold of his dhoti and interjected, "How can you wash it!" But no service was too small for Yogiji Maharaj. When something had to be done he would put his shoulder to the wheel. Yogiji Maharaj humbly replied, "How can I have the privilege of serving a blessed *mahamukta* like you who has served Shastriji Maharaj?"

In the Service of Devotees

The 85th birth anniversary of Shastriji Maharaj was being celebrated at Atladra. A lot of people had come from different places and finding a place to sleep was a problem. At 11.00 p.m.

C.T. Patel, who had come from Mombasa, was looking for a spot to sleep. The clock struck 12 midnight and he still had not found a space to lie down. He then reached the kitchen where he found Yogiji Maharaj sitting and telling beads. As he went up to him Yogiji Maharaj asked, "Have you not slept?"

"It is all right, but why are you awake? You look tired and yet why are you staying up late?"

Yogiji Maharaj smiled and said, "You see we are celebrating a festival. And devotees may come late at night, so one has to serve them." Saying this he got up and found a place for C.T. Patel to sleep.

Happy to Serve

On another occasion Yogiji Maharaj went to Ramod at the invitation of the devotees. As it was a special occasion because of Yogiji Maharaj's presence, the devotees decided to include laddus in the menu. Matam Swami started the cooking. Yogiji Maharaj was delivering a discourse.

A lot of smoke was produced in the kitchen because of wet firewood. To make matters worse there was no proper ventilation. Matam Swami could not stand the smoke which began to irritate his eyes. He left the kitchen, went upstairs, wrapped himself in a blanket and went to sleep. After completing his discourse Yogiji Maharaj went into the kitchen to see how things were. He was surprised not to see Matam Swami, who was supposed to have finished the cooking. Yogiji Maharaj went up and found Matam Swami sleeping. He woke him up and asked him as to why he was sleeping instead of cooking.

"I will not cook! The smoke is too much for me," he replied. Then Yogiji Maharaj asked with affection, "What about Thakorji's *thal*? We have to offer him food on time."

Matam Swami replied in an angry tone, "If you want to offer *thal* to Thakorji then you can do the cooking. I shall not enter the kitchen." Without a word Yogiji Maharaj plunged into work after washing his hands and feet. In no time delicacies like laddus, rice and vegetables were prepared. Then a devotee of Ramod, Mohanbhai, came to the kitchen and on seeing Yogiji Maharaj preparing the food asked, "Where is Matam Swami?"

Yogiji Maharaj was choking in the smoke. His eyes had become red. But still in his usual cheerful mood he said, "After a long time I got an opportunity to prepare Thakorji's *thal*. I am grateful to Matam Swami who has offered me an opportunity to serve."

It is no wonder after reading all this that the picture of Yogiji Maharaj that comes before one's mind is that of dedicated service, service to please Shriji Maharaj, his guru Shastriji Maharaj and the devotees.

43 POSITIVE ATTITUDE

Sadhu Vivekjivandas

The life of Yogiji Maharaj reveals his transparent and profound divinity. He was the highest wisdom and ultimate experience in the most tangile and perceptible form. His personal sacrifices, unflagging spirit to serve, fathomless love for God and his radiant, inexhaustible joy was unique. He lived for others. His eventful life of sacrifice was charged with a positive attitude, and even in the most unfavourable and conflicting of situations he remained positive, undisturbed and happy.

Respecting Shriji Maharaj

Once, Yogiji Maharaj was in Atladra. Thakorji's *murti* was placed in a silver-plated *hindolo* (a small swing). The *hindolo* had figures that played the cymbals and drums when it was rocked. But when Yogiji Maharaj gently rocked the *hindolo* the figures did not move and play the musical instruments. On seeing this, he said, in a spirit of glory, "They (the figures) are respecting Maharaj."

The fact was Yogiji Maharaj ignored that the figures did not move due to some technical fault and chose to see it as a sign of respect and reverence for God.

Our Service!

In July 1956, Yogiji Maharaj was travelling by train from Surat to Mumbai. As there was a sudden downpour the train stopped at Palghar and could not proceed further. Thousands of passengers from six trains were stranded. There was no way the trains could reverse. And there were no arrangements for food or water at Palghar station either. Everyone was upset and mad with rage. Yogiji Maharaj, however, enthusiastically began chanting the bhajan, *"Sãmbhal beni Hari rijhyãni ritdi..."* The clapping of his hands and the radiant, divine expression on his face took the tension out of the situation. Then Mota Swami narrated some incidents from Shastriji Maharaj's life.

During this time, Zinabhai (of Donja) and Sheth Bhogibhai, who lived in Palghar, came for Swamishri's darshan. They were so impressed by his serenity that they requested him to have lunch and stay at their place. Swami and the sadhus stayed for two days. Both Zinabhai and Sheth Bhogibhai asked Yogiji Maharaj to initiate them into Satsang.

On returning back to the station, some school children were amused on seeing the saffron-clad sadhus. They began teasing the sadhus. Hakabhai Khachar scolded the boys.

"What happened Hakabhai?" Swami asked.

"Oh, these monkeys (referring to the boys) were laughing at you."

"At least they were not crying," Yogiji Maharaj added.

"They should not cry. If they were amused on seeing a sadhu, then we have been of service to them."

"They Never Bite!"

Yogiji Maharaj was in Vaghodiya village near Vadodara. After finishing his morning routine, Yogiji Maharaj entered his room. He saw that Dhirendrabhai Vinchhi, a youth travelling with him, was picking something from his bed and putting it in a cup. Swami went near him and, genially placing his hand on Dhirendrabhai's shoulder, said, "Today I slept very well."

"But how could you have slept soundly! While making your bed I found many bugs," Dhirendrabhai exclaimed with surprise. He showed the 20-25 bugs he had deposited in the cup and added, "I found these many now and I wonder how many more must have bitten you in the night!"

"Guru, don't say that," Swami replied.

"But Swami these bugs bite!"

"Now there you go again! These bugs are *satsangis* (devotees). They never bite!" said Yogiji Maharaj.

"But Swami, how can they be *satsangis*?" Dhirendrabhai argued.

"Now, if you say it again then you will have to fast for the day."

And so Yogiji Maharaj cut short the conversation and defused any opportunity of fault-finding even in a trifling thing like a bed bug.

"One Way. Road Closed!"

On 31 March 1960, Yogiji Maharaj and a few sadhus were travelling in Zambia. One evening, they left from Lusaka for Broken Hill. Rajnibhai was driving the car. After a while they came across a diversion sign. The original road was blocked with barrels. Rajnibhai stopped the car, got down, removed the barrels and drove on.

"Guru, why did you get down?" Yogiji Maharaj enquired.

"Bapa, sometimes these workers block the road with barrels even after repairing it. So I got down to remove them."

"I don't think so! They must have kept them because the road is really closed. Take our car along the diversion road," Yogiji Maharaj suggested.

"Bapa, don't worry, nothing will happen. We will go along this main road," Rajnibhai spoke with confidence.

Yogiji Maharaj did not insist again.

After travelling a mile, the road ahead was broken. There was no way of going ahead. Since the road was very narrow and above ground level, there was no way to turn the car or take it down the road. There was only one alternative and that was to go back in reverse gear.

Swamishri then asked, "Now what has happened?"

A crestfallen Rajnibhai spoke, "Bapa, there is no way we can drive the car ahead and neither can we turn it around."

Yogiji Maharaj joyfully raised his hand and single finger and said, "One way! Road closed! Likewise the road to Akshardham is one way. One should not look at or find faults in others; always see the virtuous side of others. One who finds faults, then his road is closed. Take the road of appreciating the good qualities in others."

A Miracle

Yogiji Maharaj was in the village of Maliya Hatina in Gujarat.

To have darshan of the mango grove where Bhagatji Maharaj had watered the 300 mango trees, Swamishri, Mota Swami and Harmanbhai got into a horse-drawn carriage. While they were going along, the wheel of the carriage suddenly broke. The carriage careened and reeled over. Everyone inside bumped into each other. Bruised and hurt, the three managed to come out of the carriage. Yogiji Maharaj, dusting the dirt off his clothes, happily stated, "A miracle has happened, isn't that so Harmanbhai?"

Mota Swami was censuring the driver but on hearing Yogiji Maharaj he exclaimed, "Oh! what miracle?"

Yogiji Maharaj replied, "We were saved!" Hearing these words, everyone started laughing.

Defusing the most painful and irritating of circumstances was a hallmark of Yogiji Maharaj. He was always positive about whatever happened and coming out alive from the accident, although hurt, was a matter of joy for him.

Two Years in One Standard

Someone told Yogiji Maharaj about a devotee who had fallen

back from Satsang. The reason was that he felt the Satsang was no longer the same as it used to be when Shastriji Maharaj was alive.

To this Yogiji Maharaj replied, "We are not doing anything wrong. We are preaching the truth that God is present in a holy Sadhu. If someone does not believe this, then it is his wish!"

A devotee then added, "Bapa, Tribhovan Gopal (a disciple of Shastriji Maharaj) had also fallen back from Satsang."

Yogiji Maharaj checked him immediately, "Guru, you should not say that. He did not fall back (or fail) but he spent two years in one standard. Then he passed and qualified. And he believed that Shastriji Maharaj was Shastriji Maharaj! He became staunch again. We too should not lapse and fall back..."

Swami's sheer positive attitude, seeing only the good in others, simply amazed and inspired the devotees.

True Character

On 23 June 1957, Yogiji Maharaj was at Keriya. He was residing at the old mandir and was preparing lunch. Two sadhus from an old Swaminarayan sect arrived and demanded that everyone leave the mandir because they wished to stay there. The devotees were enraged. "You can stay upstairs and these sadhus will stay here below," the devotees roared. Yogiji Maharaj calmed the devotees and stopped them from saying anything further.

After lunch, Yogiji Maharaj, Sant Swami, Sanatan Swami and Vinu Bhagat left by bullock cart for Sarangpur. When the cart reached Ningala, Yogiji Maharaj got down to take a break. He saw the two sadhus, who had insulted him in Keriya, standing by the station. Yogiji Maharaj greeted them, saying, "Jai Swaminarayan," but the two sadhus twisted their face in contempt and turned away. In spite of this Swami told Vinu Bhagat, "Go and say, Jai Swaminarayan, to them and bow at their feet." Though Vinu

Bhagat did not wish to go, he went at the instruction of Yogiji Maharaj. The sadhus paid no attention at all.

Yogiji Maharaj then proceeded towards Sarangpur. The road was rough, the wind was strong and turbulent and there was a steady drizzle. The bullock cart was open to the sky and despite the discomfort, Yogiji Maharaj did not utter a single word of complaint. They reached Sarangpur at 2.30 a.m. The next day was Ekadashi (fast) and Yogiji Maharaj got up as usual, attended the *mangala arti* and performed his puja. Then he added, "Because they (the sadhus) told us to leave we got the chance of having the darshan of *mangala arti* in Sarangpur; otherwise how could it have been possible? Because we tolerated them we got this great benefit!"

The acme of Yogiji Maharaj's divinity was that he saw the good side of even those who opposed him.

HEALTH

44 WHY VEGETARIANISM? I

Sadhu Mukundcharandas

Vegetarianism has been a topic of widespread discussion among doctors, health specialists and hygiene societies. In the past several years, mounting evidence has clearly shown that man is essentially a vegetarian. It is assumed that meat eaters are stronger and healthier compared to vegetarians. Researchers have found that this is not so. Let us see how.

After tobacco and alcohol, the consumption of meat is probably the greatest single cause of death in the Western world, especially the United States. World health statistics have consistently shown that countries consuming the most meat have the highest rate of diseases (heart, cancer, etc.).

What the Records Say

During the Second World War meat became scarce in Denmark due to a food shortage caused by the British blockade. The Danish government introduced food rationing and its people were forced to live on fruits, vegetables, grains and dairy products. In the first year of rationing the death rate fell by 1.7%. When the Norwegians adopted a vegetarian diet due to the same blockade, there was a similar drop in death rate from circulatory diseases. However, after the war, when both countries were able to resume their meat diet, their death rate due to heart disease reverted to pre-war levels.

The *Journal of the American Medical Association* had commented in 1961, "A vegetarian diet can prevent 90-97% of our coronary occlusions." Blocking of blood vessels in the heart occurs when layers of cholesterol and other fats are gradually deposited in the walls of arteries, causing the diameter to get smaller and smaller thus allowing less and less blood to flow through. This places a great burden on the heart which has to pump harder and harder to send blood through the clogged vessels. This results in occurrence of high blood pressure, strokes and heart attacks. Scientists at Harvard found that the average blood pressure of vegetarians was lower than that of a comparable group of non-vegetarians.

During the Korean War, 200 bodies of young American soldiers with an average age of 22 years, were examined after death. Almost 80% had hardened arteries, clogged with cholesterol from eating meat. Korean soldiers of the same age group were found to be free of this damage as they were basically vegetarians.

Experiments on mice have shown that a high-protein diet throughout their life shortens life expectancy. Rapid growth and a shorter life go together.

Meat is a high protein food and when used in large quantities appears to be non-conducive to long life. Dr William Collins, a scientist at the New York Maimonedes Medical Center found that meat-eating animals have an "almost unlimited capacity to handle saturated fats and cholesterol." But when half a pound of animal fat was added daily over a long period of time to a rabbit's diet, after only two months its blood vessels became clogged with fat and atherosclerosis developed. And man has a digestive tract similar to the rabbit's.

Process of Meat Production

Animals reared for the slaughterhouse are fattened with chemicals such as nitrates, hormones and antibiotics in huge amounts. These chemicals are absorbed by those who eat their meat. Incidentally, when animals are killed, their bodies undergo *rigor mortis* – a rock-like hardening of the whole body. It takes about two weeks to soften the meat. Meat, which is several days old, turns a grey-green colour. In order to mask this discolouration, the meat industry also adds nitrites and other preservatives. These make the meat appear red. Nitrites combine with other nitrogen containing compounds found in innumerable foods in the natural state to produce carcinogenic agents called nitrosamines. These are known to cause cancer in the bladder as well. (ref. *Pathologic Basis of Disease* by S.L. Robbins, MD, and R.S. Contran, MD). The United States Government is now limiting the amount of nitrites used in animal products.

Just as our bodies become ill during periods of intense rage, anxiety, fear, etc., the biochemistry of animals which are going to be slaughtered, undergoes profound changes. The levels of hormones, especially adrenaline, change radically. They remain in the meat and later poison human tissue. Just consider the statement made by the Nutrition Institute of America, "The flesh of an animal carcass is loaded with toxic blood and other waste by-products." A cancer researcher at the Oak Ridge National Laboratory in Tennessee, USA, Dr William Lijinsky, even went as far as to say, "I don't even feed nitrate-laden foods to my cat!"

Diseases Due to a Meat Diet

Meat has been linked with processes which have a potential for causing cancer. It was found that in one kilogramme of charcoal-broiled steak, there was as much benzopyrene (a carcinogen) as in the smoke from 600 cigarettes. When mice were fed benzopyrene they developed stomach tumours and leukaemia.

Other studies showed that Americans consuming a mixed Western diet (high in meat) had four to five times more production of bile acids than did Seventh Day Adventist vegetarians and other American, Japanese and Chinese vegetarians.

And it has been shown that certain bile acids enhance colon tumour formation.

Colon cancer is the second leading cause of cancer deaths in the United States and occurs 8 to 15 times more frequently than in countries where the population live on a largely unrefined (unprocessed) diet with greater fibre content. People in countries where there is a high colon cancer rate tend to produce more bile acids than those living in countries where colon cancers are rare. Legumes, oats and pectin consist of fibres which help lower serum cholesterol thus reducing the potential for coronary heart disease. Dr U.D. Register, Chairman of the Dept. of Nutrition at Loma Linda University in California, performed experiments in which a diet rich in beans and peas actually reduced cholesterol, even while the subjects were eating large amounts of butter.

Visual inspection of meat is of no value and microscopic examinations are rarely made. If and when cancer is found it is just removed and the remainder of the animal is sold for food. Salmonellosis is a bacterial infection derived from contaminated animal food products. In the US an estimated 2,000,000 cases occur annually costing the people $300,000,000. Except for infants, the sick and the aged, who may die, the infection is not fatal. The American Academy of Science could only say, "Reluctantly, we are forced to recognize the impossibility of eradicating salmonellosis at this time."

Trichinosis, another infection also occurs. It is due to larvae of trichinae which originate in the pig. This has been shown to be transmitted by using the same knife used to cut beef that has been used to slice pork. Hence, "From what is known about disease transmission in meat and meat products, and what is suspected but as yet unverified, renders meat a highly questionable food for use in a health-promoting diet," concludes Dr John A. Scharffenberg, Associate Professor of Applied Nutrition at Loma Linda University.

45 WHY VEGETARIANISM? II

Sadhu Mukundcharandas

One consequence of a meat diet with its high protein content is the increase in urinary excretion of valuable bone calcium. It has been established that calcium levels in the blood are maintained at the expense of bone calcium and over a long period of time, it results in diminution of bone mass and osteoporosis, thus weakening bones (Anand C.R., Linkswiler, H.M. *Journal of Nutrition* p.104. 1974).

A non-vegetarian also accumulates more nitrogenous wastes such as urea and uric acid. An American physician analysed the urine of meat-eaters and vegetarians and found that the kidneys of meat-eaters have to work three times harder than those of vegetarians, to eliminate poisonous nitrogen compounds. With age, the kidneys become inefficient and the unexcreted uric acid is deposited throughout the body. There, it is absorbed by the muscles like a sponge soaking up water and later it hardens to form crystals. When these collect in the nerves, neuritis and sciatica result; in the joints the painful conditions of arthritis and rheumatism result. People afflicted with these conditions are now advised by many doctors to stop meat altogether.

Nutritional Considerations

Some non-vegetarians argue that meat is a complete food in itself whilst one would need to spend a long time combining the right vegetables to get enough protein everyday to maintain a balanced diet.

First, meat is not a 'perfect' food and contains, at the most, about 30% protein. The net protein utilization (NPU) - the amount which is actually digested and absorbed by the body for the following foods is:

Source of Protein	NPU
Milk	82%
Cheese	70%
Meat	67%
Mung beans	67%
Whole wheat	60%

Weight for weight the above foods may have less protein than meat but because their NPU is high, by eating more or a combination of them one can easily meet one's daily recommended protein intake.

Second, protein is not the only body requirement. Elements such as calcium, magnesium, potassium, iron and vitamins like A, C and the B-complex group are also found in vegetables and fruits and, excepting iron, are almost invariably absent in flesh foods. Not surprisingly, good nutrition is difficult on a meat diet.

One important factor for efficient functioning of the intestines that is absent in meat is fibre - roughage. This results in poor elimination - a common complaint of meat-eaters. Vegetables provide the bulk and fibre which retain water and bind the waste for easy passage. The British Health Education Council is of the opinion that, "Lack of fibre seems to be connected with various other disorders of the bowel including piles and a serious inflammation called diverticulitis."

Anatomical Characteristics

Isn't it natural for humans to eat meat because we have been doing it for ages? Recent studies by researchers have concluded that our early ancestors were vegetarians who ate meat only during extreme environmental conditions such as during the Ice Age. Comparing the body structures of man, wholly meat-eaters (carnivores) and herbivores also reinforces man's natural diet.

Carnivores such as lions, dogs, cats, etc. possess a very simple, and short digestive tract. Since flesh decays very rapidly, the products of this decay quickly poison the body if they remain too long in the gut. They have stomachs which produce 10 times the amount and 20 times the concentration of hydrochloric acid than non-carnivores to facilitate digestion of tough fibrous tissue. Their saliva is acidic whilst that of herbivores and man is alkaline. Herbivores have a longer digestive system since vegetable matter takes longer to be digested and there is no question of decay products poisoning the body.

Length of Digestive tract relative to length of body	**Nature of Saliva**	**Method for liquid intake**
Carnivores: 3 times	Acidic	Lapping
Herbivores: 10 times	Alkaline	Sucking
Man: 12 times	Alkaline	Sucking

It is also interesting to note that non-flesh eaters drink water by sucking as opposed to lapping it up with their tongues, which is what all meat-eaters do. The latter also sweat through their tongues and not through sweat glands in the skin as in non-carnivores.

The type of dentition present also gives an idea about the diet of animals. All meat-eaters have to kill their food using claws and teeth. To pierce tough skin and tear flesh they are equipped with powerful jaws and long, pointed canine teeth. They do not have molars - flat back teeth which vegetarian animals have - for grinding their food. Flesh, unlike vegetable matter, does not need to be chewed, hence it is swallowed in small pieces. And no wonder their jaws have very limited side to side mobility unlike herbivores which use it for grinding.

Human physiological characteristics are very similar to herbivores. The digestive system is twelve times the length of the body. Sweating occurs through millions of pores in the skin, liquid is taken up by suction, the tooth and jaw structure is undoubtedly a sure sign of a vegetarian and the saliva is alkaline.

Even by instinct we humans are non-carnivorous. One scientist has stated, "A cat will salivate with a desire for hunger at the smell of a piece of raw flesh but not at all at the smell of fruits. If man could delight in pouncing upon a bird, tear its living limbs apart with his teeth and sucking the warm blood, one might conclude that nature provided him with the meat-eating instinct. On the other hand, a bunch of luscious grapes make his mouth water, and even in the absence of hunger, he will eat fruit because it tastes so good." Most people have other people kill their meat for them and would be sickened if they had to do the killing themselves. So we do not even possess the killing instinct let alone the eating which follows it.

Economic Facts

Meat is a gross waste of natural resources. Land which is used to produce food crops for direct human consumption feeds 14 times as many people as land used to grow food to fatten animals for slaughter. Plants yield 800,000 calories per acre for direct human use, but only 200,000 when these same plant foods are first fed to animals. The remaining 600,000 are used up by the animals themselves. 'Meat animals' are poor converters of energy for human consumption and meat thus represents the greatest food energy loss.

Energy Loss in Use of Land for Meat Production

Land Use	**Food Product**	**Calories**
1 Acre Wheat	Bread	800,000
1 Acre Grazing	Meat	200,000
Energy Loss	-	**600,000**

Energy is lost by animals in the form of respiration, excretion, reproduction, motion, etc.

Animals are also wasteful of protein itself. Of the protein that animals consume:

23% is returned as milk

15% is returned in the form of pork and

10% is returned in the form of beef.

Compared to this, soya beans, on average, produce 17 pounds of protein per acre compared to 2 pounds for milk and 1 pound for beef by cows.

Another way of examining the economics is by comparing the production of Standard Nutrition Units (SNU) per acre. A single SNU is defined as 2,500 calories per person per day.

Diet	**SNUs Produced Per Acre**
Meat & Milk	1.3
Wheat & Bread	4
Rice & Beans (Japanese style)	7

From the above table it is evident that a simple vegetarian meal can be nutritious and economical.

46 WHY VEGETARIANISM? III

Sadhu Mukundcharandas

"Truly man is the king of beasts, for his brutality exceeds them. We live by the death of others. We are burial places! I have since an early age abjured the use of meat, and the time will come when men will look upon the murder of animals as they now look upon the murder of men."

- Leonardo da Vinci

"It is in my view that the vegetarian manner of living, by its purely physical effect on the human temperament, would most beneficially influence the lot of mankind."

- Albert Einstein

"Animals are my friends... and I don't eat my friends."

"This is dreadful! Not only the suffering and death of animals, but man suppresses in himself, unnecessarily, the highest spiritual capacity - that of sympathy and pity towards living creatures like himself - and by violating his own feelings, becomes cruel."

- George Bernard Shaw

Vegetarians Have More Stamina

It is often argued that vegetarians tend to have weak and pale bodies - but this couldn't be further from the truth. Various studies have shown vegetarians to be stronger, more agile and possessing greater stamina than those who eat meat.

Endurance tests conducted by Dr J. Loteyko and V. Kipani at Brussels University revealed that vegetarians were able to perform two to three times longer than meat-eaters before complete exhaustion, and they took one fifth the time to recover from fatigue after each test than the meat-eaters.

A Swedish scientist gave nine athletes bicycle endurance tests after three-day periods on various diets. All athletes were tested after periods on each diet so that differences in endurance could be accounted for only by differences in diet (Astrand P, *Nutrition Today* 3: No. 2, 9-11, 1968).

Diet Effect on Glycogen Stores and Physical Endurance

	Glycogen Content Per 100 g Wet Muscle	**Maximum Work Time**
Normal Mixed Diet	1.75 g	114 minutes
Fat and Protein Diet (meats, fats, nuts)	0.63 g	57 minutes
High Carbohydrate Diet	3.51 g	167 minutes

The vegetarians showed almost 3 times greater endurance than others. This is partly due to the higher and more sustained sugar (glycogen) content of muscle, resulting from a higher carbohydrate content in the diet.

It is also interesting to note that the world's most powerful and some of the longest lived animals are herbivores. The elephant, buffalo, ox, camel, and horse all have large, healthy bodies. Their stamina and phenomenal strength enables them to carry massive loads. No carnivore can stand up to such strain and can never qualify to be a beast of burden.

What the Scriptures Say

The early Christians and Jews were also vegetarian. The Bible says, "And God said, 'Behold, I have given you every herb-bearing seed, which is upon the face of the earth, and every tree in which is the fruit of a tree yielding seed; to you it shall be for meat' " (Genesis 1:29). Further, in Genesis 9:4 it says, "But the flesh with the life thereof, which is the blood thereof, shall ye not eat."

Hindu scriptures have long advocated a vegetarian diet for man. Bhagwan Swaminarayan in his Shikshapatri, the code of conduct for his followers, has pointed out, "None shall kill animals such as goats even for the purpose of performing sacrifices or for propitiating a deity, for non-violence in itself is held as the highest ethical code" (12). "None shall ever eat flesh, be it the remnant of offerings in a sacrifice..." (15).

Harvesting crops for food is permitted by the scriptures but not the killing of fully sentient animals such as cows, pigs, etc. Incidentally, eggs, even if non-fertilized, are classified as flesh - animal material originally intended for the creation of a fully sentient animal. On the other hand, milk, though of animal origin, is a secretion like sweat, and its origin lies in the love of the mother towards its newborn. One does not have to kill the mother to obtain milk, no *himsa* is thus committed.

There is also one other important aspect worth considering. Shri Krishna in the Bhagavad Gita (17.8-10) has categorized food into three types:

(a) Those that promote life, vitality, strength, health and joy are sweet, firm and nourishing and agreeable to good men *(sattvic)*.

(b) Foods that are bitter, sour, saltish, pungent, astringent, pain producing and grief causing are liked by the passionate *(rajsic)*.

(c) Foods which are stale, tasteless, putrefying and unclean are liked by men of darkness *(tamsic)*.

Flesh is *tamsic* because it will always be in a state of decay as Bhagwan Swaminarayan reveals in his *Dharmamrut: Nishkami Vartman*, "Even the respectable class in society, out of sheer passion, indulge in the consumption of undesirable non-*sattvic* foods as fish and other flesh, meats, alcohol..." (12).

Sattvic food is ideal for man - having no adverse effects on his behaviour. For the aspirant who is treading the path to self-realization and God-realization, control of his body's natural instincts is a must. *'Āhār shudhau sattva shuddhihi'* - 'If your diet is pure then your thoughts will be pure' (Chandogya Upanishad 7.26.2).

An aspirant should always keep his body's requirements as *sattvic* as possible; and to offer pure devotion to God he must abide by the scriptures with absolute faith. Recent scientific studies in the USA have revealed that human behaviour is determined by the nature of the food eaten.

Towards the end of the 19th century, a physician in the United States, Dr James C. Jackson writing in *The Laws of Life*, stated, "I have found it impossible to cure drunkards while I allowed them the use of flesh-meats. I regard animal flesh as lying right across the way of restoration. Besides, from its nutrition, it contains some element or substance which so excites the nervous system as in the long run to exhaust it, to wear out its tissues, and to render it incapable of normal action."

Pythagorus says, "Those who kill animals for food will be more prone than vegetarians to torture and kill their fellow men."

Albert Einstein was a staunch vegetarian and he believed, "It is my view that the vegetarian manner of living, by its purely physical effect on the human temperament, would most beneficially influence the lot of mankind."

Clearly then, vegetarianism is the diet for man, for which his body is suitably adapted.

Summary

Next to tobacco and alcohol, meat is the greatest single

cause of death in the United States. Meat wastes energy when conservation is necessary. Meat is deficient in two major essential food components - carbohydrates and fibre; it is more economical for the individual and the society to be vegetarian. And from the point of view of karma, vegetarianism is innocent whereas non-vegetarians invariably have to pay heavily for the violations they commit. Finally, vegetarianism is absolutely mandatory for true bhakti-yoga.

Some Famous Vegetarians

Pythagoras, Socrates, Plato, Sir Isaac Newton, Charles Darwin, Leo Tolstoy, Henry David Thoreau, Ralph Waldo Emerson, Benjamin Franklin, John Milton, H.G. Wells, Rabindranath Tagore, Albert Schweitzer, General William Booth, Mahatma Gandhi, George Bernard Shaw, Paul Newman, Upton Sinclair, James Coburn, Bob Dylan,

47 THE CRACK IN THE EGG

Kaushik Joshi

More and more people the world over are becoming acutely conscious of the diet-health relationship. The medical profession, however, is not yet decided on the best foods for the body. The last ten years have been the decade of the egg. Millions are now eaten everyday as a source of protein, vitamins and other nutrients.

This article explores the truth behind the egg. Not surprisingly, cracks have appeared, in an otherwise smooth shell!

Why Do People Eat Eggs?

The widespread use of eggs is partly due to medical prescription in matters of diet. The nutritional formula adopted by doctors is HPD (High Protein Diet) plus two eggs. It is intriguing to note that eggs have invaded the diet of once staunch vegetarian households in India. They don't eat meat or fish, just eggs, yet they don't like to be branded as non-vegetarian.

The media blitz is largely responsible for promoting the use of eggs. All forms of communication are used to drive home the point that eggs are part of a wholesome diet, nutritious and unadulterated, and that (surprisingly) they are vegetarian.

A common equation used is that 2 eggs provide as much protein as would 2 glasses of milk, 6 kg of apples or 1¼ kg of tomatoes.

All this leaves the gullible consumer mesmerised, and turns him into a devoted egg eater. It is time we subject such assertions to test and reflect upon them. It is only apt to ask: Wasn't the Indian vegetarian diet wholesome before the arrival of eggs? The craze for eggs is such that there are 60,000 poultry farms in India alone.

Brave New Chicken

The animals raised for meat, dairy products and eggs are being subjected to ever more deplorable conditions and treatment. Merely to keep the poor creatures alive under these circumstances even more chemicals have to be pumped into their bodies. The worst drug pushers don't walk the city streets, they operate today's 'factory farms'.

Millions upon millions of people are merrily eating away, unaware of the pain and disease they are taking into their bodies with every bite.

The raising of chickens today is not a process which overflows with compassion for these birds. Nor is it anything like the backyard operation that comes to mind when we imagine the lives of chickens. Formerly, chickens were free-range birds, scratching and rooting around in the soil for grubs, earthworms and grains. But today all this has changed. The raising of chickens has become completely industrialized. We live now, in the era of the assembly-line chicken.

Happy Birthday Male Chick

Male chicks, of course, are of little use in egg production. How are the little fellows greeted then, having pecked their way out of their shells, expecting to be met by mum? What happens is vividly described by J. Mason and P. Singer in their book *Animal Factories*.

"They are, literally, thrown away. We watched at one hatchery as chicken pullers weeded males from each tray and dropped them into heavy duty plastic bags. Our guide explained, 'We put them in a bag and let them suffocate.' "

It's not a picture to bring joy to a mother's heart, but over half a million little baby chickens are 'disposed of' in this fashion every day of the year in the United States.

And they are, perhaps, the lucky ones. For, those that are allowed to live, life is truly a nightmare.

Auschwitz of the Poultry World

Chickens are highly social animals. In the natural setting they develop a social hierarchy, known as the 'pecking order'. Studies published in *New Scientist* reveal that this pecking order can only be maintained in flocks with up to 90 chickens. Beyond 90 birds, however, things can get out of hand. In today's chicken factories flocks tend to be much larger than the 90-bird limit. How much larger? The figures run into thousands, depending on the factory.

In such mechanized hells the birds are unable to establish any kind of social identity for themselves. The cooped-up animals constantly fight with each other. They are driven berserk by the lack of space and the complete frustration of their primal need for a social order. They peck viciously at each other's feathers, frequently try to kill one another and even try to eat each other alive.

The experts have of course responded. They have to do something, because if very many of the birds kill each other money is lost. What is done? The conditions are made even more unnatural. A part of the chicken's beak is cut off! The experts and factory managers are of course not disturbed by the fact that the chicken is caused intense pain and is crippled for life. For them, profits must be kept up.

Further, irregular beak growth prevents the birds from eating and drinking water. The result is death from starvation and thirst, within inches of food and water.

Today's chickens are allowed no expression of their natural urges. The result is panic. In their panic, the birds will sometimes pile on top of each other and some will be smothered to death. Not to be outsmarted for profits, experts have decreased the problem by crowding the chickens so tightly into wire cages they can hardly move. The wire cages have created further problems. With no solid ground to wear the nails down, they become very long and get permanently entangled in wire. Needless to say, those birds who get stuck in the back of the cage starve to death.

Breakfast with a Conscience

The life of an egg-laying chicken in the modern world demands attention. Those who enjoy an egg for breakfast, or indulge in even an occasional omelette, should give a thought to the tortured chicken who supplied the egg.

Are Eggs Vegetarian?

Those who harbour the thought of vegetarian eggs should know that these eggs are only unfertilized eggs. They have not been fertilized by the male. Hence, no egg can be called a vegetarian egg. The ovum is very much there in such eggs. The same egg could be fertilized if allowed to blend with sperm cells. If such an egg is hatched, it could produce a chick.

The ovum is a living animal cell that breathes, inhales oxygen and exhales carbon dioxide. The egg yolk and the egg white are for the protection of the foetus, in case the egg is fertilized. The advocates of eggs or vegetarian eggs should understand the simple biological phenomenon that occurs every month in women but takes place every 22-24 hours in the case of hens. The egg that the hen lays is only an ovum. The difference between the growth of a human foetus and that of a hen is that the latter grows in an egg. Thus an egg, fertilized or unfertilized, is either menstrual secretion (ovum) or both, ovum plus sperms.

Eggs Versus Milk

Some erroneously equate milk with eggs. The comparison

between eggs and milk is also out of place. While eggs are the result of the reproductive system, milk is a secretion of the nutritional mechanism. Eggs are for procreation while milk is for nutrition. Milk is food, eggs are not. An egg is a living animal cell. Milk is lifeless.

Eggs – A Healthy Diet?

How nutritious are eggs? Is there really no substitute for eggs in our vegetarian diet? What are their effects upon our health? We should spare a thought on all this.

To augment the sale of eggs, ad campaigns are launched which blow the value of eggs out of all proportion. For example, the National Egg Co-ordination Committee advertised some time ago that eggs contain more protein than apples and tomatoes. And that two eggs provide us with more protein than 6 kg of apples and 1¼ kg of tomatoes put together. This is bluntly misleading. Can you really compare the pugilist Mike Tyson with maestro Ravishankar? The comparison is indeed out of place.

Dr Vasant Jai who has been working as a nutritionist at the Haffkeine Institute in Mumbai, says, "Apples are consumed more for their minerals, vitamins and carbohydrates than for their protein content." He further questions whether the supporters of eggs have ever thought of the vitamin C content of fruits as against eggs? One would require 200 eggs to have 100 mg of vitamin C. The same quantity of vitamin C can be had from one *amla* or a quarter kilogramme of oranges or tomatoes!

Dr Jai even asserts that nutritionally eggs have 95 per cent ill-effects.

What are these negative points? Let us begin with the protein content. There are two schools of thought on getting the most protein out of eggs. One school favours raw eggs while the other favours boiled eggs.

Leslie and Susannah Kenton write in their work *Raw Energy* that avidin in the egg white of a raw egg blends with biotin; this prevents the biotin from reaching the bloodstream. They cite the example of a youth who, after eating raw eggs, lost appetite, became anaemic, developed nausea, anorexia and muscle pains. Also, the albumin which blends with blood without being digested causes several types of allergies.

The boiled or fried egg is also not without its hazards.

In their best seller called *Fit For Life,* Dr Harvey and Dr Marilyn Diamond say that cooked eggs are without amino acids as the heat destroys them. There is also evidence that egg protein, on heating, combines with important minerals, making them unavailable for use by the body.

Even if they are eaten raw, eggs are laid by hens that are fed arsenic to kill parasites and stimulate egg production, and hence some of that virulent poison is ingested. Eggs also contain much sulphur, which puts a heavy strain on the liver and kidneys.

Thus, eggs eaten for protein cause health hazards when eaten raw, and when cooked the protein is destroyed. The egg eater is so faced with the devil's alternative.

Protein Versus Eggs

It is erroneously believed that protein gives energy. But, says Dr Diamond, "Protein does not produce energy, it uses it." He cites the example of a carnivorous lion that sleeps 20 hours a day against a herbivorous Urangutang that sleeps just six hours a day.

It is apt to note the observation in this regard that appeared in 1978 in the *Journal of the American Medical Association (JAMA)*, "Those athletes who take a wholesome diet need not take protein-rich items like eggs for muscular growth. They need as much protein as do non-athletes. But protein does not give strength. Actually, lots of energy is wasted in digesting extra protein intake which also causes dehydration, loss of appetite and diarrhoea."

A report published in 1961 in the same journal said that a vegetarian diet goes a long way in preventing heart disease.

This reveals that eggs and meat contain a high amount of cholesterol. Says Dr Catherine Nimmo in *How Healthy Are Eggs?*, "You can certainly do without more of eggs. One egg contains 4 grams of cholesterol. And greater doses of cholesterol cause heart ailments, high blood pressure, and gall bladder and kidney stones. Fruits and vegetables do not contain any cholesterol."

Some doctors advise eggs to anaemic patients. But in the case of anaemia it is iron that is needed; and eggs contain little iron, while green leafy vegetables are rich in iron; containing 7 to 10 times more iron than eggs. Millet, kidney beans and grams contain four times more iron and jaggery five times more iron than eggs. An egg prescription, therefore, is totally out of place.

Some people have the mistaken idea that only eggs and meat contain vitamin B12 and that vegetarians therefore suffer from its deficiency.

This is blatantly untrue and fabricated.

Actually, pernicious anaemia is found among patients in Western countries. It is hardly evident in India. We only need vitamin B12 in minute quantities. One milligram could be enough to meet your requirement for two years. Interestingly, most healthy persons have enough B12 to last for 5 years. One is tempted to ask where the hen got her B12 from!

An Overall Health Hazard

Eggs and meat, as is well known, do not contain fibre which is much needed for the smooth disposal of faeces. Wheat, grams, soya beans, kidney beans, groundnuts and leafy vegetables contain ample fibre.

Extensive research is also increasingly labelling eggs as a

prominent cause of ill health. Dr Robert Grass thinks that eggs could lead to tuberculosis and dysentery. Whilst Dr J.M. Wilkins states that they cause ulcers.

Extensive research in Florida has also revealed that DDT, an insecticide extensively used in poultry farms, enters the eggs and thus egg-eaters are threatened with potential health problems.

Hens are also given hormones to boost egg production. These hormones, when ingested by humans could cause breast cancer, high blood pressure and jaundice. They also affect the fertility of men. Dr Grass says eggs could even be responsible for eczema and paralysis.

A report that appeared in *JAMA* in 1988 says that eggs are largely responsible for food poisoning. The report was the result of a study of cases of diarrhoea, vomiting, fever and severe headache. The bacteria *Salmonella enteritis* was identified as the cause. Salmonella is found abundantly in eggs.

And so, eggs are not all that they are made out to be. Should we include them in our diet? For all morally minded and health-loving individuals the answer must surely be a firm 'No!'

48 WHERE MEDICINES FAIL, FASTING TRIUMPHS: I

Sadhu Mukundcharandas

People rarely believe that fasting is a great cure for many common and chronic ailments. In any case, abstinence from good food intake once every 15 days is beneficial for health. The spiritual implications and benefits of fasting are a lot more profound, helping to discipline and elevate the senses, mind and soul.

In 1958, a 28-year-old American food specialist named Dr Jack Goldstein developed diarrhoea accompanied with bleeding and intestinal spasm. As the months progressed and the symptoms persisted, he consulted his physician, who, after a series of examinations and tests, diagnosed ulcerative colitis, which is a serious disease of the large intestine. The treatment prescribed by his first physician consisted of various modern drugs. The condition worsened and he had to be hospitalized. With a dose of new drugs he showed signs of improvement. Indigestion and stomach upsets were some of the side-effects of the medication.

In the winter of 1960 he suddenly had a frightening reaction which forced the doctor to reduce the dosage. Other side-effects included dryness in the mouth, headaches, blurred and double vision, nervousness, mental slowness, a chronic low grade fever and weakness. His physician finally gave up after treating him for two-and-a-half years. Early in 1961, Dr Goldstein consulted another specialist. Drugs were once again changed and his prescribed diet consisted of eggs, milk, meat, whole wheat bread, all of which were too difficult for him to digest. His bowel movements increased to between 12 and 15 a day. Another complication also developed - haemorrhoids (piles).

By early 1962, he had an infection in the large intestine and a persistent fever. Fed up, he went to another specialist. Dr Goldstein was re-hospitalized for five weeks but the side-effects continued.

Later, the steroid prednisolone was used in heavy doses. Although his condition seemed to improve, this remission only lasted for two months, after which the fever returned and the bowel movements averaged 15 per day. The steroid dose was then reduced. Soon he suffered from muscle spasms and cramps in his limbs. He started gaining (unhealthy) weight, resulting in a puffy face and water and fat being deposited along the back of the neck. The bowel movements increased to 20 per day. His entire body was now suffering.

In 1963, he was 33 years old but felt twice that age. The bowel movements increased further to an astonishing 30 per day with increased spasm and bleeding. The haemorrhoids returned causing unbearable pain and local injection therapy proved unsuccessful. He was so sick he seriously contemplated suicide. By the end of the year, three of the haemorrhoids had turned gangrenous. These were surgically removed.

In the late spring of 1964, after six years of treatment and tremendous suffering, he paid the last visit to his physician who offered him two choices. One was to do nothing and die. The other was a total colectomy, which is the removal of the entire large intestine and the connection of the end of the small intestine to an opening in the abdominal wall. The body wastes would continually empty into a bag attached to the outside of the body. Statistics from the National Foundation for Ibitis and Colitis (USA) showed that about 25% to 35% of patients operated upon could develop further complications and need more surgery of the bowel higher up if the disease progressed. Neither choices appealed to him.

After a long mental battle he turned to Natural Hygiene in the late summer of 1964. If this failed surgery was always there. He entered a nature hygiene institution and lived only on water for six weeks under medical supervision. His pre-fast weight was 140 lbs.

During the first ten days the intestinal inflammation and the fever disappeared. The frequency of the bowel movements decreased to around five a day.

By the 22nd day the bowel movements averaged two per day and he felt "on top of the world physically, mentally and spiritually." This was all achieved without drugs.

On the 33rd day he had no bowel movements! His skin and gums were 're-conditioned' and he experienced an extreme mental alertness and tranquility which he had not experienced for the past six years.

He broke the fast on the 43rd day weighing 108 lbs; a loss of 32 lbs. For the next four weeks his vegetarian diet was meticulously supervised, after which he weighed 138 lbs. He felt 60% better than when he had come to the institution. After returning home, his family adopted a wholly vegetarian diet.

Thereafter, every year he fasted for a period of four to five weeks at the institution. By 1976 he felt 95% normal.

One of Dr Goldstein's room-mates was afflicted with Brights disease – a kidney disorder with high blood pressure, protein in the urine and obesity. The 68-year-old was chronically ill and after fasting for 52 days there was a distinct improvement in his condition. He shed excess weight, his prostrate problem had cleared, the blood pressure came down and protein disappeared from the urine. After a few weeks' treatment he returned home rejuvenated.

Another room-mate, a man in his seventies was

overweight, had high blood pressure, arthritis and a locked hip joint. He was constantly in pain, especially in the joints of his hands. He undertook a fast for four weeks. By the fifth day of the fast his pain subsided, without drugs. After conclusion of the fast his weight and blood pressure had come down and his joints functioned more freely. The locked hip joint became a little more mobile - the erosion of the joint renders the process irreversible. He was then instructed to follow a basically raw vegetarian diet.

Historically, fasting is of early origin. Religiously, partial or entire abstinence from food or from certain kinds of foods during specific seasons prevailed in Assyria, Babylon, Greece, Rome, Persia, India, China and among the American Indians. Moses is said to have fasted for more than 120 days on Mount Sinai. The Bible has 74 references to fasting. Plutarch said, "Instead of using medicine, fast a day." Avicenna, the great Arab physician, often prescribed fasting for three weeks or more. Mark Twain in *My Debut as a Literary Person* (1899) had this to say of fasting, "A little starvation can really do more for the average sick man than can the best medicines and the best doctors. I do not mean a restricted diet; I mean total abstention from food for one or two days. I speak from experience, starvation has been my cold and fever doctor for 15 years and has accomplished a cure in all instances."

It is well to emphasize the difference between fasting and starvation.

Fasting means abstaining entirely or in part and for longer or shorter periods of time from food and drink or from food alone. Under ordinary circumstances, the food reserves of man and animal are able to maintain the daily functioning and maintenance of the body for a considerable time without more food being consumed. These reserves are stored for use when environmental and/or bodily conditions are adverse. Dr George

F. Cabill Jr. of the Howard School of Medicine has said, "Man's survival is predicated (dependent) upon a remarkable ability to conserve the relatively limited body protein stores while utilizing fat as the primary energy-producing food."

Starvation, on the other hand, is 'the deprivation of nutrition to the tissues,' which they require and is invariably accompanied by harmful effects. Fasting starts with the omission of the first meal and ends when natural hunger returns, because during a properly conducted fast there is no hunger. Starvation starts if food is not eaten after the return of natural hunger and will end in death due to destruction of vital tissues. The former process merely expels the body's wastes and useless fatty tissue. In starvation there will be very little tissue fat, the heart is always smaller than normal and there will be marked anaemia. A number of English soldiers died at Aldershot after eight hours of manoeuvres in an English summer after being denied food for only eight hours. It is said that they died of starvation. A British physician, A. Rabagliati, asserted, "They did not and could not have died of starvation," and contrasted these soldiers with patients of his who had fasted and whose fasts had lasted not for hours or days, but for weeks, after which, in numerous cases patients had recovered from severe and chronic illnesses.

49 WHERE MEDICINES FAIL, FASTING TRIUMPHS: II

Sadhu Mukundcharandas

Did you know that the Alaskan fur seal bull goes without food and water for three months during the breeding season each year?

Did you know that a species of crocodile goes without feeding for over a year during dry periods?

Did you know that the African snail, *Helix desertorum,* remains in a dormant state for as long as five years?

We all know that a sick or wounded animal will retire to a secluded spot for rest, avoiding food until it gets well.

The ability of an animal to fast, even for long periods, is a vitally important factor in survival. It is nature's solution for dealing with certain physiological and biological problems. An animal can fast because it has adequate internal food reserves, and man is no exception.

Now we will look into how fasting works, the benefits and the role of fasting to cure drug addiction.

Mechanism of Fasting

The following explanation is based on experience by renowned practitioners of fasting.

In physiology, autolysis is the process of self-digestion of tissue by enzymes. (Enzymes are chemicals ,which control chemical reactions.) The food reserves of the body are stored as complex chemical substances. Before these can be utilized or circulated, they must be acted upon by enzymes to be converted to simpler forms. A severely wounded animal will not eat and yet its wounds heal. This is because the reserves are first autolysed (broken down) at the site of storage. This then mixes with the blood and large amounts of blood which represent 'food' are sent to the site of the wound to repair the damaged tissues. Throughout fasting and starvation autolysis is rigidly controlled by the body.

This autolysis extends to abnormal tissues such as tumours, deposits, outgrowths, etc., and is not confined to the normal tissues of the body during fasting. The abnormal growths possess a deficient nerve and blood supply and thus do not have the support of the organism as do normal growths. This lack of support makes them the ready victims of autolysis.

One of the first indications of illness is failing appetite. The desire for food decreases a few days before any significant symptoms appear. Researchers have shown that 'hunger contractions' of the stomach are absent in gastritis, tonsilitis, influenza and colds. Pain, inflammation, fever, headaches, mental disturbances, etc., take away the appetite, inhibit secretion and impair digestion. Nature is trying to conserve energy and direct it elsewhere. This is why the digestive functions are temporarily suspended. Any undigested food will either be vomited or will decay and cause further discomfort. In certain disorders the stomach cannot digest even light food and therefore the best solution is to give it a rest. The stomach, intestines and colon are given a complete rest by a fast and are helped to repair the damage.

Fasting and Drug Addiction

Any form of drug addiction is an escapist's way of seeking 'relief' from the day-to-day pressures of life. Those who have good healthy habits seek no 'soothing' poisons. The alcoholic 'relieves' his headache with more of the alcohol that induced it. The same applies to smoking and the consumption of hard drugs.

Alcoholism usually starts in youth when the body's ability to detoxify poisons is at its peak and any amount of indulgence seems safe. The habit becomes a chronic illness and places great stress upon the family of the alcoholic. Man is a habit-forming animal. Drugs are termed 'habit forming', but it is man that forms the habit and not the drug. Macfadden in his *Encyclopaedia of Physical Culture* says, "There is no better method of giving a victim of alcoholism an opportunity to gain secure control of himself, at least in the beginning of the treatment, than can be suggested by a complete fast."

Fasting has helped heavy smokers to shun their habit. It allows the body to re-adjust itself and quickens the elimination of poisons such as nicotine, tar, etc.

The thickening of the lining of the mouth, throat and stomach which occurs in a heavy drinker and the substantial loss in taste and smell in a heavy smoker all disappear during fasting and a thin sensitive lining appears.

The craving for drugs will positively die out of the ex-addict. The same is true of cocaine and morphine addicts, though care has to be taken to combat the withdrawal symptoms.

Benefits of Fasting

Fasting:

1. Provides the vital organs a rest.
2. Stops the absorption of foods that decay in the gut.
3. Empties the digestive tract and facilitates elimination of wastes.
4. Promotes the breakdown and absorption of diseased tissues, deposits and other abnormal growths.
5. Increases the powers of digestion and assimilation (the usage of food).
6. In itself does not remove toxins. This is done by the excretory organs.

7. Re-establishes normal body chemistry and secretions.
8. Creates an environment which allows organs to perfect their work.
9. Improves mental powers generally, e.g. the ability to reason is increased and attention and association are quickened when fasting. The Romans believed that 'a full stomach does not like to think'.
10. Tends to increase one's control over all appetites and passions.
11. Is ideal for meditation.

What Magazines and Journals Say

For those who are overweight *Time* magazine suggests, "Fasting is the oldest, the surest and the quickest way to get rid of excess fat." *Vogue* described fasting as "The newest and yet the most ancient practice, a historic mode of cleaning, a conditioner for meditation." The *Journal of the American Medical Association* is of the opinion that fasting provides the best method of self-discipline needed by the obese, "one that can be safely repeated with beneficial effect." The *New England Journal of Medicine* echoes that fasting is "a valid experience for any otherwise healthy person who has failed to relieve the weight problem by every other method."

Even a one-day fast is beneficial. In an article entitled, 'Live Better Naturally' in a London-based magazine *Doctor's Answer* (July 1982), the following advice appeared, "A one-day fast is an excellent way to rest our digestive system... and leave you refreshed... The intake of liquid should be stepped up to assist the process of flushing out the body's toxic wastes."

Charak, a renowned ancient practitioner of Ayurveda, the old Hindu practice of combating diseases, had said that, *'Langhanam paramaushadhum'*, i.e., Fasting is the ultimate medicine.

The entire philosophy of Ayurveda, which has its roots in the Vedas, rests on the foundation that self-restraint of the senses leads to tranquility and puts forth one fundamental principle that without karshan (fasting), tarpan (nutrition) is never possible.

Bhagwan Swaminarayan describes the ultimate fast as when the ten *indriyas* (senses) and the eleventh mind are withdrawn from their respective sense-objects. Control over the *ekadash indriyas* by checking their rampancy is the correct method according to the scriptures for observing *ekadashi vrat*. One who remains cautious and rejects the frivolous calls of the *indriyas* is blessed with the grace of God.

How to Break a Fast

So much for abstinence. What about breaking the fast? A one-day fast may preferably be broken initially by slowly sipping a glass of fresh fruit juice only without any solid food. About an hour later another glass can be sipped and if necessary a very light meal of natural food should be taken. Canned foods, soda type drinks, overcooked, fried, oily and spicy foods, sweetmeats and chocolates should all be strictly avoided. An example will suffice to illustrate the consequence if the above is not adhered to: A 24-year-old man who had suffered from chronic constipation and indigestion fasted for 27 days after reading a health article. He broke the fast by eating beef-steak, potatoes, bread and butter with coffee! Result? He suffered violent vomiting spells and could not tolerate even a teaspoonful of water. The invariable craving to overeat without proper mastication should be avoided. A sudden above normal distension of the stomach with heavy foods can only led to harm in the long run if frequently repeated. Any fasting programme should not be started without medical advice and medical supervision.

There are conditions in which fasting or extended fasting is inadvisable. There is an art and a science to fasting and under experienced hands it is very safe. As Dr Herbert M. Shelton in *Fasting Can Save Your Life* says, "The fast should not be misused but the results of its misuse should not be used to condemn the whole process."

50 DEFYING NATURE

Sadhu Mukundcharandas

When man defies God's laws or nature's natural systems, the consequences are dire and destructive. One can never hope to profit, no matter how apparent it may be, by flouting nature's laws. The repercussions of several such cases described in this researched article reflect the futility and danger of transgressing nature's laws.

In journalism, 'Dog bites man' is considered a mere incident. However, 'Man bites dog' is news! Something similar has been observed in the Western food industry in the past two decades. It is considered normal for man to eat animal flesh. Certain African and New Guinea tribes relish human hearts and brains. An even more bizarre act of cannibalism occurred in the civilized world during World War II when Nazi officers ate cooked flesh of Jewish prisoners in one concentration camp! Perhaps less known to the public is that to accelerate weight gain in the shortest time possible, cows were fed cows! To maximize profits, after beef is packed, the cows' remains, such as bones, horns and hooves, were powdered and mixed with cattle feed. This gruesome practice prevailed till the late seventies and eighties before nature struck back with a vengeance.

In 1984, in the South Downs of England, a farmer named Peter Stent noted mysterious symptoms in one of his cows. These included drooling, arching back and repeated sideways waving of the head. The cow also became aggressive, would lose balance and began losing weight. Six weeks later she died. Prior to this, Stent noticed telltale symptoms in some of his other cows. From his farm's name, vets labelled the disease 'Pitsham Farm Syndrome.'

In 1992, in the coastal village of Caernarfon, north Wales, the father of 22-year-old Alison Williams suddenly observed a change in her personality. She stopped attending college and stayed indoors all day, staring inanely out of the window for hours on end. By 1995, she became paranoid and lost bowel and bladder control. She soon became blind, slipped into a coma and died. Medical authorities then scrambled to identify the cause of her illness.

After their findings they labelled the Pitsham Syndrome as 'bovine spongioform encephalopathy' (BSE), commonly known as mad cow disease. It has wiped out over 200,000 cows in England and Europe. Researchers named Alison Williams' illness as 'variant Creutzfeldt Jacob Disease' (vCJD), the human variant of BSE, which claimed 94 lives. This resulted from eating infected beef. One theory attributes the cause of infection to 'prions', which are neither bacteria nor virus, but rogue protein molecules. Nobody knows for certain where they originated. They are so resilient that strong acids and extreme temperatures fail to destroy them. The human immune system, too, is unable to combat them. Prions somehow eat up the brain, forming holes, as in a sponge – hence the name 'spongioform'. Mad cow disease has so terrified the medical fraternity that *Newsweek* described it as, "the creepiest in a family of disorders that can make Ebola look like chickenpox." BSE did mobilize the authorities, which banned contaminated beef byproducts for cows at home. Yet it allowed the meat industry to export byproducts of BSE infected cows as feed to over 80 countries for eight years, from 1988 to 1996. The ramifications of this unethical and criminal practice is too horrifying even to contemplate. Millions of consumers in Europe, Russia and south-east Asia ate cattle, pigs and chickens raised on this feed!

Not surprisingly, in 1994, BSE surfaced again in England, killing many cows and humans. This finally forced the government to ban all meat-based cattle feed and spend millions on destroying cows. A monumental backlog still awaits disposal; 500,000 tons of ground-up cattle remain stored at 13 sites in England, awaiting incineration. Today an average of 30 new cases are reported each week, down from over a 1000 in the early '90s.

As cited earlier, BSE arose from the unnatural practice of feeding cows to cows, to maximize production for fast financial returns.

Another notorious practice by the meat industry is to use hormones to speed the growth rate of livestock. This too causes grim side effects. In 1978, a horrified mother in Milan, Italy, visited a physician with her 6-year-old son who was developing female characteristics. This did not shock the physician, for in recent months he had seen 1,100 such cases. He traced the cause to diethyl stilboesterol (DES), a powerful growth hormone which greedy farmers use to fatten their veal calves. All the affected children had eaten meat of these animals. In 1979, a hospital in Puerto Rico witnessed the disorder in 8-year-old boys. Besides premature sexual development, DES induced premature aging in young children.

DES was first used in the 1950s to promote fertility in women with reproductive failure, but was banned when side effects surfaced 29 years later. However, meat producers in the US and Europe routinely use DES in livestock, otherwise they estimate a loss of $30 per cow and over $40 million per year.

Another disorder resulting from flouting nature's laws is illustrated by the Fore tribe of Papua New Guinea. In the 1950s, Dr Carleton Gadjusek encountered a peculiar disease among them. The Fore women and children suffered from *kuru*, meaning shivering. The symptoms included unsteadiness, slurred speech, tremors and coma, leading to death within 16 months. He discovered the cause to be diet-related. While the men ate tubers, beans and meat from forest game, the women and children ate their dead relatives. Specifically they ate only those women who died from *kuru* and not those from dysentery or leprosy which they considered unclean. Richard Rhodes described this as "deadly feasts" in his book.

When Gadjusek sent brain autopsy samples of the *kuru* victims to his colleagues in the USA, they reported holes, known as vacuoles, in the brain, similar to those who suffered from vCJD! More disturbingly, researchers later discovered that eating such infected flesh was not the only method of transmission of such diseases.

In the 1960s endocrinologists discovered hormones in the pituitary gland of the brain. Of these, they extracted the human growth hormone (hGH), which could help dwarves reach normal height. From 1963, researchers began to extract hGH from human cadavers, treating 8,200 children over the next 20 years.

Everything seemed stable until 1984, when a worrisome effect surfaced. Normally, vCJD affected people over 50. However, those children who had received the growth hormone exhibited the disease in their 20s. This meant that the bug had tagged along with the hormone. In April 1985 authorities banned the practice of injecting the hormone. Yet 27,000 of the world's children had already received it. In the US, new cases are still being recorded every year. This is the high tech 'civilized' equivalent of the Fore's deadly feasts.

After the BSE, vCJD and hGH experiences, one assumes that man would have learnt his lesson; to respect nature by following its laws. However that was not to be.

Foot & Mouth Disease (FMD)

No sooner had the BSE terror subsided, when another

plague struck the British countryside. Besides cows, it affected sheep, pigs and threatened wild animals in zoos and safari parks. On 20 February 2001, a vet inspector detected the first case of foot and mouth disease in a slaughterhouse in Essex. However, the outbreak is attributed to a pig farm in Northumberland, where swine were apparently fed swill made from waste food, which may have contained contaminated meat. The contagion is the O Pan Asia virus which causes blisters in the mouth and feet of animals. It does not kill them and they recover within a short period. However, they do lose weight and yield less milk. Though not a biological threat to humans, FMD has become a monumental economic disaster. The contagion also spread to Ireland, the Netherlands and France.

Today's agri-business practices, bent on high yields and cheap foods, have been forced into mass culling of the infected and innocuous livestock! According to a British scientist, no country abroad will accept British meat if it might be infected with FMD. A loss of £8 million per week is estimated because of a ban on meat exports.

Killing Frenzy

In the previous mass outbreak of foot and mouth disease in 1967, only 2,364 cases were confirmed, yet to stem the contagion, over 442,000 animals were slaughtered within a span of 6 months. From 20 February 2001 to 24 April 2001, 1,448 cases were detected. This prompted a scientist to describe the slaughter as "a manic killing frenzy" on an apocalyptic scale; On June 12, the goverment's MAFF database, recorded the slaughter of 3,290,000 animals - 519,000 cattle 2,645,000 sheep, 124,000 pigs and 2000 goats. However, according to *The Times* of June 11, the Government gave the official figure as 4.2 million, omitting 2 million lambs, calves and piglets. Whatever the age factor, the fact remains that a staggering 6.2 million have been slaughtered.

Compared to the killings, disposal of the carcasses has caused an even greater headache. Initially they were incinerated on pyres stretching up to 2 km, lighting up the British countryside for days on end. Public outcry against air pollution from dioxin forced the authorities to opt for burial. Since the rate of culling outpaced burial, scores of carcasses bloated and burst after lying in the countryside for up to 2 weeks. *The Times* (UK) of 21 April 2001 reported 174,660 carcasses lying across Devon.

Ironically, this led to a horrible stench in the air due to rotting carcasses and groundwater contamination from the liquid leakage! Phenol based disinfectants to combat the outbreak also threatened wildlife and fish in streams. Tourists who usually trekked through the countryside were banned for fear of spreading the virus. The BBC estimated losses from rural tourism alone at £100 million a week.

Positive Feedback

Whatever the financial losses to industry, the draconian slaughter affected the general public on two levels. When humanitarians voiced concern over the method of culling, the authorities quickly pointed out that it was humane. However, the facts revealed a different story. Slaughtermen either used a single-shot handgun which fired a lead bullet in an animal head causing concussion, or a captive-bolt pistol whose bolt penetrated the skull. After withdrawing the bolt, the slaughtermen inserted a flexible rod or wire through the hole and macerated the brain and spinal cord! For dangerous livestock such as bulls, vets injected a sedative before culling. They used lethal injections for lambs and piglets.

The second effect directly concerns meat eaters. In a land raised on Beatrix Potter's animal stories, such news and gruesome images of animals being killed and flung around, and piles of slaughtered lambs, pigs and burning cattle so upset children and adults, especially the aged, that thousands opted to stop eating meat. Singer Chrissie Hynde, a vegetarian, said it was good that people were finally seeing the reality of slaughter. A campaign group, Viva, dressed in lamb costumes outside Liverpool Street tube station with banners saying, "If killing 'healthy' lambs upsets you don't eat them." The Vegetarian Society of UK reported being 'inundated' by calls from people who considered the FMD outbreak as 'the final straw' and sought advice about a vegetarian diet. BBC News-on-line of 28 March 2001 reported, "Animal culls spark veggie surge!" About 5000 people per week in UK are becoming vegetarians. In 10 years the total number has doubled to 4 million.

Though the outbreaks of BSE and FMD have jolted many consumers into changing their food habits, the meat industry will invariably continue its intensive practices for financial gain, with little regard for human health, animal welfare and the environment.

The following story well illustrates the mentality of those at the industry's apex who wield ruthless power. Over the past quarter of a century, inhabitants of Padre, a village in the Kasaragod block of Kerala, south India, have suffered mutely. They have borne the brunt of the state government's aerial spraying of endosulfan on its cashew nut groves, located 1.5 km away on nearby hills. The chemical leaches into a nearby stream, which is the only source of drinking water for the villagers. They suffer from a hideous array of disorders, such as, cerebral palsy, mental illness and retardation, malformed limbs, epilepsy, congenital defects, skin and genital disorders, abortion, tuberculosis, cancer and suicide! By 20 January 2001, a local physician recorded 197 members in 123 families afflicted by one or more of these disorders. Besides human suffering, cows give birth to malformed calves. Many bird species and wildlife, too, have disappeared from the adjacent jungle. The state government vehemently denies that endosulfan is the culprit, claiming it is innocuous, despite the fact that it has been banned in many countries worldwide. The state government further argues that failure to use endosulfan would result in a loss of Rs. 20 million every season!

Despite awareness of the destructive consequences to himself and the environment, man continues his profit-before-safety practices, on his wanton march to sense gratification. Whether it is BSE, vCJD, FMD, AIDS, Salmonella, Campylobacter, E.Coli O157, usage of DES, GM foods, deforestation, groundwater depletion or human cloning, all are symptoms of a warped humanity; greed, taste and lust gone over the edge. Man now has two options. Either he curbs the instincts to experience peace and harmony with himself and nature, or prepares himself for the next Doomsday scenario; when nature strikes back with another insidious bug from its inexhaustible storehouse.

As he sows so shall he reap.

Source References:

1. *Newsweek* – 12 March 2001 (USA)
2. *TIME* – 12 March 2001 (USA)
3. *The Times* – 15 March, 3, 24 April, 11 June 2001 (UK)
4. *BBC News-on-line* – 28 March2001 (UK)
5. Official Govt. website: www.maff.gov.uk
6. *The Ecologist* – May 2001 (UK)
7. *Down To Earth* – 28 February 2001 (New Delhi)
8. *Unfit for Human Consumption*–Richard Lacey, 1991 (UK)
9. *Problems with Meat* – John Scharffenberg, 1979 (USA)

GLOSSARY

A

ahamkar	ego
akshar-rup	form of Akshar. That which has qualities similar to those of Akshar. Used to describe the spiritual state of *akshar muktas*. Highest level of faith or spiritual status is to become aksharrup and worship Purushottam
amla	hog-plum
amrut	immortalizing nectar
ankush	a small sharp weapon to control an elephant. To restrain
annakut	offering of many food items before the *murti* of God
antahkaran	the complete mind which comprises *man, buddhi, chitt* and *ahamkar;* where the *man* generates thoughts and desires; the *buddhi* consolidates thoughts, makes decisions and resolutions, forms convictions or discriminates; the *chitt* repeatedly contemplates or focuses; and the *ahamkar* forms a sense of being. Normally used in the singular since all four are aspects of the one *antahkaran,* but also often referred to as being four different *antahkarans*
apara vidya	worldly knowledge
apaurusheya	not man-made (normally referred to Vedas)
arti	Hindu ritual of waving lighted wicks before the *murti* of God as an act of worship
asat	untruthful, perishable

atma	soul
atmarup	one who has realized true self as *atma*
atma-shakti	power of *atma*
atmic	related to *atma*

B

bhakti-yoga	to commune with God through bhakti
bhav	good feeling
brahmachari	one who observes brahmacharya and whose *indriyas* are immersed in God
brahmanise	to make one *brahmarup*
brahmarup	form of Brahma. Possessing qualities similar to those of Brahma
buddhi	intellect

C

chameli	type of flower
champa	type of flower
chandlo	auspicious vermilion mark applied on the forehead
chitt	consciousness

D

dagli	upper garment
dakshina	gift given by host
dal	spicy soup of dissolved pulses
dandvat	prostration
devi	minor goddess
diwan	minister

E

ekadashi	special religious observance of fasting performed on the 11th day of the bright

	and dark halves of a lunar month
ekta	unity

G

gana	member of Lord Shivaji's army
gopi	milkmaid of Vrundavan who was devoted to Shri Krishna
gor	molasses
guna	quality, innate nature
guru parampara	succession of God-realized gurus
gurukul	residential school
gutka	a kind of tobacco

H

himsa	injury - by mind, action or speech
hindola	swing

I

indriya	the senses; five of physical action - hands, feet, mouth, anus, and genitals; and five of perception - eyes, nose, ears, skin and tongue

J

jalebi	a sweet delicacy
janoi	sacred thread
jap	mantra recitation
jiva	soul. One of the five eternal entities
jivan yatra	life's journey
jivanmukta	redeemed during this very life
jnan	spiritual knowledge leading to enlightenment, in particular, the knowledge of one's atma and the form and greatness of Paramatma

K

kaupin	undercloth for sadhus
keyur	bracelet
khes	upper garment
kundal	ornament to decorate deity's ears
kuru	shivering
kusang	evil company

M

mahamantra	a great mantra
mahamukta	a great realized *atma*
maharathi	expert charioteer
man	mind
manan	repeated thinking, reflecting
mangala arti	first *arti* of the day, performed at sunrise
mansi puja	mental worship. Form of worship in which one devoutly performs puja, offers *arti, thal,* etc., to God mentally
manvantar	306,720,000 human years
maya	anything that deviates one from the worship of God. Instrument or power of God used as the fundamental 'substance' of creation.
mayik	of, or pertaining to *maya.* Opposite of divine.
mesub	a sweetmeat - regarded as the king of sweets
mogra	type of flower
moksha	liberation; deliverance of the *jiva* from recurring births and deaths
mukta	a liberated soul
murti	sacred idol of God that is revered and worshipped

N

nag	snake
nam-jap	chanting God's holy name
nididhyas	constant contemplation. Repeated deep reflection
nirlobh	vow of non-covetousness
nirman	vow of humility
nishkam	vow of absolute celibacy
nissneh	vow of detachment
nisswad	vow of non-taste

P

para vidya	spiritual knowledge
paramhansa	A male sadhu of the highest order, characterised by his ability to discriminate between *sat* and *asat* - just as swans were traditionally considered to be able to distinguish between milk mixed with water. The highest order of ascetics
parshad	renunciant wearing white robes
pativrata	chaste wife
pran	vital airs, derived from verb-root 'pran'– to breathe. Collective term referring to the principle life force or energy flowing within the primary life-currents of the body, called *vayus,* which control crucial bodily functions. There are five main *vayus:* (1) *pran* - exhaled breath (2) *apan* - inhaled breath (3) *saman* – equalizing breath (4) *udan* - ascending breath (5) *vyan* - retrained breath and five subordinate *vayus:* (1) *nag,* (2) *kurma,* (3) *kukal,* (4) *devadatta,* and (5) *dhananjay*
prasad	sanctified food

pratyaksh puja	offering of worship in person
pujan	ritual of worship with materials such as kumkum, sandalwood paste, rice, flowers
punya	a measure of spiritual merit, opposite to sin

R

rajogun	quality of passion
rajsic	related to *rajogun*
raksha	to protect; protection
rangoli	traditional design made on festive days with special coloured powder
rath	chariot
rathi	owner of chariot
reto	*Feto* with silky, decorative edges woven with golden or silver threads. Tied around the head or waist, or left to rest upon the shoulders
rotla	a basic unleavened bread-like staple food of many parts of Gujarat, made generally of millet flour that is kneaded and patted into a flat, circular shape before being cooked on an earthen or metal hot plate

S

sadhana	spiritual endeavour by an aspirant
samp	unity
sansar	course of mundane life, worldly existence
sanskar	virtuous impression
sant samagam	to associate with a sadhu by listening to discourses, etc.
sarthi	chariot-driver
sat	truth, imperishable

sati	a woman who immolated herself on the cremation pyre of her dead husband. Also a woman who is chaste *(pativrata)*
satsang	the practice of spiritually associating with the Satpurush, fellow *satsangis,* one's own *atma* and the sacred scriptures of the Satsang fellowship
satsangi	member of the Satsang fellowship One who practises satsang
sattva	part of *maya. Sattvagun* is the attribute of clarity and purity of thought, excellence, mental poise.
sattvagun	quality of goodness
sattvic	one who is under the influence of *sattvagun*
sensei	master
seva	spiritual service
shami	type of tree
shlok	verse
shravan	listening, derived from verb-root 'shru' – to listen
sifu	teacher or master of martial art
sud	bright half of the lunar month
suhradbhav	spirit of friendship, cooperation, fraternity
surval	trouser-like garment worn by men

T

tamogun	quality of darkness, ignorance
tamsic	related to *tamogun*
thal	food devotionally offered to God as a form of bhakti, which in turn consecrates the food, turning it into *prasad*
tilak	U-shaped mark made with sandalwood

	paste on one's forehead
trilok	three worlds

U

upasana	'sitting near', derived from 'upa' + verb-root 'ās' – meaning to sit near. Philosophical framework outlining the fundamental principles of a doctrine. Philosophical understanding of the nature of God as well as the mode of worship of God

V

vad	dark half of the lunar month
vairagya	detachment; an aversion or strong, persistent dislike for the world and its pleasures
vishay	sense pleasure
vivek buddhi	mental power of discrimination
vrat	vow or spiritual observance

Y

yagna	sacrificial worship. Ceremonial ritual performed as a form of worship to seek the good favour and receive the blessings of the deities